Unlocking the English Language

Unlocking the English Language

ROBERT BURCHFIELD

With an introduction by

HAROLD BLOOM

 HILL AND WANG

A division of Farrar, Straus and Giroux

Library of Congress Cataloging-in-Publication Data

Burchfield, R. W.
    Unlocking the English language / Robert Burchfield. — 1st
American ed.
        p.   cm.
    Includes index.
    1. English language.   I. Title.
PE1072.B795   1991   420—dc20   90-43282   CIP

In memory of my parents

Frederick Burchfield (1891–1979) and
Mary Lauder Burchfield (1894–1974)

Contents

List of figures

Preface

In 1979 I wrote a preface to a facsimile edition of Dr Johnson's *Dictionary of the English Language* in which I said:

> In the whole tradition of English language and literature the *only* dictionary compiled by a writer of the first rank is that of Dr Johnson. The muses spared him a while from his main literary work before letting him return to his poems, his essays, and his tracts. If Dryden in the seventeenth century, Macaulay in the nineteenth, and T. S. Eliot in the twentieth had found it possible to withdraw from their main pursuits for a similar interval, and diverted their own 'intolerable wrestle with words' to the realm of lexicography, the result would very likely have been as beguiling, and as influential.

The first four chapters of this book are based on the four T. S. Eliot Memorial Lectures that I gave at the University of Kent at Canterbury on successive evenings from 7 to 10 November 1988. They are interspersed with references to T. S. Eliot and his writings, and it hardly needs to be said that in this case reference means reverence.

The rest of the book is made up of eight essays on English lexicography and grammar first printed in a variety of books and journals. A few minor corrections have been made, and the essays are arranged here in the chronological order of their first publication (between 1973 and 1987).

The linking theme is the attempt I have made during the last thirty years to render our complex language more accessible to its users, to unlock many of its mysteries. A prudent nation looks to the preservation and recording of its linguistic past and present, and it has been an enormous privilege to be able to play a part in this process.

It will be abundantly apparent that I favour a diachronic or historical approach to the unravelling of philological problems. To some extent this has meant my working against the spirit of the age. During the last thirty years linguistic scholarship has been dominated by those who favour synchronic or descriptive techniques. This clash of views is brought out in several of the essays in this book, and a resolution of the opposing views does not seem to be at hand.

For much of the present century, the general public, perplexed by what is judged to be a lack of sensitivity towards traditional grammar and towards some other aspects of word usage, has tended to see the language as entering a period of serious decline. I do not share this pessimistic view. All languages are subject to perpetual change and English is no exception. The rate of change in the twentieth century is not substantially different from that of earlier centuries, except in the sense that overseas varieties of English, in the United States, Australia, and elsewhere, are steadily moving away, in small matters and large, from Standard English, and from one another, at a somewhat accelerated rate. Such slow severances and departures from what was once regarded as a prized norm are bound to happen in countries that are so widely dispersed, and when the number of speakers involved – some 300 million – is so large.

I should like to thank the various institutions in this country and abroad that have been the venue of the lectures and essays collected here, and in particular Dr Shirley Barlow, Master of Eliot College, University of Kent, for the impeccable arrangements she made for my wife and me in Canterbury a month ago. My greatest debt in the writing of this book is to my wife. Retirement from the *OED* Department has brought me away from the burdens of administration but has taken me to a new stage in my life where hardly a week goes past without a publishing deadline. It is exciting but quite wearing, and someone has to take the strain. I suspect that it is my wife.

R.W.B.

Sutton Courtenay, Oxfordshire

December 1988

Introduction

Dr Samuel Johnson, lion of literary critics and of lexicographers alike, taught us that the essence of poetry is invention, in the sense of discovery. Robert Burchfield, Johnsonian lexicographer, teaches us that invention also is the essence of language, though this is a teaching that does not altogether console him or us:

> The English language is now at an uneasy stage of its development and expansion: the sheer voluminousness and complexity of the network of the language throughout the English-speaking world place almost insuperable obstacles in the path of those whose job it is to set down an accurate record of all of its varieties.

Burchfield, though wary of a future in which lexicographers may be replaced by clerks, refuses to be the elegist of his craft. If the reader seeks Borgesian parables of the last lexicographer, that quest must be fulfilled elsewhere. Politics and social movements shadow the lexicographer as they do the literary critic, and Burchfield accepts new pressures upon his enterprise, sometimes ruefully, but always with a stoic grace. His balanced defense of the lexicographer caught between bitter camps is manifested most forcefully in the essay 'The Turn of the Screw: Ethnic Vocabulary and Dictionaries', where the key words are *'Jew, Palestinian, Arab, Pakistan, Turk, Asiatic, Muhammadan,* and *Negro'*. With a sad dignity, Burchfield murmurs that 'dictionaries cannot be regulative in matters of social, political, and religious attitudes'. As a literary critic, I want to assert as much for criticism, if it is to remain the realm of aesthetic description and judgement, but like Burchfield I sense the encroachments of our Age of Resentment.

As the editor of the four-volume *Supplement to the Oxford English Dictionary* (final volume published in 1986), Burchfield gave nearly thirty years to his Johnsonian task, and emerged from it with a Johnsonian literary humanism enhanced. He is a diachronic or historical philologist, which is to be a dissident in an era dominated by synchronic or descriptive linguistics, whether in the mode of Saussure or in that of Sapir and Bloomfield. A critic who takes (as I do) a diachronic or historical view of rhetoric, as opposed to the synchronic theory of Paul de Man, is bound to be attracted by Burchfield's principles. What vanishes in deconstructive criticism, as in the linguistics of Saussure, is the pragmatic distinction between denotation and connotation, upon which poetry depends. Saussure sets a bar between signifier and signified, but then cannot tell us on which side of the bar connotation is to be discovered. Without a sense of connotation, the reader would be tone-deaf, and all figurative language would become a form of irony, as it does in de Man's formulations. One of the uses of Burchfield's meditations is to restore an understanding of trope that is diachronic. The skilled lexicographer shows us that the irony of one age is the noble synecdoche of another, and helps us also in seeing how the prestige of metaphor rises and falls with that of sublimation, as we move from one age to another.

Burchfield's most fascinating essay, for me, is the dryly wicked performance 'The Genealogy of Dictionaries', which might be retitled 'The Anguish of Contamination among Lexicographers', or even 'The Anxiety of Influence in the Making of the *Oxford English Dictionary Supplements*'. But Burchfield's emphasis is properly upon his precursors: Dr Johnson, Noah Webster, and Dr J. A. H. Murray (crucial editor of the *Oxford English Dictionary*). Himself a medievalist, Burchfield sagely reminds us that plagiarism is a relatively modern legalism:

Medieval European authors took it as axiomatic that their main purpose was to 'translate' or adapt the great works of their predecessors. The word *plagiarism* itself is first recorded in 1621, but the association of *plagiarism* with guilt and furtiveness came rather later.

One could notice that Chaucer himself delights in giving credit to fictive authorities, while slyly translating Dante and Boccaccio, but it remains true that all strong literature is a kind of theft. Emerson cheerfully affirmed that 'the Originals were not original', and literary originality generally has little to do with origination. Burchfield traces the 'path of descent' from the *American College Dictionary* (1947) down to its British and Australian derivatives, and the more surprising reliance of *Webster's Third New International* upon the *OED*. By the time he has shown us Dr Johnson quietly cannibalizing one Nathan Bailey, Burchfield is ready to suggest that we 'take the word *plagiarism* right out of the subject as an unnecessarily delicate consideration in the provision of information for mankind.' The word 'delicate' is crucial there, and so is 'information'. If you are going to unlock the language, whether through philology or criticism, you need to take help wherever you can get it.

Contrasting his project to that of his direct precursor Murray, Burchfield remarks that Murray averaged one quotation per century for any given meaning, whereas the *Supplements* aim for at least one quotation per decade. This raises the image of future supplements giving one quotation for each year for each meaning, and suggests that dictionaries beyond that may touch their apocalypse, with fresh quotations being required each month as meanings swerve toward the end of our time, presumably in the year 2001. Beyond even that will be the quotation per day, and lexicographers will have to accept the choice of extinction or madness. Unlocking the English language will become equivalent to rebuilding the Tower of Babel, a Kafkaesque exercise without restraint, a Borgesian excursion into an endlessly upward-mounting labyrinth.

Burchfield's book is too cheerful and pragmatic for such a vision, and that is certainly part of its value. Rereading it tends to put me into an elegiac mood, which is very contrary to Burchfield's purposes. But I suspect that my mood is more than personal, and that Burchfield, like Dr Johnson, Noah Webster, and J. A. H. Murray, belongs to the Giant Race before the Flood. A great dictionary, in another decade or so, is likely to seem a grand monument rising out of the compost heap of a universal electronic culture. We will resort to that monument in the way that the librarians worked at the Museion in Hellenistic Alexandria, hoping to preserve what needs to be preserved, in the coming times of the Fire and the Flood, knowing that conservation needs to be the mode of our New Alexandrianism.

HAROLD BLOOM

Acknowledgements

The essays in Part II first appeared individually in the following publications:

'The Treatment of Controversial Vocabulary in the *Oxford English Dictionary*' in *Transactions of the Philological Society, 1973*, pp. 1–28. 'The Turn of the Screw: Ethnic Vocabulary and Dictionaries' in the *Listener*, 13 April 1978, pp. 454–6. 'The Point of Severance: British and American English' in *Encounter*, October 1978, pp. 129–33. 'The Fowlers: Their Achievements in Lexicography and Grammar' published as the 1979 Presidential Address to the English Association, 1 Priory Gardens, London W4 1TT. 'The Genealogy of Dictionaries' first given as a lecture at the University of Toronto on 27 March 1984 and subsequently printed in *Encounter*, Sept./Oct. 1984, pp. 10–19. 'The *Oxford English Dictionary* and Its Historical Principles' in *Lexicography: an emerging international profession*, edited by Robert Ilson; copyright © 1986 the US-UK Educational Commission; reproduced by permission of Manchester University Press; pp. 17–27. 'The End of the Alphabet: Last Exit to Grammar' in *The English Reference Grammar*, edited by Gerhard Leitner, Max Niemeyer Verlag, Tübingen, 1986, pp. 45–55. 'The *OED*: Past and Present' in *Dictionaries of English: Prospects for the Record of our Language*, edited by Richard W. Bailey, University of Michigan Press, 1987, pp. 11–21.

List of abbreviations

a	*ante*, before
AV	Authorized Version (1611) of the Bible
c	*circa* (with dates)
CGEL	*A Comprehensive Grammar of the English Language* (Longman, 1985)
COD	*The Concise Oxford Dictionary*
G., Ger.	German
IPA	International Phonetic Alphabet
L.	Latin
modE.	modern English
NEB	New English Bible
New OED	computerized version of the *OED* and *OEDS* (merged in one alphabetical series), prepublication title of the second edition of the *OED* (1989)
OE.	Old English
OED	*The Oxford English Dictionary* (12 vols, 1884–1928)
OEDS	*A Supplement to the Oxford English Dictionary* (4 vols, 1972–86)
OUP	Oxford University Press
Phil. Soc.	Philological Society
POD	*The Pocket Oxford Dictionary*
RP	Received Pronunciation
sc.	*scilicet*, that is to say, namely
S.P.E.	Society for Pure English
¹Suppl.	Supplement (1933) to the *OED*
²Suppl.	= *OEDS*
TPS	*Transactions of the Philological Society*
*	Used conventionally in modern grammatical work to indicate an unacceptable construction, as *three my children* (instead of *my three children*)

Part 1: The T. S. Eliot
Memorial Lectures, 1988

1 Linguistic Milestones

The beginning of harmless drudgery

And, turning the past over and over,
You'll wonder only that you endured it for so long.

Unidentified guest in *The Cocktail Party* (1950)

For twenty-nine years, from 1957 to 1986, I was engaged on the greatest search and most arduous task of my life – the preparation, with the assistance of many colleagues and with guidance from many outside scholars, of the four volumes of *A Supplement to the Oxford English Dictionary*. When I embarked on the project in July 1957, I had little idea of the complexity and immensity of what I had taken on. I shall begin by trying to give some idea of the milestones that marked the journey from the first baffling, dreamlike day in July 1957 until 8 May 1986 when the final volume was published.

How did it all begin? Towards the end of 1956, a fixed-tenure lecturership that I held at Christ Church, Oxford, had almost run its course. I was approached by the Secretary to the Delegates of the Clarendon Press, Mr C. H. Roberts, and the Assistant Secretary, Mr D. M. Davin, to edit a new Supplement to the *OED*. The latter asked me (9 November 1956) for a curriculum vitae: 'Can you let me have a sheet of paper which will record your virtues rather than your vices?' I obliged, and said that I was 'well satisfied with a salary of £1,500 p.a.', the amount they had offered me. The Dean of Christ Church, John Lowe, said that he was 'glad a suitable post had offered itself'. My father, in distant New Zealand, was interviewed by his local newspaper about me:

With a family of three children and work on the supplement ahead of him, there seemed little chance of his being able to return to New Zealand for a long time, said his father, Mr F. Burchfield, Pitt Street, Wanganui, today.[1]

I left Christ Church, where my main colleague had been the scholar and novelist J. I. M. Stewart, set aside a vast piece of work I had undertaken on the *Ormulum* (an immense set of versified sermons written in a semi-phonetic script circa AD 1200 by an Augustinian canon named Orm), and started out on my lexicographical career. Stewart remarked that I would need to establish a new pattern of work: 'the afternoons will seem long', he warned.[2]

In the first 'long' days I perused some old Clarendon Press files. Kenneth Sisam, a former Secretary to the Delegates of the Clarendon Press, had been the person responsible for the administration of Oxford dictionaries from the 1920s to 1947. I held him in high esteem. He was a distinguished medieval scholar, a fellow countryman of mine, and also, like me, he had been lured to the University of Oxford by a Rhodes Scholarship. He had set down (28 September 1952) a splendidly autocratic memorandum on the way to proceed. He proposed a one-volume Supplement of about 1,275 pages to be completed within a period of seven years.

> Collectors of quotations . . . must be warned to avoid nonce-words; rare technical words . . .; pure slang, dialect, transparent and unlimited kinds such as negatives in *un-*, or proper noun adjectives in *-ian*, *-an*, . . . I think USA words of a certain status and permanence must go in, even if not in the collections from English authors, because so many American books are printed or current in England, and one must please the Americans . . . I should be cautious of American constructions (often non-English in origin) unless they are fully naturalized in England . . . I don't think a good editor would need more than a clerk-typist at first, and later on a young man who could be trained to succeed.

The first milestone

A few weeks after I began work on the Supplement, I went down to the Isles of Scilly (12–15 August 1957) to seek up-to-date advice from

Sisam. My working notes about the visit have survived. His advice to me was simple: set yourself a time limit. 'Say seven years and get it out in ten.' The completion of the project would be like swimming the Channel: make the crossing before the tide turns or you will never get across.

The image was a powerful one. But similes are one thing, policy matters another. Must I be bound by the length of the book he wanted, namely a single volume of 1,275 pages? How could I tell whether seven, or even ten years would be sufficient? The prospect ahead was worrying.

I returned to Oxford and continued to read through the correspondence files since 1933. I found numerous suggestions of antedatings, omissions of individual words, and other quite useful offerings, and these were carefully indexed and filed away in the quotation boxes. It seemed that small matters of linguistic detail inflamed the population at large rather than broad matters of policy. For example, I found in the files a letter of 28 July 1952 from Mr (now Sir) Peter Saunders, which ran as follows:

Dear Sirs,
   I am producing a play called 'The Mousetrap' and I should be grateful if you would kindly inform me whether the word 'mousetrap' is one word, two words or hyphenated.
         Yours faithfully,
   (signed)   Peter Saunders

Mr Saunders was the producer of Agatha Christie's famous play. Mr Davin replied (12 August 1952)[3] as follows:

Dear Sir,
   Thank you for your letter of 28 July to which I am sorry not to have replied before. The *Concise Oxford Dictionary* gives mousetrap as one word and I think you would be quite safe in following it. The question of when a hyphen between two words of this kind can be dropped is always a difficult one but where as in this case the combination is thought of as being a single entity we think it could easily be printed as one.
         Yours truly
   (signed)   D. M. Davin

Another type of inquiry – demand would be a more accurate word – with important consequences for all dictionaries, came from the Irish statesman Eamon de Valera (17 September 1956) complaining that

> you give gratuitous circulation to the statement that the Fianna Fail Party 'took the oath' on entering Dail Eireann in August 1927. No oath was taken, nor was an oath demanded by the official in charge, and many witnesses are available to prove this.

He demanded that the definition of Fianna Fail be corrected. He was right and the entry was duly amended in the *Concise Oxford Dictionary*. This letter, and some later ones about other political terms, soon taught me that in our turbulent age political and ethnic issues are more brittle, more explosive, and more sensitive than any others.

Meanwhile in Oxford I saw a great deal of Dr C. T. Onions, the last survivor of the four editors of the original *OED*, and his advice, like that of Sisam, was also deeply cautionary. From a note I made of a conversation we had on 1 August 1957, I see that he told me, for example, that professional scholars should be consulted only when all other sources had failed. 'They are admirable if asked to criticize a provisional entry, hopeless if asked to do all the work.' In other words, members of staff should prepare entries, and the entries should be shown to outside scholars only at that stage, not earlier. As to members of staff, 'You will need one or two itinerant lexical assistants. They must not be men with degrees, or anyone seeking advancement or higher pay.'

It will be clear that the first milestones I passed were all admonitory. The path ahead was made to seem very tortuous indeed.

As soon as an opportunity offered itself I began to draft some experimental entries for various classes of words. I buried myself in the Radcliffe Science Library for a while to try to get the measure of the problems facing anyone drafting entries for scientific words. Sisam had urged me to keep to technical and scientific words that were 'fairly easy to date and define': he mentioned *poliomyelitis*, *nylon*, and *jet* as examples. The first word I chose to work on was *radiocarbon*, a term very much in the air then (as now, witness the Turin shroud). I found it relatively easy to establish its history – the technique is, roughly, 'follow the footnotes in the relevant articles in learned journals' – and also the history of derivatives or synonyms like *radiocarbon dating* or *carbon-14 dating*, but much less easy to define them. Against the advice of Sisam and Onions, and against the whole tradition of the *OED*, I decided that scientifically trained staff would be needed in due course.[4]

In a leaflet distributed in 1957 describing the immediate needs of the Supplement, I listed twenty-one key-words that I thought would help us to unlock the language of the twentieth century. They were:

action painting	meson	self-service
automation	morpheme	skiffle
chain-reaction	myxomatosis	sound-barrier
cybernetics	nylon	trafficator
disinflation	paratroop	Welfare State
ionosphere	penicillin	
jet (-engine)	plutonium	
megaton	radar	

These seemed to me to be the words of the age. If we could prepare satisfactory entries for them, all would be well with the rest. Or so, misguidedly, I thought at the time.

Literary language

At an early stage I set about forming a policy for the collecting and treatment of the vocabulary of modern creative writers and the complex metalanguage of literary critics. I consulted first an Oxford colleague, the late J. B. Leishman of St John's, for his views 'on how best to collect the evidence for recent literary vocabulary'. He replied (19 March 1959): 'I must confess that I have no definite views about how to collect evidence for recent literary vocabulary.'[5] He inclined to the view that a Supplement should in effect be a collection of Addenda and Corrigenda for the original *OED*. I replied (20 March 1959) that 'It will be possible to insert a limited number of literary words (or senses), particularly those of the nineteenth century, . . . but I'm afraid there is no hope at present of correcting mistakes in the O.E.D. or of printing earlier quotations for words already in, desirable though this would be.' I went on, 'Our main effort must be directed towards such modern terms as *commitment* (in the literary sense).'

I had made a start even if it was a somewhat negative one. Piece by piece, discussion by discussion, a broad policy emerged. The main literary sources – the entire works of writers like Eliot, Auden, Joyce, Lawrence, and many others, needed to be indexed in the manner that the readers of sources drawn on for the *OED* had indexed the works of Chaucer, Malory, Marlowe, Shakespeare, Milton, Johnson, and all the other famous writers of the past. It is important to bear in mind that there were no computers in the late 1950s, only primitive photocopying machines (not accessible to us), and very little at all to take the pain out of the collecting of the evidence. A retired schoolteacher from Faversham in Kent, Mr R. A. Auty, undertook the task of reading the entire works of James Joyce, except for *Finnegans Wake*. Like a medieval scribe he copied in his own handwriting many thousands of 6×4 inch slips on which he entered illustrative examples for any word or meaning that occurred in Joyce and was not already entered in the Dictionary. He was one of about a hundred readers, among them several from the University of Oxford, including Douglas Gray and Emrys Jones (both now professors), and several from the University of Birmingham, including D. S. Brewer, E. G. Stanley, and Mrs Elsie Duncan-Jones. Shortly afterwards the main team of readers was joined by the most prolific and creative of them all, the late Miss Marghanita Laski. The quotational evidence soon built up, but it took longer to discover what my editorial policy would be.

Despite occasional setbacks, this early period was immensely enjoyable. For a time it looked as if the thoroughly domestic project that the Clarendon Press had urged me to embark on would be completed in a thoroughly domestic manner. Some important entries had been drafted – those for all words with *radio-* or *tele-* as first elements, for example – quotations were pouring in from the outside readers, and most of the outside consultants were adding a touch of polish to the entries we showed them. Some were even amused. For example, when J. I. M. Stewart improved the definition of the expression *archetypal pattern*, he quipped

> Bung
>   This bunk
> Under Jung
>   (Or Iunk).[6]

It hardly needs saying that I referred continually to the twelve volumes of the *OED*, and found my admiration for James Murray growing every day. He had imposed a shape on the dictionary which not only stood the test of time but was followed as a model by historical lexicographers all round the world. When his grand-daughter's biography of him, *Caught in the Web of Words*, was published in 1977, I found a great deal to sympathize with in the story of his struggle to complete his enormous task. He died in 1915, thirty-three years after he had sent the first instalment of copy to the printer and thirteen years before the publication of the last volume. Lexicographers are generally long-lived – they need to be – but many fail to complete their course. This was a threat that haunted me for twenty-nine years.

The 'decline' of the language

While I was immersed in the study of medieval literature at Christ Church I was unaware that a certain unease about the state of the language was beginning to be expressed in many quarters. Once embarked on my task of mapping the vocabulary of the twentieth century, I quickly discovered deeply pessimistic statements about the way the language was tending. The statements did not come from professional scholars but from some creative writers, from many journalists, and from some sections of the general public. In the April 1946 issue of *Horizon*, for example, George Orwell began a piece called 'Politics and the English Language' as follows:

> Most people who bother with the matter at all would admit that the English language is in a bad way, but it is generally assumed that we cannot by conscious action do anything about it. Our civilization is decadent, and our language – so the argument runs – must inevitably share in the general collapse.

Orwell believed that 'the decline of a language must ultimately have political and economic causes', and he also thought that the process of decline was reversible:

> Modern English, especially written English, is full of bad habits which spread by imitation and which can be avoided if one is willing to take the necessary trouble. (*Ibid.*)

I believe that Orwell's views are broadly representative of those of many educated, very literate, but linguistically unprofessional AB-type people since the 1939–45 war. It was in the climate of such views, constantly repeated in public writings, that the Supplement was prepared.

A similar view was imaginatively expressed in 1982 by Max, a character in Tom Stoppard's play *The Real Thing*:

> I thought you liked me showing an interest in your work. *My* showing. Save the gerund and screw the whale.

'Save the whale', 'save the rhino', more recently 'save our planet' – the particular and the general fossilized subjunctive slogans of our age – were quite soon joined by cries of 'save the gerund', 'save the word *gay*', and, after 1968, 'save us from the word *hopefully*'. A broad belief emerged that the language is somehow at risk, a species threatened by predators and barbarians.

Doom-laden linguistic prophecies of this kind were commonplace while my colleagues and I prepared the *Supplement to the OED*. The period also coincided with the arrival in the higher realms of linguistics of what I have called 'linguistic burial parties', that is, scholars with shovels intent on burying the linguistic past and most of the literary past and present. I refer, of course, to those who believe that synchronic (or descriptive) treatments of a language are theoretically sound and diachronic (or historical) treatments theoretically unsound. Since the 1950s, great marauding bands of scholars have sought out the complex semantic and grammatical rules that govern our language by using new techniques of observation and evaluation. The new techniques involve the rejection of evidence from past centuries and the ditching of quotational evidence from modern written texts. You will easily discern that I regard such work as the linguistic equivalent of walking around partly blindfolded.

As a result, the period 1957 to the present day has been marked by the establishment of the linguistic equivalent of Benjamin Disraeli's two nations:

> Two nations; between them there is no intercourse and no sym-pathy; who are as ignorant of each other's habits, thoughts and feelings, as if they were dwellers in different zones, inhabitants of different planets.
>
> (*Sybil; or, the Two Nations*, 1845)

There is little doubt that the *Supplement to the OED* was prepared in an age when other stars were in the ascendancy, at any rate stars in the Rummidge-like studies of synchronic linguistics and their deconstructing colleagues in literary departments of many universities.

A specimen page

By 1961, the collecting process had reached the point when it seemed desirable to prepare a specimen page. I selected a sequence of words in the middle of the alphabet – from *Lo* to *lock-up* – and prepared entries for them. After long discussions and experimentation with typefaces the specimen was printed. It occupied three pages and it settled the layout for the whole of the project.[7] The scholars to whom the specimen was sent objected principally to the inclusion of technical and scientific words, American and Australian slang, and to quotations from modern poetry. My publishing overlords within OUP seemed to hold the same views.[8]

The Australian slang objected to was the expression *to lob in*, 'to arrive':

> Scrubby lobs in one sundown while Old Dave is over with the storekeeper. (*Bulletin* [Sydney], 12 Dec. 1934, 25/2)

And the American, *lobby-gow*, 'An errand-boy, messenger; a hanger-on, underling, especially in an opium den or in the Chinese quarter of a town':

> I ain't gunna have her think Stevey's tied up with a bunch of lobby-gows. (G. Bronson-Howard, *Enemy to Society*, 1911, ix. 295)

Neither qualified for admission on grounds of familiarity – they were both unknown to me – but printed evidence for both lay in the quotation boxes. I was playing the game by the book with little idea of the size of the problem that the inclusion of such items was to produce.

Under *loam* I had included, for example, an undefined phrase from T. S. Eliot's 'East Coker':

> Lifting heavy feet in clumsy shoes,
> Earth feet, loam feet, lifted in country mirth.

Thousands of such undefined poetical phrases had been listed in the *OED*. I saw no need to change the policy that James Murray had devised, though it irked me that the critics seemed to be unaware of this minor corner of Murray's policy. I retained the entry and all the more so as Donald Davie, perhaps directly influenced by Eliot's line, had used the same expression:

> Come with me by the self-consuming north
> (The North is spirit), to the loam-foot west
> And opulent departures of the south.

(Brides of Reason, 1955, 28)

At the time, with J. C. Maxwell, I was editing *Notes & Queries*, and most of the literary notes that we were printing in it were details of Shakespearian, Miltonic, etc., 'echoes' found in later writers. At the very least, my entry for *loam foot* would obviate the need for such a note in some future issue of *Notes & Queries*.

From this trifling example and from one or two other remarks made about poetical items in the specimen page, it became apparent to me that the key to the problem was one of proportion. The solution lay before my eyes in the pages of the *OED* itself. Increase the coverage of every realm of English vocabulary throughout the English-speaking world, and poetical combinations of the *loam foot* kind would be mere golden specks in the whole work. Another significant milestone had been reached and passed. To their everlasting credit the senior officers of the Press did not intervene, and the editing continued on the basis of the specimen together with my newly formed principle of swamping somewhat unpopular items, or rendering them semi-invisible, by enlarging the whole structure. It was the moment, I now realize, when the one-volume Supplement that had been planned inevitably turned into a four-volume work.

Before I leave the subject of the specimen, I recall that Mr Davin told me informally that the Delegates of the Press, to whom it had been briefly shown, expressed great pleasure at the first item. The word was *Lo*, a noun meaning 'an American Indian', humorously derived from a line in Alexander Pope's *Essay on Man*, 'Lo, the poor Indian', and illustrated by numerous quotations from American sources from 1871 onward. For example:

On Florida's shield stands a placid and buxom Mrs Lo, with fringed skirt falling to the knee. (*N.Y. Evening Post*, 6 August 1904)

It is not always easy to inject humour into a dictionary. The gods favoured me on this occasion. With the good-humoured blessing of the Delegate the Supplement went ahead.

By 1972, when the first volume of the Supplement was published, I was able to describe my policy about literary vocabulary in a fairly decisive manner:

> Whereas the *O.E.D.* adopted a policy of total literary inclusiveness for the earlier centuries, with the result that all the vocabulary, including *hapax legomena*, of such authors as Chaucer, Gower, and Shakespeare, was included, we have followed a somewhat more limited policy, namely that of liberally representing the vocabulary of such writers as Kipling, Yeats, James Joyce, and Dylan Thomas. The outward signs of the working of this policy may be observed in entries like those for the following words: *apatheia* (a medical word used by Beckett), *athambia* (*hapax legomenon* in Beckett), *Babbitt* (name of a literary 'hero'), *bandersnatch* (a 'Lewis Carroll' word), *bang, sb.*[1] 2 (used allusively after T. S. Eliot's line), *barkle, v.* (dialectal use in D. H. Lawrence), *baw-ways* (dialectal use in James Joyce), *ectomorph* (anthropometric term adopted by R. Fuller, C. P. Snow, W. H. Auden, etc.), and *elf, sb.*[1] 6 (further illustrations in Walter de la Mare, J. R. R. Tolkien, etc., of obvious combinations).[9]

The policy prospered and, I believe, brought fruit during the next fourteen years while Volumes 2 to 4 were being prepared. Inevitably some items were overlooked. A dictionary editor at the level of the *OED* is at the mercy of his readers. If a reader fails to observe a new or unrecorded word or meaning in his source that item will normally fail to appear in the dictionary.

Behind the scenes

A dictionary is judged by its contents. When it is completed and printed and stands on the shelves, it is too late to speak about the mishaps and adversities that have occurred on the way to the destination. Quite properly dictionary users are entitled to ignore the circumstances in which the work has been prepared, and simply use it as a work of reference. Now that a decent interval has passed since the publication of the final volume of *OEDS* in May 1986, however, it might not seem inappropriate to mention some of the setbacks that happened behind the scenes, as it were.

Kenneth Sisam's advice about the turning of the linguistic tide was confirmed just four years after I began work on the Supplement. I was scarcely out of Dover, in a sense, and a calm crossing seemed likely, when in 1961 *Webster's Third New International Dictionary* released for public inspection and appraisal an unprecedented number of current English words. The sheer quantity and range of the material included in *Webster's Third* made it ominously obvious that I had seriously underestimated the task of collecting modern English vocabulary. Our sources needed to be vastly increased in number and retrawled so that we could match the inclusiveness of this huge new dictionary. Discussions about the merits of *to lob in*, *lobby-gow*, and *loam foot* became sideline issues. Nothing less than a full-scale analysis of the Englishes of every English-speaking region would enable us to produce a work that would be as compendious as *Webster's Third*. The reading programme had to be sharply increased.

The second main rip of the tide came from within OUP itself. The smaller Oxford dictionaries, which had from the beginning been edited in the homes of the editors concerned – on Guernsey, at Twickenham, at Exmouth, and so on – were gradually brought together in Oxford so that they should all be edited under the same roof. Severe competition from other dictionaries of similar size made it imperative that the Oxford dictionaries were made less subject to the whims and biases of far-flung editors. The new concept was to see them as a powerful family of closely related books. I was placed in charge of a huge defensive operation. In 1957 there were just four main Oxford dictionaries (other than English Language Teaching ones), namely the *Concise Oxford Dictionary* (first published in 1911), the *Pocket* (1924), the *Little* (1930), and the *Shorter* (1933). Over the years they had drawn apart both in their conventions of presentation – pronunciation systems, abbreviations for old languages, methods of transliteration of foreign alphabets, use or non-use of the swung dash, and so on – and, much more importantly, in their selection of vocabulary and in the regularity with which definitions had been kept up to date. The lexicographical group concerned with the preparation of the *Supplement to the OED* was joined by numerous other groups and sub-groups preparing new editions of the smaller dictionaries, and also some brand-new dictionaries. Between the years 1957 and 1984, in which year my role in the governance of the smaller dictionaries came to an end, the five mainline Oxford dictionaries turned into more than twenty. It was a necessary task of great magnitude if the Oxford dictionaries were to remain pre-eminent. It also produced a great deal of revenue for the continuation – I almost said the survival – of OUP's policy of publishing bevies of valuable but unprofitable scholarly monographs. But rewarding and exciting though the whole operation was, it was at the same time a distraction of indescribable proportions from my main work on the *Supplement to the OED*.

The creation of new dictionaries siphoned off some of the best of the *OEDS* staff. Everyone wanted to have a project of his or her own, and some agonizing choices had to be made. I also discovered very soon that it was impossible, in the economic conditions of the 1960s and 1970s, to retain some other very able members of staff. Dr Onions had been right, or very nearly right, when he had warned me that, as to members of staff, 'they must not be men with degrees, or anyone seeking advancement or higher pay'. One of those who left was the novelist Julian Barnes. A profile of him printed in the July 1980 issue of a publication called *Over 21* set down his reasons for leaving the staff of the Supplement in 1972 after a three-year stint:

> Imagine yourself as a lexicographer on the *Oxford English Dictionary* . . . Your job is to find the first example of the word appearing in print. One of your areas is sex words. Words like 'penis' or 'condom' are old hat; the words you are after are ones like 'blow job' and 'bang'. You sift successfully through the zappy American writers circa 1960 – Miller, Mailer, Burroughs – for most of your quotations. But, dammit, . . . there is one word which no amount of medical books, sex manuals, soul or body-baring women's novels or modern American poetry will yield. You *know* it exists but after three weeks of continuous searching there is still no trace: 'Germy.' It is as if 'germy' had vanished into thin air. This was just one . . . measure of the exasperation which led the young Julian Barnes to abandon lexicography.[10]

He went on to write *Metroland, Flaubert's Parrot,* and other novels.

The loss of Barnes and of some other very able members of staff taught me that there is an area of academic and creative territory from which it is not possible to attract and retain suitable editorial assistants. At regular intervals, and especially at the time of publication of the separate volumes, some of the more ambitious of my colleagues, seeing others in the Department as career-blockers, went off to appointments and projects elsewhere.

One minor curiosity of the project was the discovery, against all expectations, that a few members of staff had no stomach for the crudities of sexual and scatological vocabulary. I had assumed from the beginning that *Homo lexicographicus* was a chalcenterous species of mankind, that is, a person with bowels of brass.[11] I don't want to overemphasize this. Lexicographers are not puritanical in an old-fashioned sense: no one ever expressed reservations about treating phrases like 'he's a boring old fart' or 'a new tabloid with plenty of tits and bums'. But when the time came for the verification in the Bodleian Library of some of the richer uses of the words *cunt* and *fuck* I was told by the library research assistant at the time that she had had 'quite enough of the kind of filth found in Partridge and other dictionaries of slang'. It seemed tactful not to insist, and I therefore had the doubtful privilege of looking out the material myself.

Another aspect of dictionary work is the necessity of setting down as faithfully as possible, without censorship or bias of any kind, the social and political circumstances and beliefs of the time. Thus, for example, the *Deutsches Wörterbuch* was right to include the ghastly terminology of Nazi Germany, not with approval but simply as a matter of record. So, too, it is lexicographically sound for present-day Chinese dictionaries to include the Communist-based vocabulary of slogans, battles, successes, and failures of the various regimes since that of Chiang Kai-shek. It is not so easy to present the language of dissent in a totally neutral and disinterested way. How was one to deal with definitions of spiritualistic terms, for example, which asserted that spiritualistic experiences and entities were not 'alleged to exist' but were actually verifiable? How also was one to prevent the sly insertion of value-laden words into definitions of pacifism and of the shady world of hallucinatory drugs.

These were real issues at one time or another, and I had to search in my heart for neutrality.

The necessity of recording the unpleasantnesses of one's own age has its own penalties. In 1971, a Salford businessman took an action against the OUP challenging its right to include unfavourable senses of the word *Jew* in Oxford dictionaries. The case was widely reported in the press and letters pro and con flowed into the *OED* Department. The businessman lost his action, but the issue remained controversial. I learned that there are sections of the community that would like to sweep the bigotries of some of its fellow citizens under the carpet. And it still chills me to think that at one point in the affair I became perhaps the first lexicographer in history to receive an anonymous death threat.

Kenneth Sisam's 1952 memorandum (see above) had laid stress on the need to avoid seeking advice from committees:

> The greatest danger would be the formation or intrusion of any Committee – the Phil. Soc. for instance – which would normally help in collecting but in practice interfere with the policy of selection and inclusion. There should be no Committee whatever that can interfere with policy. Cannan [*sc.* a former Secretary to the Delegates of the University Press] proved that production of dictionaries makes no progress under Committees, and the American dictionary projects have usually been wrecked by them . . .

It seemed, and still seems to me, the wisest of advice. He himself had the committee of Delegates of the Press to turn to, of course, but they were dons, sagacious beings above the day-to-day commercial fray, professorial gurus, and the history and traditions of Delegacies in Oxford had established very civilized relationships between them and the University Departments they advised.

In the last decade of the *OEDS* project, from 1976 onwards, I had to grow accustomed not so much to a Committee but to a profusion of committees. The process, familiar now to most people, is called corporate management. Outside management consultants were brought in to ask my colleagues and me to describe in detail exactly what we did from day to day in order to 'write' (as they called it) dictionaries. Job descriptions were prepared on which carefully balanced committees of publishing staff were to ponder and set a grading value. The exercise was further complicated by the fact that it coincided with the establishment of a trade union affiliation (at that time with the ASTMS) for members of publishing and dictionary staff. OUP found its own village Arthur Scargills, Ron Todds, and Eric Hammonds. The union was not a closed shop. Old friendships were put at risk, time was lost, and projects were delayed as the rough justice of grading and other battles proceeded. When disputes arose, as they did from time to time, the *OED* Department was picketed by some of its members of staff, or, sometimes, by publishing staff from other departments of the Press. Sometimes dictionary staff were absent from their desks picketing elsewhere in disputes unrelated to dictionary work. It was a dispiriting experience for which the cloistered life of a don in the University of Oxford had not prepared me at all. One of the greatest rewards of retirement is the freedom it gives one from the sight of such ignoble skirmishes, as distant as anything could be from older realms of scholarship. I often wondered what James Murray would have thought of it all. One thing was certain. He was often locked into conflict with the senior officers of the Press – and so was I – on matters to do with space, time, and money. But it was a battle between himself alone and gentlemen publishers. Members of Murray's staff were not involved at all, and went on quietly with their work. That, I concluded ruefully, was the difference between Murray's time and mine. Murray and his colleagues were for the most part able to keep their attention on linguistic milestones. I had also to consider procedural points.

Conclusion

James Murray and I lived in very different times. His was a pioneering work of staggering proportions that set down the vocabulary of the English people from Anglo-Saxon times to 1900 and a little beyond. I saw my task in much more relative terms:

> When Murray began, a computer was very much a person who worked with ledgers, an abolitionist was anti-slavery, not anti-capital punishment, and a silo, quite innocuously, stored wheat, not Cruise missiles . . . And trolleys were the kind of thing pushed by coalminers, not by you and me in Waitrose . . . We have gained many words since 1884, but lost hardly any. One hundred years is only just

over the span of a person's life and words take much longer than that to die out.[12]

Sir James Murray was the Hamlet of historical lexicography. As for myself, like J. Alfred Prufock,

> No! I am not Prince Hamlet, nor was meant to be;
> Am an attendant lord, one that will do
> To swell a progress, start a scene or two, . . .
> Deferential, glad to be of use,
> Politic, cautious, and meticulous;
> Full of high sentence, but a bit obtuse.

A large dictionary project is marked by numerous milestones. One of the last things I did before leaving *OEDS* behind me was to write to Anthony Burgess on 12 May 1986, four days after the publication of the final volume. Of all the reviewers of all the volumes he seemed to me to come nearest to understanding the problems that I had overcome. It was my turn to compliment him and thank him:

> You have a perfect awareness of the never-ending raggedness, stretching away into the darkness, of our language at the perimeter of what we can manage to put in our largest dictionaries.[13]

I am glad to have left the lexicographical stage, that this particular curtain has come down. In the next chapter, I shall report on a new performance, this time on a grammatical stage. I shall name parts and give an account of how the perception of the nature of English grammar developed from 1586 to the present day.

> On *this* stage the linguists come and go
> Boasting of *descriptio*.

Notes

1. *Wanganui Chronicle*, November 1956 (precise date not noted).
2. It had long been a convention in Oxford to teach and lecture only in the mornings and in the early evenings from 5 to 7 pm, thus leaving the undergraduates free to participate in games, theatrical rehearsals, and so on, in the afternoons.
3. Both letters preserved in the archives of the *OED* Department.
4. In fact it was not until 1968 that the first science graduate, Mr A. M. Hughes, joined the staff.
5. 'Men of Letters' file in the archives of the *OED* Department.

6. *OED* Department archives 26 April 1965.
7. And, incidentally, for the *Oxford Latin Dictionary* (1968–82).
8. A more detailed account of the reactions of both the outside scholars and the publishers is set down in my Threlford Memorial Lecture, 'The End of an Innings but not the End of the Game', in *The Incorporated Linguist*, summer 1984, pp. 114–19.
9. Preface to *OEDS*, Volume 1.
10. In fact examples of the word were found after Barnes left the dictionary and an entry for the word *germy* (1912–) appeared in *OEDS*, Volume 1.
11. See the entry for the word *chalcenterous* in *OEDS*, Volume 1.
12. *Standard*, 31 January 1984, p. 6.
13. Private letter, 12 May 1986.

2 The Naming of Parts

Before the serjeant begins to teach young soldiers their *exercise* of the musket, he explains to them the different parts of it; the butt, the stock, the barrel, the loops, the swivels, and so on; because, unless they know these by their names, they cannot know how to obey his instructions in the handling of the musket. Sailors, for the same reason, are told which is the tiller, which are the yards, which the shrouds, which the tacks, which the sheets, which the booms, and which each and every part of the ship . . . This species of preliminary knowledge is absolutely necessary in all these callings of life; but not more necessary than it is for you to learn . . . how *to know the sorts of words one from another.*

William Cobbett addressing his son in
A Grammar of the English Language (first British edition, 1823),
Letter III, para 12

This chapter is about the naming of parts of speech, about the tortuous journey from the preparation of the first English grammar four hundred years ago – when everything seemed obvious when viewed in a Latin mirror – to the complex descriptions of English grammar in the later part of the present century. The earliest grammarians inspected English grammar with, so to speak, low-strength magnifying glasses. Inevitably they felt it incumbent upon them to analyse the results in the same manner in which they had analysed Latin grammar at their schools and universities. The best modern grammarians, by contrast, work with linguistic microscopes. The parts of speech, the manner in which they are used, the permissible and the impermissible orderings of words, the tenses and the modalities, are now being scrutinized with unparalleled minuteness, and with vast arrays of competing terminology. This chapter is about the multiplication of grammatical concepts as the endless quest goes on for keys to unlock the English language, to find out how it works.

The study of grammar stood in the forefront of the medieval disciplines of the trivium – grammar, logic, and rhetoric. The categories and distinctions of Aristotle, Priscian, and other ancient grammarians were subjected to endless analysis and re-examination. One category of words was that of the *syncategoremata*, that is, words which had meaning only in conjunction with other words. In medieval Latin, for example, the *syncategoremata* included adjectives like *omnis*, *ambo*, and *nullus*, verbs like *est* and *incipit*, adverbs like *non* and *tantum*, and the conjunctions *si*, *nisi*, *et*, and *vel*. Such words often determined the relationship between subject and predicate; many of them governed the structure of subordinate clauses.

The first English grammarian, William Bullokar, was naturally greatly influenced by these and other grammatical distinctions. In his *Bref Grammar for English* (1586), for example, with his mind turning on the grammar of Latin, he declared that since the subjunctive mood in Latin appears in subordinate clauses preceded by conjunctions, therefore both types *if we be idle* and *when we use diligence* contain a subjunctive. As G. A. Padley puts it, he 'foreshadows a long English tradition of willingness to ascribe purely notional categories to words that are not formally marked for them'.[1] The account that follows details the way in which category errors have slowly been identified, and even more slowly been rooted out, during the last four hundred years. The process is far from over. The nature of standard English grammar is certainly better understood now than at any time in the past. But our language is being subjected to intricate strains and pressures throughout the English-speaking world as it continues to divide and subdivide into scores of distinguishable varieties. There is no shortage of research work being done and remaining to be done. It all seems to be something of a losing battle. An entirely adequate description of English grammar is still a distant target and at present seemingly an unreachable one, the complications being what they are.

Paradigm ecstasy

With the coming of *perestroika*, Eastern European countries like Poland and Hungary are said to be bristling with groups and grouplets raising almost every flag, slogan, and aspiration of the political spectrum: populists, reform economists, radical sociologists, smallholders, evangelical sects, youth groups, Solidarity, syndicalists, and so on.[2] Hungarian political scientists have coined the term 'paradigm ecstasy'[3] to cover this state of affairs.

My theme here is more or less the same – paradigm ecstasy or terminological ecstasy – but the context is of course that of linguistics, not that of politics.

Since the 1960s groups and grouplets of grammarians, in America, Britain, and elsewhere, have transformed the nature of the subject. English grammar has continued to move slowly on its historical axis, but the examining eyes of grammarians have detected patterns and shapes not noticed by earlier scholars, and have applied to these patterns and shapes a bewildering array of competing nomenclatures.

I turn first to the notion that English grammar is continuing to revolve slowly on its historical axis. It is self-evident that present-day English grammar in its standard form is fundamentally different from the system revealed to us, for example, in the writings of King Alfred in the ninth century. At that time English was a language with three-fold grammatical gender in the nominal system, with adjectives that agreed in number and gender with the nouns they qualified, and with a verbal system in which the so-called strong verbs of the *helpan/healp/holpen* type (modE. *help/helped/helped*) held sway over all the others. Most major features of Old English, that is, of the English language spoken and written before 1066, have been substantially modified or abandoned as the centuries passed. The earliest recorded version of our ancestral tongue is now virtually a foreign language. To acquire a working knowledge of its rules and procedures, native English speakers need to regard it as if it were as unEnglish as, say, modern Flemish or Swedish or German.

Grammatical variation outside England

The most radical changes to English grammar seem to have happened before 1776, that is, in the period of about one thousand years between the surviving records of English circa AD 740 and the declaration of American independence. Since then there has been no series of cataclysmic events, no linguistic equivalents of Hurricane Gilbert. Instead a gradual process of splinterings and splits has nudged the main varieties of English apart until now scholars speak of 'Englishes' in the plural, not just of 'English'. One of the best-known learned journals in the field was called *World Language English* from 1982 to 1984, but *World Englishes* since 1985. Its subtitle is 'Journal of English as an International and Intranational Language'. Among the titles of articles in the most recent number (Vol. 7, No. 2, 1988) are 'Developing discourse types in non-native English: strategies of gender in Hindi and Indian English', 'The development of the expression of temporality in the written English narratives of monolingual American and bilingual Mexican pupils', and 'A cross-cultural study of ability to interpret implicatures in English'. The grammatical front line of our language is now as often in far-flung bilingual territories – Mexico, India, Korea, and so on – as in London, Boston, or Sydney. A second front of research is the comparative study of grammatical concepts that English shares with other languages. For example, most Indo-European languages have a passive voice that is normally distinguishable from the active voice. Many non-Indo-European languages do not. The passivity, so normal and ordinary a verbal concept to us, contrasts sharply with other procedures, especially ergativity, in many non-Indo-European languages, among them North American Indian languages and the languages of Australian Aborigines. Linguists from MIT, the Australian National University, and elsewhere, are scrutinizing such things. It is partly a matter of asking 'How do such things work in foreign languages?', and partly a matter of studying unrelated foreign languages to see if they can throw additional light on the strange irregularities of the English language.

Grammatical deviation among the main standard varieties of English tends to be comparatively minor. For example, no standard speaker in England is perplexed by the stage Welshness of one of the characters in Mary Wesley's *Jumping the Queue* (1983):

It says in the *Daily Mirror*, look you.   (ch. xv, p. 105)

or when another in Bernice Rubens' *Mr Wakefield's Crusade* (1985) is reported:

> 'There's posh it is,' she said. 'And I'm not a bit surprised, knowing as
> I do, where all the money comes from.'   (ch. vii, p. 90)

A standard speaker from Canterbury or Cheltenham would just shrug off such minor deviations as distinctive but unpuzzling features of Welsh English.

Similarly almost any modern Australian novel will yield examples of a not-quite-standard Australian use of the conjunction *but*. Placed at the end of a phrase or a sentence it means 'though, however, no doubt about it':

> He's a champion swimmer but. Bronze medal![4]

> Yes, I told 'im. Not the whole of it, but.[5]

In such constructions the conjunction *but* has been put to use as an adverb. Curiously, exactly the same phenomenon has been noted in South African Indian English, clearly as an independent development:

> That was a lovely cat, but.[6]

> It's nice and quiet here, but.[7]

In standard English the conjunction *but* seems to have developed only two new uses since 1776:

(i) (First noted in 1887) Used to give emphasis to something that follows, with the sense of 'indeed': 'I believe you would do it if I asked you!' he said. 'But, of course.' (Marie Corelli, 1887); I'm goin' fix that man, but good. (Ian Fleming, 1965)

(ii) (First noted in 1920) Introducing an emphatic repetition: She knew what it was to be in love, but-in-love. (Katherine Mansfield, 1921); And about everything I talked to her: but everything. (D. H. Lawrence, 1928)[8]

In all other respects, as far as one can tell, the conjunction *but* has kept within the traditional bounds of its use. Grammatical change in the period since 1776 seems to be much slower than either lexical change or phonetic change.

Before moving to my main theme perhaps I may mention an example of a different kind, something which might be called an example of the creaking-gate syndrome. In among the myriad constructions of the noun *use* is a relatively rare one in which the noun phrase *no use* is followed by a *to*-infinitive. I came across it while re-reading T. S. Eliot's *The Family Reunion* (1939):

So it's no use to telephone anywhere.   (p. 65)

The construction is listed in the *OED* (sense 20c) with just one illustrative example from a letter written by Shelley in 1820:

Alas! it is no use to say, 'I'm poor!'

My grammatical files yielded another example from a work of 1980 written by an Australian novelist, Elizabeth Jolley:

I am so overtired it is no use to try to sleep.[9]

In its small way this somewhat unusual construction draws attention to the potential instability of English grammar. Thousands of such constructions stand at the borders of the language, waiting, so to speak, for a jolt to bring them into common use or else to expel them from the language for ever.

But it is time to return to my main theme: that while English grammar has progressed from being a prototypical early Germanic system to one that is sharply distinguishable from that of other Germanic languages, the terms used to describe its nature have proliferated in an astonishing way. Selection is inevitable. My evidence is drawn mostly from the grammars of Ben Jonson (1640), James Greenwood (1722), Joseph Priestley (1768), and Randolph Quirk *et al.* (1985).

Ben Jonson

I begin with Ben Jonson. His grammar, which is no more than a pamphlet of fifty-four pages, was published in 1640. The title-page reads *The English Grammar, Made by Ben. Iohnson. For the benefit of all Strangers, out of his observation of the English Language now spoken, and in use.* It begins with a commendation of the subject itself:

The profit of *Grammar* is great to Strangers, who are to live in communion, and commerce with us; and, it is honourable to our selves. For, by it we communicate all our labours, studies, profits, without an Interpreter.

Above all, he claims, a knowledge of grammar protects us from barbarism, brings out the relationship of English to other languages, and advances the knowledge of our children:

> Wee free our Language from the opinion of Rudenesse, and Barbarisme, wherewith it is mistaken to be diseas'd; We shew the Copie of it, and Matchablenesse, with other tongues; we ripen the wits of our owne Children, and Youth sooner by it, and advance their knowledge.

His Preface contains numerous instructive quotations from the works of Quintilian, Marcus Terentius Varro, Cicero, Julius Caesar Scaliger, and others. Obviously his role model is Latin.

He leads off by systematically comparing the sounds of English with those of Latin. For example:

> R. Is the *Dogs* Letter, and hurreth [vibrates] in the sound; the tongue striking the inner palate, with a trembling about the teeth . . . And so in the *Latine*.

The Latin authors he cites describe the letter *r* in very similar terms:

> Vibrat tremulis ictibus aridum sonorem
> (This harsh sound vibrates with a trembling impact)
>> Terentianus Maurus

> Sonat hìc de nâre caninâ
> (This letter has the sound of a dog's nose)
>> *Litera* Persius Flaccus

More than a third of Jonson's *Grammar* is devoted to pronunciation, something that would be inconceivable now. Part of this section is concerned with the placing of the stress in such pairs as *désert* (noun) and *desért* (verb), *óbject* (noun) and *objéct* (verb). He gives prominence to the fact that many English nouns like Latin ones are stressed on the antepenult – for example, those ending in *-ty*, as *verity*, *charity*, and *simplicity*. Latin, it would seem, governs everything in English.

Jonson says (ch. 9) that there are eight parts of speech in English as in Latin:

Noune	Adverbe	Participle
Pronoune	Conjunction	Interjection
Verbe	Præposition	

'Only,' he says, 'we adde a ninth, which is the *Article*: And that is two-fold,

> *Finite*, as *The*.
> *Infinite*, as *A*.'

The adjective is not regarded as a separate part of speech but rather as a special kind of noun. Nouns, for Jonson, were either 'Nounes Substantive' or 'Nounes Adjective'.

Since Latin nouns fell into declensions, Jonson obviously felt it incumbent on himself to find nominal declensions in English. He decided that there were six:

> *First*, the *Masculine*, which comprehendeth all *Males*, or what is understood under a *Masculine species*: as *Angels, Men, Starres*: and (by *Proso[po]pœia*) the *Moneth's, winds*, almost all the *Planets*.
> Second, the *Feminine*, which compriseth *Women*, and *femal species*: *I'lands. Countries. Cities.* And some *Rivers* with us: as *Severne, Avon*, &c.
> Third, the *Neuter*, or *feined Gender*: whose notion conceives neither *Sexe*; under which are compriz'd all *inanimate* things; a *ship* excepted: of whom we say, *shee sayles well*, though the name be *Hercules*, or *Henry*, the *Prince* . . .
> Fourth, the *Promiscuous*, or *Epicene*, which understands both kindes: especially, when we cannot make the difference; as, when we call them *Horses*, and *Dogges*, in the *Masculine*, though there be *Bitches*, and *Mares* amongst them . . .
> Fift, the *Common* or rather *Doubtfull gender*, wee use often, and with elegance: as in *Cosin, Gossip, friend, Neighbour, Enemie, Servant, Theefe*, &c. When they may be of either Sexe.
> Sixt, is the *Common of three* Genders: by which a *Noune* is divided into *Substantive*, and *Adjective*. For a *Substantive* is a *Noune* of one only

Gender, or (at the most) of two. And an *Adjective* is a *Noune* of three Genders, being alwayes infinite.

It is intellectually chastening to think that generations of children in seventeenth-century grammar schools were encouraged to think that English nouns, like Latin ones, could be classified into genders.

Jonson treated pronouns in a very summary manner: he saw them simply as 'irregular nouns'. He makes no mention of the possessive pronoun *its* though we know that it was firmly in existence during his lifetime. For Jonson (ch. 16), verbs were not 'transitive' and 'intransitive' but 'active' (*love, hate*) and 'neuter' (*pertaine, dye, live*). He recognized that one could not say **he is pertained, *he is died, *he is lived*,[10] though he did not express the distinction between active and neuter verbs in quite that way.

At that time the apostrophe had no possessive force, but was instead a device used to indicate that elision had occurred. As Jonson put it,

> *Apostrophus* is the rejecting of a Vowell from the beginning, or ending of a Word. (Syntaxe, ch. 1)

His examples included *th' outward* (showing the elision of *-e* in *the*), *Moneth's* (in which a final *-e* has been elided), and *I'lands* (showing elision of *s*).

Jonson was aware that certain auxiliaries (*will, doe, may, can, shall, dare*, and in certain circumstances *must* and *lett*) govern a plain infinitive (they 'receive not the sign *to*'). By contrast *ought to* behaves differently:

> When two *Verbes* meet together, whereof one is governed by the other, the latter is put in the infinite,[11] and that with the signe *to*, comming betweene; as *Good men ought to joyne together in good things*.

The concept of modality as applied to verbal auxiliaries like *will/would, can/could, must*, and so on, had not emerged. It would seem that Horne Tooke, in his *Diversions of Purley* (1798), was the first to use 'modal' in a grammatical sense.[12]

Keeping to his mirror-image of Latin, he naturally saw past and future time in English as replicas or translation equivalents of Latin: 'the *futures* are declared by the *infinite*, and the *Verbe, shall*, or *will*: as *Amabo*: *I* shall, or will *love*.'

Clearly in Jonson's *Grammar* we are looking at a museum piece. The parts of speech that are named at all are named in a Latinate manner. All round him the language was showing its unstable hooks and claws. The dramatist in Jonson realized this and his plays show the English language at its abundant best. As a playwright he was a lord of the language but as a grammarian just an obsequious footman.

James Greenwood

Almost a century later, James Greenwood, Sur-Master of St Paul's School, in his *Essay Towards a Practical English Grammar* (2nd edn, 1722),[13] put the subject on a much more professional footing. His aim was 'to excite Persons to the Study of their Mother Tongue'. He was also concerned

> To give such a plain and rational Account of *Grammar*, as might render it easy and delightful to our *English* Youth, who have for a long time esteemed the Study of this Useful Art very irksome, obscure and difficult . . . My *third* Aim [he continued] that I had in the writing this Treatise was, to oblige the *Fair Sex* whose *Education*, perhaps, is too much neglected in this Particular.

Greenwood, like Jonson, believed that English had eight parts of speech. Adjectives, not being one of these, are still called 'Nouns Adjective' (p. 55). *Its* is a routine part of the pronominal system (p. 116). Jonson's six-gender system for nouns has been abandoned. He shows only routine interest in the pronunciation of the letter *r*: it is simply listed with several other consonants which 'have the same Sound with us, as they have for the most part among other Nations' (p. 252). He has much of interest to say about the auxiliaries or 'helping verbs', as he called them (*do/did, can/could*, etc.), and he notes that while they themselves change form the verbs that they 'assist' remain the same: '*I do burn, Thou dost burn, He doth burn*, &c.' (p. 137).

Apostrophes are still regarded as an indication of elision, 'for quicker Pronounciation' (as he spelt the word, I'm afraid). But he was perhaps the first grammarian to record that the apostrophe in such uses as 'Milton's Poems' represented a lost inflexion in *-es* 'in plain imitation of the *Saxon* Genitive Case' (p. 68), something that he had acquired from 'the Learned Dr. *Hicks*' (i.e. the Anglo-Saxon scholar George Hickes,

1642–1715), and that it was not a reflection of a hypothetical construction *Milton his Poems*.

Greenwood was also one of the first grammarians to present a list of irregular verbs. His list[14] is instructive in that it includes paradigms that are now obsolete:

Present Tense	Preter Tense
Dare	Durst or Dared
Dig	Dug and *Digged[15]
Drink	*Drank or Drunk
Fraight	Fraught
Ride	Rid or Rode
Shine	Shined & shone
Thrive	Throve and *Thrived
Win	Won and *wan

Past tenses like *digged*, *shined*, *thrived*, and *wan*, and a present tense like *fraight* are reminders that a great many irregular verbs have continued to be unstable up to the present day. We should not be surprised, therefore, when *snuck* is beginning to pose a threat to *sneaked* in some modes of modern English speech, and also *dove* to *dived*.

Greenwood was a schoolmaster, and in good schoolmasterly fashion he ends his book with a section written by 'Mr. Dennis' entitled 'A Praxis on the Grammar'. It was a straightforward set of exercises in parsing. 'In these Sentences following,' he says, 'tell me what Part of Speech every Word *is* and *why*.' The second Praxis is the Lord's Prayer, and it starts like this:

> *Our*] Is a Pronoun Possessive put for the first Person of the Plural Number . . .
> *Father*] Is a Noun Substantive . . .
> *Which*] Is a Relative . . . It is spoken both of Things and Persons, (tho' chiefly of Things) as *who* and *whom* are used when we speak of *Persons*, . . .

Thus, by 1722, the scene was set for the next two centuries during which schoolchildren sat at their desks and struggled to name the parts of speech with varying degrees of success.

Joseph Priestley

The polymath Joseph Priestley, discoverer of oxygen, forerunner of Bentham's principle of Utilitarianism, philosopher and radical politician, wrote perhaps the best of all eighteenth-century grammars. It was published in 1761[16] and was called *The Rudiments of English Grammar.* In many respects it is conservative but there are some quite startling innovations.

He begins (p. vi) by rejecting the terminology of Latin grammar when speaking of English:

> I own I am surprized to see so much of the distribution, and technical terms of the Latin grammar, retained in the grammar of our tongue; where they are exceedingly aukward, and absolutely superfluous.

He therefore rejects the notion of a future tense in English (p. vii):

> A little reflection may, I think, suffice to convince any person, that we have no more business with *a future tense* in our language, than we have with the whole system of Latin moods and tenses; because we have no modification of our verbs to correspond to it; and if we had never heard of a future tense in some other language, we should no more have given a particular name to the combination of the verb with the auxiliary *shall* or *will*, than to those that are made with the auxiliaries *do, have, can, must*, or any other.

In a good scientific manner, he defines the grammar of a language as 'a collection of observations on the structure of it, and a system of rules for the proper use of it' (p. 1). His illustrative examples are drawn, he says, 'from modern writings, rather than from those of Swift, Addison, and others, who wrote about half a century ago' (p. xi). 'By this means,' he says, 'we may see what is the real character and turn of the language at present' (p. xi). In practice this seems to mean that he drew his evidence from authors like Bolingbroke, David Hume, Samuel Johnson, and Smollett. The dates fit, but as a matter of fact he also quoted extensively from seventeenth- and early eighteenth-century authors.

The adjective is at last judged to be an independent part of speech, but the number of such parts remains at eight. He added the adjective but discarded the participle. Much traditional terminology was retained: for example, he must have been one of the last grammarians to call the past tense of verbs the 'preter' tense. He might have been a radical politician but as a grammarian he can be classed only as semi-radical. This halfwayness is underlined by the fact that he divides verbs into those that are 'transitive' and those that are 'neuter': in other words his terminology is a medley of the new and the old.

His list of irregular verbs (pp. 47–52) differs in several respects from that of James Greenwood, though he was writing only forty years later.

Radical form	Preter Tense	Participle pret.
dare	durst*[17]	dared
dig	dug*	dug*
drink	drank	drunk
ride	rode	ridden
shine	shone	shone*
thrive	throve	thriven
win	won	won

Digged, fraight, shined, thrived, and *wan* have disappeared. The conjugational system has moved on a cog, its permanent state of instability once more confirmed.

The second part of the 1768 edition is made up of 'Notes and Observations, For the Use of those who have made some Proficiency in the Language'. This section turns out to be one of the earliest attempts at compiling a usage manual.

> Sometimes [he says] we find an apostrophe used in the plural number, when the noun ends in a vowel; as in *inamorato's, toga's, tunica's, Otho's, a set of virtuoso's*. Addison on Medals.

> The *idea's* of the author have been conversant with the faults of other writers. Swift's *Tale of a Tub*, p. 55.

Priestley simply reports the use and does not condemn it. A hundred years later Henry Alford, Dean of Canterbury, in his fully-fledged usage manual *The Queen's English* (1864), regarded this practice with puzzlement:

> 26. There seems to be some doubt occasionally felt about the apostrophe . . . One not uncommonly sees outside an inn, that '*fly's*' and '*gig's*' are to be let. In a country town blessed with more than one

railway, I have seen an omnibus with 'RAILWAY STATION'S' painted in emblazonry on its side.

27. It is curious, that at one time this used to be, among literary men, the usual way of writing the plurals of certain nouns. In the 'Spectator,' . . . Addison writes '*Purcell's opera's*' with an apostrophe before the '*s*'. And we find '*the making of grotto's*' mentioned as a favourite employment of ladies in that day.

Modern grammarians firmly reject this use as incorrect:

it is incorrect (though not uncommon in shop notices) to use '*s* for plurals that are not genitives (*1 lb of tomato's*).[18]

But it looks like being ineradicable.

Priestley goes on to consider all manner of things which are associated with writers like H. W. Fowler: the plural of words of foreign origin ('some people write *criterions*, others *criteria*', p. 58); the choice between *the two Miss Thomsons* and *the two Misses Thomson*; grammatical concord used after nouns ending in *s* like *oats*, *odds*, *measles*, *shambles*, *tidings*, *vespers*, and many others; the use by tradesmen of *twenty pound* (not *pounds*), one of various uses, he comments, that some might think 'a very harsh ellipsis, but custom authorizes it'. It is all very illuminating, and in its way quite chastening, to find that discussions about such matters have been going on for more than two hundred years, and that most of them are still unresolved.

Priestley was one of the first grammarians to notice the possessive gerund, though he did not call it that. He regarded 'I remember *its* being reckoned a great exploit' as more elegant than 'I remember *it* being reckoned a great exploit' (p. 70). He also identified the double genitive:[19]

In some cases we use both the genitive and the preposition *of*; as, *this book of my friend's*. Sometimes, indeed, this method is quite necessary, in order to distinguish the sense . . . *This picture of my friend*, and *this picture of my friend's*, suggest very different ideas . . . Where this double genitive, as it may be called, is not necessary to distinguish the sense, and especially in grave style, it is generally omitted.

(pp. 71–2)

Most memorably, perhaps, he drew attention to incorrect concord in the use of pronouns (p. 102):

> Contrary, as it evidently is, to the analogy of the language, the nominative case is sometimes found after verbs and prepositions. It has even crept into writing. *The chaplain intreated my comrade and* I *to dress as well as possible.* World displayed, vol. I, p. 163. *He told my Lord and* I. Fair American, vol. I, p. 141.

He was the first grammarian, of those whose works are familiar to me, to draw attention to this erroneous use. It is sad to think that after two centuries of condemnation the erroneous use is still very widespread. The defending troops are becoming a little weary of the battle.

A partial survey

I have drawn attention to the way in which grammarians addressed themselves to the problem of analysing English grammar between 1586 and 1768. The outline pattern is one of a reluctant recognition that Latin paradigms were far from ideal models for the English language. Quite primary connections remained: both languages, for example, depended on a Subject/Verb/Object system even if the arrangement of the elements was more flexible in one language than in the other. Give or take a name or two, the names given to the parts of speech, to cases of nouns, to verbal moods (subjunctive, indicative, imperative, infinitive), were broadly similar. But Priestley's *Rudiments of English Grammar* was a privotal work. Its rejection of the terms of Latin grammar took the subject into a more natural climate. His treatment was in a broad sense descriptive, not prescriptive, though the intellectual shackles of his age are still visible in parts of his work. A monograph on the history of usage manuals – something not yet attempted by anyone – would find his *Rudiments* a useful starting-point. Landmarks that lay ahead of him included the grammars and usage books of William Cobbett (1823), Henry Alford (1864), Henry Sweet (1892–8), Otto Jespersen (1909–49), and a great many others. Step by step the magnitude of the task of ascertaining the rules and assumptions of English grammar became apparent.

The relatively small portion of the subject that concerned itself with the public awareness of uses and constructions that were arguably either 'correct' or 'incorrect', or were at any rate 'debatable', fell into the hands of writers like Henry Alford, H. W. Fowler, Ernest Gowers, Eric Partridge, and, most recently, Robert Ilson, Sidney Greenbaum, and Janet Whitcut. Similar guides were written by Americans like William Strunk and E. B. White, by William and Mary Morris, and a good many others. The major publishing houses issued their own guides to house style, among them *Hart's Rules for Compositors and Readers at the University Press Oxford*, *The Oxford Dictionary for Writers and Editors*, and *The Chicago Manual of Style*. There is a public hunger for such prescriptive books that is never quite satisfied.

As for grammar, the new mode, since the 1960s, is decidedly descriptive, rather than prescriptive. Revolutionary new methods of parsing have been presented in monograph after monograph. The names of Noam Chomsky, M. A. K. Halliday, and Rodney Huddleston are now writ large in nearly all grammatical work. Historical approaches have been thrown out or side-lined. Algebraic symbols and other traffic rules of Symbolic Logic have been imported into formal descriptions of English grammar. Written evidence from novelists, poets, and playwrights plays no part in this new style of grammar. The examples are neatly drawn from the fertile brains of the grammarians themselves, or at best from tape-recorded informal speech. To those of us brought up in a more literary and humane tradition, much of this new work is 'like dead flowers in a dry landscape'.[20] But there is no doubt at all that to the present generation of students in our universities the new techniques seem more attractive and more convincing than the old ones – grammatical semantics, computational linguistics and cognitive science hold sway. Historical linguistics is everywhere in retreat.

The naming of parts has become an industry of unparalleled proportions. It is in no way surprising that this has come about. Closer scrutiny of English grammar, an examination of all the normalities and all the constraints, has revealed seams and streaks in the language all round us that were previously ignored or not noticed at all. And these new seams and streaks need names.

In the most ambitious practical grammar of our age, *A Comprehensive Grammar of the English Language* (1985), edited by Professor Sir Randolph Quirk and three colleagues, certain kinds of adjectives, some pronouns, and the articles are placed in a group called *determiners*. These *determiners* are divided into predeterminers (*double* the sum), central determiners (half *my* salary), and postdeterminers (my *three* children). We are reminded that any alteration of the order of elements would change the meaning (the *double* sum, my *half* salary) or would produce an unacceptable construction (**three* my children). Obviously, invisible constraints are at work. The positioning of such elements was not noticed, or was not thought significant, by the grammarians whose works I have described earlier.

To the early grammarians, pronouns were just pronouns and their position in the sentence was presumably regarded as something not worth commenting on. In *CGEL*, pronouns, and some other parts of speech, are designated as *anaphoric* (backward-looking) or *cataphoric* (forward-looking): (anaphoric) *John bought* a bicycle, *but when he rode* it *one of the wheels came off* / (cataphoric) *On* his *arrival in the capital*, the Secretary of State *declared support for the government*.

Adverbs and adverbial phrases are divided into four groups called *adjuncts, subjuncts, disjuncts*, and *conjuncts*, a real enough gang of four, though, because of borderline cases, the new grouping will inevitably be seen in the new General Certificate of Secondary Education syllabus as a newly contrived form of mental punishment. Adjectives are divided into customary groups, according to whether they can be naturally used in both the attributive position and the predicative, or whether they are normally restricted to one or the other position. But they are further divided into *emphasizers* (a *true* scholar: note that it is not idiomatic to say **as a scholar he is true*), and *amplifiers* (a *complete* fool).

The new terminological mood is confirmed when *many* and *a few* are called *multal* and *paucal quantifiers* (6.53), and in the frequent use of terms like *approximator subjunct, ditransitive construction*, and *ingredient preposition*.

One of the topics discussed by Rodney Huddleston in his *Introduction to the Grammar of English* (1984) is the nature and behaviour of modal verbs. Drawing on that branch of Logic that deals with modality, he distinguishes two kinds of possibility and necessity, which he calls *epistemic* and *deontic*. These types are set down in tabular form (p. 166):

	Epistemic	Deontic
Possibility	i *You may be under a misapprehension*	ii *You may take as many as you like*
Necessity	iii *You must be out of your mind*	iv *You must work harder*

His is the authentic voice of the 1980s. This is an epistemic and a deontic age, an age characterized by plain sentences filleted into complex metalanguages, and one in which literary works have become banned books in the studies of Professors of Linguistics.

Traditional grammarians have enormous respect for the insights of modern grammarians like Rodney Huddleston, but wonder why the evidence cited must always be so threadbare. For example, Huddleston shows how the verb *to be* has the power to highlight or focus attention on a particular statement, producing what he calls 'cleft' and 'pseudo-cleft' constructions (p. 459):

i. *A faulty switch caused the trouble*   (not highlighted)
ii. *It was a faulty switch that caused the trouble*   (cleft construction)
iii. *What caused the trouble was a faulty switch*   (pseudo-cleft construction)

A traditional grammarian would illustrate the same types of construction from a verifiable source:

i. *Country lords know the country*   (not highlighted)
ii. *It is we country lords who know the country* (T. S. Eliot, *Murder in the Cathedral*, 1935, p. 31)   (cleft)
iii. *What country lords know is the country*   (pseudo-cleft)

Illustrative examples for cleft and pseudo-cleft sentences abound in written works as well as in spoken English:

It is we who are inappropriate. The painting was here first. (Penelope Lively, *Moon Tiger*, 1987, p. 149)   (cleft)
What he [sc. Bernie Grant MP] concedes the House has done is to increase his status, nationally and internationally. (*Listener*, 6 Oct. 1988, p. 16)   (pseudo-cleft)

It is a far cry from the simple portraits of English grammar sketched in the sixteenth and seventeenth centuries to the substantial, 1,800-

page *Comprehensive Grammar of the English Language* published in the middle of the 1980s. The rules and structures governing the complex ways in which we go about forming sentences are better understood now than at any time in the past. The task is nowhere near finished, though, if only because of the restructuring of the English language in all the areas where it is spoken and written abroad. There are many points in our language where the structure itself is unstable. Brittleness lurks at the boundaries of the language and in some of its central systems too.

Notes

1. G. A. Padley, *Grammatical Theory in Western Europe 1500–1700. Trends in Vernacular Grammar II*, 1988, p. 237.
2. Timothy Garton Ash in *New York Review of Books*, 13 October 1988, p. 3.
3. See Rudolf L. Tökes, 'The Science of Politics in Hungary in the 1980s', in *Südosteuropa*, Vol. 37, 1/1988, p. 15 and *passim*.
4. M. Pople, *The Other Side of the Family*, 1986, p. 15.
5. D. Malouf, *Antipodes*, 1985, cited from 1986 paperback reprint, p. 141. The earliest example of this construction in *The Australian National Dictionary*, 1988, is one of 1853, but it does not seem to have come into regular use in Australia until the 1930s.
6., 7. Both examples cited by R. Mesthrie in *English World-Wide*, 1987, VIII. 272. In subsequent discussions I was informed by several people that the construction is commonly used in northern counties of England, in Scotland, and in Ireland.
8. All four examples are taken from *OEDS*, Volume 1.
9. *Palomino* (p. 40 in a 1984 paperback reprint).
10. The asterisk used here is the usual modern convention to indicate that the construction in question is meaningless or unacceptable.
11. This example antedates the earliest one (1871) listed in the *OED* s.v. *Infinite* adj. 7. The use of *infinite* as a noun in a grammatical sense is not listed in the *OED*.
12. *OED Modal* adj. 5.
13. I was unable to consult the first edition of 1711, but my comments do not hinge on the difference of dates between the two editions.
14. Greenwood actually gives two separate tables. Some of the forms quoted here are from Table I and some from Table II.
15. Greenwood added an asterisk to forms that 'are not proper or usual'.
16. My quotations are drawn from a revised edition of 1768.
17. Priestley says that 'when the regular inflection is in use, as well as the irregular one, an asterism is put' (p. 47).
18. *Longman Guide to English Usage* (1988), p. 50.
19. Priestley's use of the expression 'double genitive' antedates the earliest example (1824) listed in the *OED* s.v. *Genitive* sb.
20. Cited from my book, *The English Language*, 1985, p. 155.

3 The Boundaries of English Grammar

Definitions

An anecdotal definition of 'grammar' is implied in a cartoon in the 7 September 1987 issue of *The New Yorker*. It shows a traffic cop issuing a summons to a van-driver. The van has the owners' name painted on the outside: ME AND WALLYS PRODUCE. And the caption reads: 'Sorry, but I'm going to have to issue you with a summons for reckless grammar and driving without an apostrophe.'

More seriously, definitions of the words 'grammar', 'syntax', and 'parsing' lie at the centre of modern computer work. My dBASE II User Manual (1984) lists numerous 'error messages' like 'BAD FILE NAME' and 'NO "FOR" PHRASE'. The advice given is stern: 'syntax error in file name' and 'rewrite command with correct syntax'. The compilers of the User Manual assume that one knows what 'syntax error' and 'correct syntax' mean. Computer-users soon learn that the miraculous powers of personal computers are based on avoidance of error.

In the *Dictionary of Computing* (OUP, 1983) there are definitions of 'syntax' and related words. A *grammar* 'consists of a set of rules (called *productions*) that may be used to derive one string from another by substring replacement'. *Syntax* is 'the rules defining the legal sequences of elements in a language – in the case of a programming language, of characters in a program'. A *string* is 'any one-dimensional array of characters'. *Parsing* or *syntax analysis* is 'the process of deciding whether a string of input symbols is a sentence of a given language and if so determining the syntactic structure of the string as defined by a grammar . . . for the language'.

An understanding of the processes involved is vital for all kinds of computer-driven operations, for example in the worlds of air traffic control, meteorology, the launching of spacecraft, and star wars technology. Errorless syntax is essential if some disaster is to be averted. Most schoolchildren now know about the technical constraints of computer software and cheerfully accept them. So do weather forecasters, air traffic controllers, and the controllers of spacecraft at Cape Canaveral.

The point of computer parsing in scholarly work is to make it possible for particular linguistic items or features to be systematically retrieved from the electronic databases of sophisticated but unintelligent computers. A computer will unerringly locate and retrieve typographical distinctions and sequences of letters or signals when commanded to do so. One must keep in mind, however, that computers are unable to 'work out' the *meaning* of even the simplest of words. A computer, even of the most powerful kind, cannot be programmed to distinguish the noun *run* from the verb *run*, or any of the senses of the word from other senses. A very sophisticated program indeed is needed to produce a command which will distinguish 'L.' used as an abbreviation of 'Latin' from the 'L.' of 'A. L. Rowse', or 'O.N.' as an abbreviation of 'Old Norse' from the preposition or adverb 'on', as I found to my dismay recently.

It looks as if the computer senses of 'grammar', 'syntax', and 'parsing' will soon become the dominant ones, as the study of linguistic grammar recedes. In practice, even now, a Polytech course with any of these words in the title is much more likely to be about the computer kind than the kind written about by Henry Sweet or Otto Jespersen.

Syntax and phonology

An area of considerable interest to modern scholars is that of syntactic influences on phonological rules. Much of the research is cross-linguistic, that is, it is concerned with searching for patterns in English that correspond to patterns in other languages. A routine example of such syntactic influence on English phonology is the rule of auxiliary reduction: *do not* → *don't*, *will not* → *won't*, but *is not* → *isn't* (i.e. no change), *are not* → *aren't* (no change), and *am I not* → *aren't I* (but often *amn't I* in Scotland and Ireland). An example of the reverse process, that is, of phonological reduction influencing syntax, is shown by such reduced forms as *wanna* (= want to), with loss of the sign *to* before a following infinitive, and *coulda* (= could have), *shoulda* (= should have), and *woulda* (=would have) followed by a past participle, in each of which the final *-a* takes the place of an auxiliary.

Phonology Yearbook 4 (1987) shows comparable processes at work in several foreign languages: tone sandhi in Xiamen (a language in China), phrasal tone insertion in Kimatuumbi (Tanzania), and fast speech rules, involving elision of vowels, in modern Greek and modern Italian. Important comparative work of this kind is particularly associated with the names of two American scholars, Ellen M. Kaisse (University of Washington, Seattle) and Elisabeth O. Selkirk (University of Massachusetts, Amherst), especially a book called *Connected Speech* (1985) by Kaisse and one called *Phonology and Syntax* (1984) by Selkirk.

As Kaisse remarks (p. 1):

> Those who have learned a foreign language word by word from books and then found themselves unable to understand the train conductor's patient explanation about which cars go to Milan (or Bangkok) will attest that, in normal conversation, words have an irresistible tendency to blur together; the last vowel of one merges with the first vowel of another, consonants assimilate or disappear altogether, the tones are not pronounced the way they are listed in the glossary, and some little words may be so reduced as to be unperceivable.

The same phenomena occur in English and a great deal of work is being done now on the syntax of connected English speech. The most important study of conversational English to be published so far is *A Corpus of English Conversation* (1980) by Jan Svartvik and Randolph Quirk. The texts they transcribe are riddled with special signs – arrows, stars, angled brackets, and so on – to indicate the end of a tone unit, the onset of a new syllable, nucleus tone symbols, relative pitch, and numerous other features of informal conversation. A typical passage is reproduced in Figure 1.

Fast speech rules are an aspect of social interaction in day-to-day transactions, and a considerable amount of research is being carried out in this area. One field being investigated is that of service encounters, for instance at a post office, a souvenir shop, or a travel agency. The researcher, who is equipped with a portable cassette recorder and two small microphones, eavesdrops on such ordinary quotidian exchanges.

B 982 and ‖very ÓFTEN∎ 983 you ‖get a ₐstudent 'who · ₐprobably ΔDÒES
understand the PÁSSAGE∎ · 984 but be‖cause he feels he ΔMÙSTN'T use the
☆words of☆ the PÁSSAGE∎ ☆☆–☆☆ 985 ‖gives

A 986 ☆《‖QUI͞TE∎》☆ 987 ☆☆《‖YĒS∎》☆☆

> B 985 you the im₎pression that he ☆ₐDÔESN'T under₎stand it∎☆ - 988 be‖cause
he's ₐused words which ₎aren't so ₐGÔOD∎

A 989 ☆‖[m̃] {‖[m̃] {‖[m̃]∎} ∎} ∎☆ 990 ‖yes QUÍTE∎ · 991 ‖YĒS∎ · 992 ‖YĒS∎

B 993 ‖ÀNYWAY∎ 994 I ‖think we've got ᐧARÌD of that at LÁST∎ 995 ‖I've been
CAMₐPÀIGNING for THÁT∎ 996 for ‖several ΔYÈARS NÓW∎ 997 and in ‖ÀNY
▷case {I ‖MÈAN∎} ∎ · 998 ‖why ΔSHÒULD we {‖test the two things
TOGÈTHER∎} ∎ · 999 we're sup'‖posed to be ₎testing ΔSÙMMARY {‖in that
QUÈSTION∎} ∎ · 1000 ‖then Δwhy introduce ΔPÀRAPHRASE∎ - 1001 we're
‖also going to get rid of those the ₎questions three and ₐFÒUR∎ - 1002 ‖that
came ÓUT∎ 1003 it'll it'll ‖have to go through the [k ði] ₐCÒUNCIL of
▷course∎

A 1004 [ə] ‖which questions ☆are you REₐFÈRRING ▷to∎☆

B 1005 ☆‖these [ɔə]☆ ₎odds and ΔSÒDS ▷questions {you ‖KNÒW∎} ∎

A 1006 you're ‖[g] Δgetting RÌD of them 《ÁRE you∎ 1007 ☆‖LÀTER∎ ·
1008 ‖GÒOD∎》☆

B 1009 ☆‖YÈS∎ 1010 [ə] it was ‖passed☆ at [ði: ?ə ði ə] ₐsub–committee Δlast
☆ΔTÙESDAY∎☆

Figure 1. Jan Svartvik and Randolph Quirk, *A Corpus of English Conversation*
(C. W. K. Gleerup, Lund, 1980), p. 51.

A recent study by a Finnish scholar, Eija Ventola, *The Structure of Social
Interaction* (1987), is a typical example of this branch of the subject. It is
a study of the conversational modes of numerous sets of people,
including one between *S* (a shop assistant) and *C* (a customer). The text
of such an encounter is reproduced in Figure 2 (p. 44).

They go on to discuss the price and to look at other kinds of mobiles.
In due course *C* buys one, *S* says 'thanks very much', *C* says 'good',
collects her things and leaves the shop.

Such service encounters make up a small Halliday-inspired corner of
semiotics. The situations are on the face of it simple, while the
metalanguage arising from them is not. The framework of analysis
involves terms like 'lexical cohesion', 'context-dependent semantic
networks', and 'speech function networks'. Such books form part of the
drift away from traditional grammars which concentrated on the written

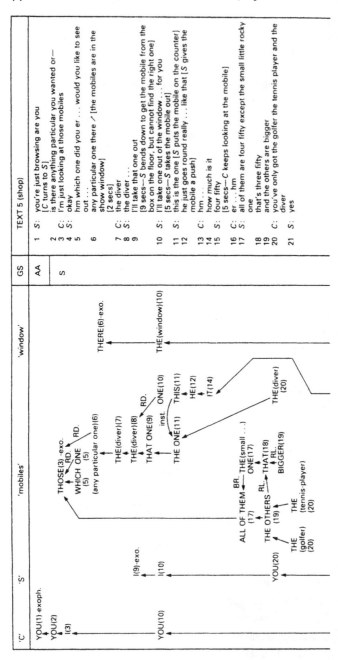

Figure 2. Eija Ventola, *The Structure of Social Interaction: a Systemic Approach to the Semiotics of Service Encounters* (Francis Pinter, London, 1987), p. 200.

language of ideal English speakers. The number of such service encounters is, of course, infinite, and the conventions change with the passage of time. It looks like being a field of research for many years to come. It is perhaps worth noting too that, because English is now an international language, more than ever before overseas scholars writing papers on aspects of the language outnumber those from this country. Eija Ventola is a Finn and her book was based on service encounters in Australia.

Philosophy and grammar

It seems a bold thing to do to place the philosophical study of grammar on the boundaries of the subject. It might have been more tactful to use expressions like 'bedrock' or 'ground of being.' But let me try to show what I mean by turning to some remarks of Wittgenstein's on grammar. In paragraph 45 of his *Philosophical Investigations* (1953) he writes:

> The demonstrative 'this' can never be without a bearer. It might be said: 'so long as there is a *this*, the word "this" has a meaning too, whether *this* is simple or complex.' – But this does not make the word into a name. On the contrary: for a name is not used with, but only explained by means of, the gesture of pointing.

The reasoning is sound, but of course he does not go on to set out the deictic uses of the demonstrative pronoun itself. He just defines its nature.

Wittgenstein sees language as a tool with an indefinitely large number of uses and relationships. Perhaps his most famous dicta concern language as a rule-governed game of great complexity: (1) The sentence 'Excalibur has a sharp blade' made sense, he says, even when Excalibur was broken in pieces, because in this language-game 'a name is also used in the absence of its bearer' (para 44); and (2) 'For a *large* class of cases – though not for all – in which we employ the word "meaning" it can be defined thus: the meaning of a word is its use in the language' (para 43). The second of these two dicta can be interpreted as a prop to the view that usage, even if 'illogical', 'untraditional', or 'believed to be wrong', is the only true guide to acceptability.

Wittgenstein is an excellent guide to the outlying boundaries and the primary assumptions of grammar. So, too, is Professor P. F. Strawson, one of the pioneers of what is called pragmatics. Strawson[1] draws a distinction between the 'essential grammar' of a language and its 'variable grammar', and he lays stress on the fact that 'a perspicuous grammar of a language is one in which the actual formal syntactical arrangements of the language are presented as realizations of the essential grammar of the language-type to which the language belongs' (p. 75f.).

One must pay all due regard to such primary statements of philosophical belief as those of Wittgenstein and Strawson, but once accepted such statements tend to recede into a kind of black hole. We know they exist but we are not quite sure how they help to interpret the cruel asymmetrical facts of a given language.

Discourse analysis and pragmatics

Service encounters in shops and travel agencies are, of course, only a part of the whole subject of discourse. A standard work on the subject, *Discourse Analysis* (1983) by Gillian Brown and George Yule, examines the strategies and techniques of ordinary conversations. Typical features of spoken language are:

(1) It contains many incomplete sentences.
(2) It typically makes little use of clause-subordination.
(3) Constructions are joined not so much by conjunctions or relative pronouns as by pauses:
    it's quite nice the Grassmarket since + it's always had the antique shops but they're looking + they're sort of + em + become a bit nicer + (p. 16)

Such language hardly responds to a traditional parts-of-speech approach. Key terms in discourse analysis are *reference, presupposition, implicature,* and *inference.* Let me briefly illustrate two of these. Brown and Yule point out that the statement *My uncle's coming home from Canada on Sunday* contains several *presuppositions* for the hearer to absorb: the speaker has an uncle, who may always have lived in Canada, or may have just had a holiday there, it is on a day before Sunday that the conversation occurs, and so on (pp. 28ff.)

If person A remarks *I am out of petrol* and B replies *There is a garage round the corner,* we have an example of conversational *implicature.*

Speaker B implies that the garage is open and selling petrol, and by adding *round the corner* is plainly implying that the problem of a lack of petrol in the vehicle or container can be solved quickly. It is an attractive subject – there are presuppositions and implicatures in virtually everything we say or write. The terminology, which is largely drawn from the work of the philosopher H. P. Grice, is gradually settling into general use among scholars who are not themselves discourse analysts.

Another subject lying in the outer suburbs of traditional grammar is *pragmatics*. The term was introduced just over fifty years ago (1937) by the philosopher Charles Morris as a branch of semiotics. He defined it as the study of 'the relation of signs to interpreters'. In Stephen C. Levinson's book *Pragmatics* (1983), the subject is redefined as 'the study of those relations between language and context that are grammaticalized, or encoded in the structure of a language' (p. 9). In practice it is concerned with the presuppositions and other elements agreed between the speakers of a language that enable them to communicate with one another. Some pragmaticists concern themselves mainly with communicative competence, others with contextual disambiguation. The arguments are heavily loaded with the terminology of the philosopher J. L. Austin, in other words with concepts like *explicit performatives*, *implicit performatives*, *locutionary acts*, *illocutionary acts*, and *perlocutionary acts*. Types of apparently simple commands or admonitions – *Shoot her!* and *You can't do that* and *I warn you the bull will charge* – need to be placed in their correct pragmatic bins. It shares many features with discourse analysis. It, too, is a world of inferences, implications, and suppositions. For example, in a conversation between a child and her mother

Child: Mummy $\left.\vphantom{\begin{matrix}a\\b\end{matrix}}\right\}$ Pre-sequence
Mother: Yes dear

Child: I want a cloth to clean the windows } The request itself

there is a pre-sequence – which is strictly unnecessary but is polite. In other contexts there are *pre-arrangements*, *insertion sequences*, *pre-announcements*, in what is said or written.

It is all a far cry from the grammatical analyses of Ben Jonson, James Greenwood, and Joseph Priestley. They were looking at the language with a telescope from a high hill. Ours is the century of the zoom lens and the electron microscope.

Diachronic and synchronic

Even when we move away from the philosophical edges or bases of grammar we need to take a further primary division into account: that between a *diachronic* (or historical) treatment of grammar and a *synchronic* (or descriptive) one. The first of these approaches held sway down through the ages, but the second is now dominant. A simple example of the difference between the two methods must suffice.

The normal plural inflexion of English words is, of course, -s or -es (*book-s, church-es*), but there is a small group of nouns with a different pattern altogether, nouns like *goose/geese, man/men, mouse/mice*, and so on. The plural forms *geese, men, mice*, etc., are explained diachronically as 'i-mutation plurals', that is, in Primitive Old English an -i- forming part of the unstressed plural inflexion caused certain vowels in the preceding stem to mutate before it disappeared itself.

Synchronic scholars, by contrast, account for the distinction by saying that words like *books* and *churches* each have two morphemes, *book* and *s, church* and *es*. A word like *book-bind-er-s* has four, *book* + *bind* + *er* + *s*. Since such partitioning is impossible in words like *geese, men*, and *mice*, synchronicists fall back on the view that each consists of two formants, *goose* + PLURAL, man + PLURAL, and *mouse* + PLURAL. For flexionless plurals like *sheep*, synchronic scholars resolve the problem by inventing the concept of a *zero morpheme*.

Traditional grammarians are predisposed to think that grammatical irregularities or surface ambiguity in sentences can be resolved by pursuing the history of a form or construction. Synchronic grammarians, on the other hand, try to solve such problems 'logically'. Thus, for example, Rodney Huddleston leads off in his *Introduction to the Grammar of English* (1984) with two diagrams that draw attention to the ambiguity of the sentence *Liz attacked the man with a knife*. Quirk *et al.* (1985, p. 570) illustrate courtesy subjuncts by a sequence of sentences that are acceptable:

Kindly leave the room
Please leave the room
Leave the room, *please*

and one that is not:

*Leave the room, *kindly*.

No modern grammarian completely merges the two approaches, though there is a certain amount of partial merging. For example the word *morpheme* (*base, bound, free, lexical, root, stem morphemes*) occurs repeatedly in *CGEL*, but nowhere, I fancy, in R. W. Zandvoort's *Handbook of English Grammar* (7th edn, 1975) or Bruce Mitchell's *Old English Syntax* (1985).

The problem of nomenclature does not end there, of course. There is not much common ground between the two approaches. In practice grammarians in the fast lane use modern terminology but usually display no knowledge of earlier forms of English and do not quote from identified printed sources. Traditional grammarians, now a disappearing group, master earlier forms of English, acquire a sufficient knowledge of influential languages like Latin and Greek, and quote freely from printed sources as well as oral sources.

The central territory of grammar

So far I have been concerned mostly with the peripheral territory of grammar. I now turn to the central ground, the rule-governed network of grammar that governs effective communication in the main standard varieties of our language. An excellent starting-point is the definition of the word *grammar* in the *OED*:

> That department of the study of a language which deals with its inflexional forms or other means of indicating the relations of words in the sentence, and with the rules for employing these in accordance with established usage; usually including also the department which deals with the phonetic system of the language and the principles of its representation in writing.

Despite the stultifyingly boring and resultless discussions by some grammarians about the 'meaning' of the word *sentence* – how it is to be distinguished from the word *utterance*, for example – and the word *word*, it is clear that the Victorian definers of the word *grammar* in the *OED* recognized that an ascertainable set of rules accounts for all, or at any rate most of, the constructions of a given language at a given time. Their definition has survived unscathed, except that 'the phonetic system of the language and the principles of its representation in writing' are now usually dealt with briefly in grammars and much more fully in separate reference works.

Standard English

What is 'Standard English', or, as it is commonly called, 'Received Standard English'? The current edition of the *Concise Oxford Dictionary* defines it as the 'form of English speech used, with local variations, by the majority of educated English-speaking people'. This makes it sound as if it is the 'speech' of a large number of people, unless we place a narrow definition on the word 'educated'. Consider the matter more closely. Take the case of an RP-speaking student returning to his college in Oxford (the centre of gravity of Standard English) from a visit abroad. Let us assume that the student is male. He leaves the plane and enters a series of RP-free zones. He passes through customs and immigration, catches a terminal bus, joins a train from Paddington, calls for milk and a Big Mac on the way to his college from the Oxford station, greets the lodge porter, and joins his fellow undergraduates in the Junior Common Room, at least 40 per cent of whom will be from northern or other pronouncedly un-RP counties. How many 'educated' speakers of Standard English will he have encountered on the journey? A touch of Jamaica here, a tinge of Cockney there, strains of Belfast or Dublin or Liverpool or Glasgow at almost every one of the stages. The point is obvious. Recognizable forms of Standard English, in speech *and* writing, are to be found in a relatively small proportion of the population of England, possibly as small a number as five million. We move round using our various dialects and idiolects surrounded by, *overwhelmed by*, walls and barriers of unmatching sounds and dissimilar constructions.

For convenience I am dealing here only with the Standard English of England. Other forms of English are left out of account. I can safely assume, I imagine, that no speaker of Standard English in England would naturally say

> You can go sit someplace else as far as I'm concerned
> (Garrison Keillor, *Lake Wobegon Days*, 1986, p. 175)

or

> We can sell this house, you can come live with us.
> (Lee Smith, *Cakewalk*, 1983, p. 227)

Such constructions of *go* and *come* followed by a plain infinitive are, of course, part of the apparatus of another rule-governed Standard, that of the United States. So, too, is the type *order* (verb) followed by an object and past participle:

> two gunmen burst into the cockpit and ordered the plane flown to Algeria.   *(Christian Science Monitor,* 8–14 June 1987, p. 16)

The construction is not opaque but Standard British English would require 'ordered the plane *to be* flown to Algeria'.

A rich cargo

I believe that it is imperative to see modern English grammar as a rich and diverse linguistic system deposited on our shores 1,500 years ago, and left with us *unweakened*, though substantially changed by the social and political events of the intervening period. I place stress on the word 'unweakened'. I also place stress on the fact that each element in our systems of grammar is a legacy from the past, with a logical and traceable history. I believe that any system of grammar that aims only to describe current English without reference to the past is intrinsically defective and potentially misleading. The process of law depends upon the listing of precedents. Scientific research depends on the tracking down and eliciting of previous experimental work. A person's adult behaviour is at any rate partly explicable in terms of his or her childhood circumstances.

I have just quoted three American constructions. It is satisfying enough, I suppose, to say that they are distinctively American without wondering how and when they became so. But how much more informative and interesting it is to observe that *go* and *come* were so used in this country from Anglo-Saxon times onward until they receded into archaistic or dialectal use; and that the ellipsis of *to be* in the type 'ordered the plane to be flown' is first recorded in the North American colonies in 1781. The etymology of grammatical constructions is as illuminating as the etymology of individual words.

We can catch glimpses of lost or dying ways of speaking by reading older works, as, for example, by turning to the increasingly unconsulted text of the Authorized Version of the Bible (1611). Let me remind you of some of the 1611 uses that live on in the AV even though they have been replaced by supposedly 'timeless' equivalents in the New English Bible. 'He *maketh* me *to lie* downe in greene pastures' (*Psalm* 23:2), a natural construction in 1611, has given way to 'He *makes* me *lie* down in green pastures' in the NEB. Other examples: 'they are *moe then* the haires of *mine* head' (*Psalm* 40:12) is replaced by 'they are *more than* the hairs of *my* head'; 'a golden reede to measure the citie, and the gates *thereof*, and the wall *thereof*' (*Rev.* 21:15) by 'a gold measuring-rod, to measure the city, *its* walls, and *its* gates'. The conjunction *for to* and the preposition *unto* ('saluation is come *vnto* the Gentiles, *for to* prouoke them to ielousie', *Rom.* 11:11) have become remembered tokens of a past age. The adverb *alway* has given way to *always*, or, in the NEB, to *unceasingly*, or some other synonym. Older forms of the verb *to be*, the commonest of all English verbs, linger on as linguistic phantoms in the AV but have otherwise passed into disuse: 'Art thou the first man that was born? or *wast* thou made before the hills?' (*Job* 15:7); 'thou being a wilde oliue tree *wert* graffed in amongst them' (*Rom.* 11:17).

I hope that for at least a century to come the ability to read and understand the AV and the Book of Common Prayer will be regarded as a test of literacy. Anyone who ignores or puts aside such landmarks is as deprived as those who know nothing of the Norman Conquest and the French Revolution, or any other military or social events of great consequence that occurred in past centuries.

For T. S. Eliot, the New Testament of the New English Bible (1961) was not even a work of distinguished mediocrity.[2] In 1979, a group of eminent writers, including Kingsley Amis, Christopher Fry, Margha-nita Laski and Iris Murdoch, expressed their deep concern about 'this great act of forgetting' which is leading to the gradual abandonment of the AV and the Book of Common Prayer.[3] Just to list some of the changes made between the old and the new versions – the deletion or replacement of words like *abiding, loe, sore afraid, vnto, tidings, yee, all at once*, and intricate small changes made in the order of words – reveals the outward signs of a devastating loss of religious mystery in the modern versions. The grammatical and linguistic semantics of such linguistic substitutions merit further study: perhaps Dr D. A. Cruse whose useful monograph *Lexical Semantics* (1986) has cleared the ground of such matters as the sense-spectrum in uses of the word *mouth*:

> John keeps opening and shutting his mouth like a fish
> The mouth of the sea-squirt resembles that of a bottle
> The mouth of the cave resembles that of a bottle
> The mouth of the enormous cave was also that of the underground
> river   (p. 72)

will now turn his attention to the sense-spectrum in the replacement of *sore afraid* by *terror-stricken* and of *I bring you good tidings of great joy* by *I have good news for you.*

Controversy at the boundaries of grammar

It is time for me to move away from the democratization of English grammar by professional grammarians – the fairly militant straining to find a fit and equal place for all varieties and levels of usage – and also from the great battles about religious language, and turn to an examination of some uses and constructions that cause endless controversy among native speakers of Standard English:

double negatives
split infinitives
nominative forms of pronouns used in the objective position

Double negatives

A plain-speaking shopkeeper explained to an interviewer from the *Sunday Times Magazine*:[4]

I run a family business and I don't want no hassle.

To him it was obviously a comfortably natural way of expressing the idea. The double negative emphasized the negativity and did not cancel it. There was no ambiguity, and communication was not impeded in any way. But in the twentieth century the construction is not Standard English, even though such sentences containing double or cumulative negation are found up and down the country in most walks of life.

Consider the history of the construction. Repetition of negatives was the regular idiom in Old English and Middle English in all dialects. Thus, in Chaucer:

> He *nevere* yet *no* vileynye *ne* sayde
> In al his lyf unto *no* maner wight.[5]

At some point between the sixteenth and the eighteenth centuries, for reasons no longer discoverable, double negatives became socially unacceptable in Standard English. Playwrights placed them in the conversation of vulgar speakers, and grammarians like Lindley Murray roundly condemned them:

> Two negatives, in English, destroy one another, or are equivalent to an affirmative; . . . 'His language though inelegant, is *not ungrammatical*'; that is, 'it is grammatical'.[6]

Double negatives lie strewn about in modern fiction and drama as surefire indications of social vulgarity or of deficient education:

> 'Clouds come up,' she continued, 'but no rain never falls when you want it.'[7]

> 'He never did no harm to no one.'[8]

> 'Don't you fancy her no more?'[9]

> 'I don't give a damn about nobody.'[10]

A double negative is now part of the standard equipment of the underclasses, and Elizabeth Jolley, Eddie Grundy, Carol Rumens, and Athol Fugard are well aware of it. By contrast, as if to distance themselves as far as possible from double negatives, Standard speakers endlessly use Lindley Murray-type self-cancelling expressions like

> It has not gone unnoticed
> I don't feel inclined to disagree
> a not unwelcome decision
> not entirely dissatisfied

It is not as though Jane Austen could not create attractive heroines.

Clearly the presence of cancellable negatives is part of the property of Standard English, and the use of double or multiple negation for emphasis a certain indication of some kind of linguistic deficit. But it was not always so and attitudes can easily change again in the future.

Split infinitives

A split or cleft infinitive of course occurs when an adverb or adverbial phrase is placed between the particle or sign *to* and the infinitive it governs. The construction was used for emphasis by a British Airways hostess on a flight that I made to Brussels in 1986:

> For your safety and comfort we do ask you *to please stay* in your seats until the 'fasten your seatbelts' sign has been switched off.

To a large section of the middle class at the present time it is a sign of uttermost degradation. But an examination of the history of the construction shows how periods of acceptance and hostility have alternated over the centuries:

a. It did not occur in the Old English period when *to*-infinitives were rare, and when in any case such infinitives were inflected as if they were nouns.
b. There are recorded instances, with the frequency increasing all the time, from the thirteenth century to the fifteenth century.
c. It was avoided between 1500 and 1800. No examples have been found in the works of Shakespeare, Spenser, Pope, or Dryden, for example.
d. From the time of Byron onwards (see *OED Infinitive* sb. 1) the construction has reappeared and has been used with increasing frequency despite the hostility of prescriptive grammarians.

The underlying causes of the advance and retreat of the split infinitive construction are not clear.

The first major grammarian to oppose the use of split infinitives was Henry Alford in his usage manual called *The Queen's English* (1864):

> 238. A correspondent states as his own usage, and defends, the insertion of an adverb between the sign of the infinitive mood and

the verb. He gives as an instance, '*to scientifically illustrate.*' But surely this is a practice entirely unknown to English speakers and writers. It seems to me, that we ever regard the *to* of the infinitive as inseparable from its verb. And when we have a choice between two forms of expression, 'scientifically to illustrate,' and 'to illustrate scientifically,' there seems no good reason for flying in the face of common usage. (p. 171)

By 1926 the mood among the experts had changed. In his *Modern English Usage* H. W. Fowler expressed a balanced view:

We maintain, however, that a real split infinitive, though not desirable in itself, is preferable to either of two things, to real ambiguity, & to patent artificiality. (p. 560)

In my view this opinion still holds good. It is one of the simplest of all tasks to collect examples of the construction in every kind of good writing:

it will have *to drastically change* its management style.
                                   (*N.Y. Times*, 18 March 1982)
David . . . allowed one eyelid *to minimally fall.*
                    (Anita Brookner, *Hotel du Lac*, 1984, p. 88)
We want *to really start* our argument with one of the principal . . . attacks on the ancient stabilities.
(George Steiner in *Bull. Amer. Acad. Arts & Sci.*, Nov. 1987, p. 15)
In face of all this Patrick managed *to quite like* him.
            (Kingsley Amis, *Difficulties with Girls*, 1988, p. 44)

Examples with more than one inserted word are less common, but do occur:

a willingness *to not always, in every circumstance, think* the very best of us.   (Philip Roth, *The Counterlife*, 1987, p. 70)

Some attempts to avoid splitting an infinitive seem very artificial:

If Mr Baker wants teachers *speedily to accept* a sensible pay and conditions package . . .   (*The Times*, 10 Jan. 1987, p. 17)
The threat of abolition enabled the Livingstone administration *briefly to ride* the inevitable wave of popular indignation it caused.
                    (*London Review of Books*, 10 Dec. 1987, p. 25)

The folklore of total prohibition is still widely believed in. The rule should rather be: place the adverb or other contextual element where it is unambiguous or where it does not seem artificial. And bear in mind that hard-core hostility to the split infinitive, if it existed at all before the mid-nineteenth century, was not expressed before Alford wrote his book in 1864. A century is a very short time in syntax.

Nominative forms of pronouns used in the objective position and vice versa: a partial reversal of roles

For some two centuries, for reasons that can only be guessed at, there has been a marked tendency to carry over the nominative forms of personal pronouns, and especially the pronoun *I*, to the objective position. A stock example:

They asked Jim and I to do the job.

And another:

This is strictly between you and I.

The construction occurs only when the pronoun is part of a compound object. No one would say

*They asked I to do the job.

This switching of cases is found among Standard speakers as well as in regional dialects:

Everyone got used to the image of Eric and *I*.
(Ernie Wise, speaking of Eric Morecambe,
            'Today' programme, BBC Radio 4, 6 May 1987)

a better, richer life than the one allotted to them by our Royal Family, the government and *we*, the taxpayers.
            (Carmen Callil in the *Listener*, 9 Apr. 1987, p. 36)

their arrival made Genia and *I* realise we were very nearly imprisoned in our own house.
            (Thomas Keneally, *A Family Madness*, 1985, p. 102)

The *OED*, s.v. *I* pers. pron. 2, notes the use: 'Sometimes used for the objective after a verb or preposition, esp. when separated from the governing word by other words. (This was very frequent in end of 16th and in 17th c., but is now considered ungrammatical.)' The entry presents illustrative examples from Shakespeare, Ben Jonson, Vanbrugh, and Thomas Hughes, among others. Clearly the tendency to use *I* in such circumstances represents just a new wave from an old ocean.

For my own part, despite the historical pattern, such uses fall outside Standard English. Nevertheless it is distinctly interesting to observe that disturbance of pronominal roles is not confined to the pronoun *I*, but is something that occurs from time to time, and in this area or that, in all kinds of circumstances. In spoken and written English the pronouns *me* and *myself* occur often enough in informal contexts at the head of clauses:

> *Me* and the teacher are going to race tonight from the school to the store. (Jim Crace, *Continent*, 1986, p. 53)
> *Me* and the bike, we're supposed to be on 'Miami Vice'.
> (*New Yorker*, 17 Nov. 1986, p. 43)
> 'We? Who's we?' . . . '*Myself* and another priest.'
> (Brian Moore, *The Colour of Blood*, 1987, p. 56)

The *OED* regarded such uses, which it illustrates from writers over a four-hundred-year period, as 'now only *dial.* and *vulgar*'. And there is not the slightest doubt that such switching of pronominal roles is fiercely opposed by most Standard speakers. But there are one or two circumstances to take into account:

a. 'It's me', in answer to the question 'Who is it?', is now standard.
b. In answer to the question 'Who's there?', the natural answer is 'Me', not 'I'.
c. After *as* and *than* there is much diversity of usage:
    He started to encounter kids as gifted as *he*.
    (*New Yorker*, 17 Nov. 1986, p. 69)
    Jim would have run the farm as good as *me*.
    (Marian Eldridge, *Walking the Dog*, 1984, p. 163)
    The men are . . . more formal and authoritarian in tone than *she*.
    (Marilyn Butler, *London Review of Books*, 25 June 1987, p. 12)
    He was five years older than *me*.
    (Evelyn Waugh, BBC TV, 'Face to Face', 1960)

    d. As a reply to another person's assertion, *me too* or *me neither* are normally used, not *I too* and *I neither*.

       'Let's talk about each other, that's all I'm interested in at the moment.' 'Me too,' says Tom.

                     (Penelope Lively, *Moon Tiger*, 1987, p. 76)

       'Oh no, I couldn't stand it!' 'Me neither!'

       (Rachel McAlpine, *Driftwood*, 1985, p. 38) (New Zealand writer)

    e. The types *Silly me!* and *Me, I go on about this all the time* are now commonly encountered in spoken English and in the dialogue of good novels.

Disturbance of pronominal roles is clearly at least a partial phenomenon in modern English. The most sensible course is to keep an eye on its progress from the uses tombstoned in the *OED* to the constructions one encounters in spoken English or in written English all the time. It is as if the first person pronouns have moved into an area of uncertainty, one that is no longer stable and predictable, one that defies simple definition or description. Why such migrations occur is uncertain, but occur they do.

Conclusion

However one approaches English syntax it is seen to be rule-abiding up to a point. The rules and relationships are immensely complex. There are edges and boundaries to be taken into account, and for the study and identification of these peripheral areas a synchronic or merely descriptive account is inadequate. No language stands still and English is no exception. The rate of syntactic change is slower than that of phonetic change or lexical change, but it can be established with the aid of the *OED*, large historical grammars like those of Jespersen and Visser, and modern computerized databases.

    My central point is that after 1,250 years of recorded use, and despite an increase in the number of speakers from under one million to more than 300 million, and despite the increasing diversity of national styles of English in the main English-speaking countries, the English language remains unweakened by the changes that have come upon it, just different from what it once was, and engagingly so.

Notes

1. *Subject and Predicate in Logic and Grammar*, 1974.
2. *Sunday Telegraph*, 16 December 1962, p. 7.
3. *PN Review 13*.
4. 12 July 1987, p. 53.
5. *Canterbury Tales*, Prol. 70f.
6. *English Grammar*, 1795, cited from an edition of 1824, p. 172.
7. E. Jolley, *Palomino*, 1980, p. 23 of 1984 reprint.
8. Eddie Grundy referring to the late Jethro Larkin, BBC Radio 4, 'The Archers', 18 June 1987.
9. Carol Rumens, *Plato Park*, 1987, p. 171.
10. Athol Fugard, *Tsotsi*, 1980, p. 35 of 1983 Penguin reprint (Black speaker).

4 Words and Meanings in the Twentieth Century

On the title-page of T. S. Eliot's *Notes Towards the Definition of Culture* (1948) someone placed an epigraph purporting to be the entry in the *Oxford English Dictionary* for sense 1 of the word *definition*. In fact it was the entry for sense 1 of the word *definition* from the *Shorter Oxford English Dictionary*, an abridged version of the twelve-volume parent work.[1] In the context the misattribution did not happen to matter. When I noticed it, I took it to be a trivial example of the way in which poets are often inattentive to, or unconcerned with, the exactness of pure scholarship as they excavate their own kind of truth. This chapter will be partly about Eliot's paltry inaccuracies – it is not enough just to praise him in an uncritical fashion – and partly about some of his enduring contributions to the language. It will also be concerned with some of the main tendencies in the spawning general lexicon of English between 1900 and the present day.

The century can be divided up in many different ways. I have decided to divide the story of twentieth-century English into three episodes. The divisions are personal to me. I shall begin by speaking about the growth of the vocabulary of English in the period from 1900 to 1923, that is, in the period before I was born. Episode two will take things forward to 1949, in which year I arrived at the University of Oxford as a New Zealand Rhodes Scholar. And the third episode will deal with the period since 1949. In the nature of things, I need to confine my attention to a selected number of broad tendencies.

Before embarking on the main theme, I should perhaps mention that my father, Frederick Burchfield, was born in the village of Halling, near Rochester, in Kent in 1891, and that he emigrated with his parents, brothers, and sisters[2] to New Zealand in his teens. The reason for the uprooting of the family was said to be the threat of unemployment to workers in a cement factory near Halling because of the discovery in Germany of a new process of making cement. My mother, Mary Lauder Blair, was born in a township called Fortrose in the province of Southland in New Zealand. She was of Scottish descent, her father, William Blair, having emigrated from Scotland.

Emigrants take their language with them, and I was therefore strongly influenced by the persistent Englishness of my father's vocabulary and the unaltered Scottishness of the language of my maternal grandfather. In the 1920s and 1930s I also acquired the typical day-to-day vocabulary used by all New Zealanders, words that are largely unfamiliar here but are part of the normal currency there: words like *bach* (beach cottage), *booay* (back country), *haka* (Maori war dance), *kowhai* (a shrub), *pikelet* (a drop scone), *toheroa* (a New Zealand shellfish), and *tui* (a New Zealand bird). All of them remain firmly in my mind some forty years after changing places, as David Lodge would have it, from Wellington to Oxford.

I. 1900–23

A great many new words came striding into the language in the first twenty-three years of the century. It was the age, for example, of the first motor vehicles. The motor cars or automobiles – note that the word still survives in Britain in the title *Automobile Association* – had features that are no longer in use or that later changed their names: they had *dashboards* (1904), *dickey seats* (1912), *mudguards* (earlier on bicycles), and *running boards* (1907, earlier on boats, locomotives, and trams). The first heavier-than-air planes took off from primitive *runways* (a term first used of the one at Boston Airport in 1923), most of them *biplanes*, and all of them driven by revolving *propellers*. British fliers could not decide whether to call these flying machines *aeroplanes* or *airplanes*, and even as late as 1927 the BBC Advisory Committee on Spoken English advised the use of *airplane*. Advisory Committees often make wrong decisions. Meanwhile, in America, *airplane* was the regular term from the beginning: in 1917–18 American warplanes were officially *airplanes* not aeroplanes. British planes landed on *aerodromes*, American ones on *airports*. It was quite some time before Heathrow, Gatwick, Luton, and other landing places came to be called *airports*.

The first decade of the century witnessed an uneasy peace, its uneasiness underlined by the appearance of the words *pacifism* (1902) and *pacifist* (1906) alongside the more or less synonymous terms *pacificism* (1910) and *pacificist* (1907). War broke out. *Tommy Atkins*, a Victorian term for a private soldier, was revived as the soldiers went into action against the *Boche*, the French soldiers' term for the Germans. The lucky ones came back to *Blighty*, an Army slang term for England, derived from Hindustani *bilāyati* by soldiers serving in India at an earlier stage. The eighteenth-century term *white feather* was taken out of the shame-upon-you cupboard. *Conchies*, apparently thus called for the first time in 1917, though the fuller term *conscientious objector* is recorded from 1899, were dispatched to Dartmoor. In the mud of Flanders and Passchendaele commissioned officers wore *Sam Browne belts* and everyone wore *puttees* (a strip of cloth wound spirally round the leg from the knee to the ankle) and *tin hats*.

On the social front, the *Alexandra limp* perhaps just survived into the first decade of the century – 'a manner of walking affected by fashionable society in imitation of the limp of Alexandra (1844–1925), wife of King Edward VII, when she was Princess of Wales' (*OEDS*). Women and girls began to wear *panties*, as they called 'short-legged or legless knickers' (*OEDS*) from 1908 onward – these were what we would call shorts, not underclothes – half a century before *blue jeans* became standard casual wear for about half the population. Sex appeal was called 'It' and so, by James Joyce in *Ulysses* (1922), was sexual intercourse:

> Gardner said no man could look at my mouth and teeth smiling like that and not think of it. (p. 747)

This use of 'it' had been around for some time in the secret language of the Victorian period, but Joyce was perhaps the first to put this meaning of *it* into wider circulation.

The well-off danced to *palm-court music* (1908), played *petits chevaux* at gaming tables, made *person-to-person* telephone calls, or went to *picture palaces*, *cinemas*, *kinemas*, or *bioscopes* to see silent *movies* or, by 1921, *talkies*.

Scientists were beginning to turn Heath-Robinsonesque laboratories into sensational sites of new discoveries. Marja Sklodowska aka Marie Curie was awarded the Nobel Prize for Physics in 1903 as a reward for her discovery of the radioactive elements *polonium* and *radium* in 1898. *Isotopes* were identified for the first time. In 1901 the familiar black-and-white *panda* was first brought to the notice of Western zoologists, and distinguished from the small red panda of Nepal known from the early part of the nineteenth century. Sigmund Freud launched the words *ego*, *id*, and *libido* and by doing so brought the study of human behaviour into a new dimension. In 1912 *Piltdown Man* was declared to be a 'primitive hominid' and given the scientific name *Eoanthropus dawsoni*. Its fraudulent nature was not confirmed until 1953.

At a more trivial level the useful phrase *pie in the sky* entered the language in 1911, *phooey* (not so spelt until 1929) was written as *pfui* (after its German original), and in the United States the name given from 1917 to a kind of supermarket chain like the modern Tesco or Waitrose was *Piggly-Wiggly*.

Acronyms

Prominent among the linguistic innovations of the period were the first acronyms, including *Anzac*, a word coined at Gallipoli in 1915 by Lt.-Gen. Sir W. R. Birdwood from the initial letters of the *A*ustralian and *N*ew Zealand *A*rmy *C*orps:

> 1915 C. E. W. BEAN *Diary* 25 Apr. 67 *Col. Knox to Anzac.* 'Ammunition required at once.'

In 1923 the Russian secret police became known as the *Ogpu*, which stood for the initial letters of the equivalent Russian words for 'United State Political Directorate'. It was the beginning of a process of word-formation that has come to have no bounds. Acronyms, of course, are sets of initials that can be pronounced as words. Routine examples include *Nato* (*N*orth *A*tlantic *T*reaty Organization, 1949), *radar* (*ra*dio *d*etection *a*nd *r*anging, 1941), and the names of trade unions like COHSE (*C*onfederation *o*f *H*ealth *S*ervice *E*mployees). The main disadvantage of such formations is that they are effectively proper names with no power to form derivatives. Thus a member of COHSE is not normally called a COHSE-er and there is no verb *to *COHSE*— "to become a member of COHSE, to act in the manner of a member of COHSE'. The type 'He doesn't COHSE about' is lying ready for use but not yet employed as far as I know.

As formations they are often ingenious – for example KWIC (*K*ey *W*ord *i*n *C*ontext) and CARE (*C*ooperative for *A*merican *R*elief *E*verywhere, a federation of US charities) – but they are barren, in that they cannot generate anything except themselves, and etymologically rootless. Each one that is formed takes the language fractionally away from its Germanic, and ultimately its Indo-European, origins. The latest example I happen to have noted is one from the 6 October 1988 issue of the *Chicago Tribune* (sect. 3, p. 6):

> . . . a medical technique designed to aid couples with fertility problems. The procedure, Zygote Intra-Fallopian Transfer, or ZIFT, was conducted at the hospital's Fertility and Reproductive Endocrinology Center.

Whether ZIFT will turn out to be a gift or the reverse remains to be seen. David Lodge makes mild fun of them, or rather of the use of sets of abbreviations, in his novel *Nice Work* (1988) by building some into a memo from the Vice-Chancellor of Rummidge University to the Deans of all Faculties:

> The DES, through the UGC, have urged the CVCP to ensure that universities throughout the UK . . .   (p. 53)

and by linking *FA* (= Faculty of Arts) with *sweet FA*, meaning you know what.

Suffragettes

One of the key words of the period was *suffragette*. The movement for the extension of the franchise to women apparently began in the mid-1880s but the word itself is first recorded in 1906. It is of interest to see that the *OED* (in an entry published in 1915, only nine years later) defined *suffragette* as 'a female supporter of the cause of women's political enfranchisement, *esp.* one of a violent or "militant" type'. The word 'militant' is placed within inverted commas because it was a new, twentieth-century, use of the word. Mrs Pankhurst was one of the first militants in a political or trade-union sense, that is, a person advocating the use of direct action, demonstrations, and so on, as a way of enforcing or obtaining political or industrial change.

Suffragette is also of linguistic interest for a different reason. It seems to have been the first word in which the suffix *-ette* is used to indicate a person of the female sex. From the end of the eighteenth century onward, the suffix *-ette* had had two main functions: (a) added to a noun to indicate something small of its kind, as *balconette* (1876), a miniature balcony, *essayette* (1877), a short essay, *novelette* (1820), a story of modest length, and *sermonette* (1814), a short sermon; (b) commonly in the names given by manufacturers to materials, especially cloth, intended as imitations of something else, as *cashmerette* (1886), *flanel-(l)ette* (1882), *leatherette* (1880), and *muslinette* (1787), cheaper imitations of the real thing.

All three types have had a precarious existence in the twentieth century. As a female suffix, *-ette* has been called on, and has more or less endured, in *usherette* (1925) and *majorette* (1941, *drum majorette* 1938). From 1919, for about thirty years, female undergraduates were occasionally called 'undergraduettes', but no longer. The suffix is having a mild revival in the world of journalism. John Naughton in the *Observer* (16 October 1988, p. 52) used the word *hackette* pejoratively of a junior member of the trade:

> The week's Foot-in-Mouth award goes to the anonymous hackette who inquired of Mrs Margaret Tebbit, as she was wheeled along the Brighton seafront, whether the place had any bad memories for her.

Private Eye (16 September 1988, p. 6) commented on 'the dauntingly beautiful "hypette" Polly Samson, . . . Publicity Director of Cape'. And the *Chicago Sun-Times* (28 April 1988, p. 2) reported that 'A Sneed snoopette spotted former national security adviser Robert "Bud" McFarlane of Irangate fame buying chocolates at the Chocolate Moose in Washington for Secretaries Week'. Other very recent examples, all having a distinct male chauvinist edge, include *awarette, editorette, voguette*, and *whizzette*.

In the sense 'something small of its kind', our century has rather grudgingly yielded a few words that look like remaining in the language, at any rate for the present: examples include *dinette* (1930), a small dining room, *diskette* (1973), a floppy disk, *kitchenette* (1910), a small kitchen, and *laund(e)rette* (1949) – this last is formed in fact from the verb *launder* (with no implication of smallness); also *Veepette* applied mockingly (= an insignificant Vice-President) to J. Danforth Quayle.

As a suffix indicating that the material is an imitation of some earlier material, -*ette* appears in *satinette* (1904, earlier *satinet*) and *winceyette* (1922). *Georgette* (1915), a thin silk or other crepe dress-material, hardly belongs, except by accident, in this group as it is simply named after Mme Georgette de la Plante, a French *modiste*, and has no antecedent as the name of a material.

Silent arrivals

At all periods of the language it is difficult to assign a beginning date to most new words and meanings. They tend to slip into the language silently, and are placed in date order only when scholars subsequently get to work. Thus, in the period 1900 to 1923, new words kept clocking in, as it were, in the United States at a prodigious rate: words like *air-conditioning* (1910), *air lane* (1921), *auditorium* (1908), *baked Alaska* (1909), *baloney* (1928), and *blurb* (1923), to take examples from the letters A and B alone. At some indeterminable later date each of these, and thousands more, made their way at a gentle pace into the customary language of Britain. The period 1900 to 1923 was one in which British English underwent its first major buffeting from American English. It was a pivotal period, in that it seems likely to have been the time when American English became the dominant form of English, at any rate in the eyes of foreigners learning English as a second language.

T. S. Eliot's early vocabulary

It was of course during this period that T. S. Eliot embarked on his literary career, and by 1923 he was a very famous writer indeed. Among his many works, *Prufrock, and Other Observations* (1917), *Ara Vos Prec* (1920), and above all *The Waste Land* (1922) had been published by 1923. It was a time when Eliot called on, and then largely abandoned, most of his American vocabulary. The birds in his poem 'Cape Ann' are all American ones:

> O quick quick quick, quick hear the song-sparrow,
> Swamp-sparrow, fox-sparrow, vesper-sparrow
> At dawn and at dusk . . .
>   Leave to chance
> The Blackburnian warbler, the shy one. Hail

> With shrill whistle the note of the quail, the bob-white
> Dodging by bay-bush.

It was during this time too that he began to pick up long-since disused words and use them in his own poetry. In the nicest possible way, poets scavenge where they can.

In

> Not by any concitation
> Of the backward devils.   *Ara Vos Prec* (1920) 12

concitation, which means 'stirring up, agitation', is a word otherwise recorded only in the sixteenth and seventeenth centuries. In the same poem he adopted Shakespeare's word *defunctive*,[3] meaning 'dying':

> Defunctive music under sea
> Passed seaward with the passing bell.   *Ibid.* 14

Other writers, including William Faulkner and Thomas Wolfe, then picked up the word, almost certainly from Eliot rather than from Shakespeare.

It was also a time when Eliot brought some new words and meanings of his own into use. For example, *anfractuous* in the sense 'rugged, craggy':

> Paint me the bold anfractuous rocks
> Faced by the snarling and yelping seas.   *Ibid.* 22

The word was not new – it had been used by many writers from the seventeenth century onwards in the sense 'winding, sinuous' – but the meaning was.

His rather unhappy formation *juvescence* also belongs to this period:

> In the juvescence of the year
> Came Christ the tiger.   *Ibid.* 11

It should have been *juvenescence*, a word already in existence (*OED* 1800–). But Stephen Spender apparently liked it and used it in a later poem:

> That kissing of steel furies
> Preparing a world's childless juvescence
>   (in *Time and Tide*, 10 Jan. 1948)

It is perhaps no worse than the word *middlescence*, recorded sporadically from 1965 onward in North America in the sense 'the period of middle age'.

In *The Waste Land*, Eliot turned to Latin for the word *laquearia*, 'a panelled ceiling':

> . . . the prolonged candle-flames
> Fling their smoke into the laquearia.

This too was not a neat fit. A better reflection of the Latin word *laqueāre*, *-is* (neuter) would have been *laqueary*, a form recorded in English dictionaries of the seventeenth century.

In 'Mr Eliot's Sunday Morning Service' (1919) we find a small group of hard words, beginning with *polyphiloprogenitive*, Eliot's own coinage, contextually linking 'the sapient sutlers of the Lord' with the 'two religious caterpillars' of Marlowe's *Jew of Malta*. It is a famous coinage, but of course its originality is limited because it is merely an extension of the nineteenth-century adjective *philoprogenitive*, which also meant 'inclined to the production of offspring, prolific'.

In the same poem, *superfetation* is an old word meaning 'super-abundant production', but in the fifth stanza Eliot produces another coinage of his own:

> The young are red and pustular
> Clutching piaculative pence.

Piaculative, meaning 'for the purposes of atonement', appears to be Eliot's own reshaping of the adjective *piacular*, a word in regular use from the seventeenth century onward.

The publication in 1971 of *The Waste Land* drafts brought two new unrecorded items to light.

1. Then we had dinner in good form, and a couple of *Bengal lights*.

Obviously *Bengal lights* were unlikely to be fireworks in the context. Valerie Eliot wrote to ask for help, and said that the only clue she could give was that the context was 'probably Boston about 1910'. Much delving in the directories of trade marks of the relevant period led to an entry for 'Bengal Lights (cigarettes and cheroots)' in *Connorton's*

Tobacco Brand Directory U.S. (1899), p. 550. A small problem had been solved.

2. Song. For the *opherion*.

Here the outcome was less satisfactory. It would appear that Eliot's word is simply an error for *orpharion*, a large musical instrument of the lute kind, much used in the seventeenth century. It was a classic example of the kind of linguistic flaw found in the work of most major writers.

Towering above this poetical experimentation with words, however, are two expressions that Eliot gave to the language of literary criticism. The first of these was *objective correlative* which Eliot used first in an essay printed in the 26 September 1919 issue of the *Athenaeum*:

> The only way of expressing emotion in the form of art is by finding an 'objective correlative'; in other words, a set of objects, a situation, a chain of events which shall be the formula of that *particular* emotion: such that when the external facts, which must terminate in sensory experience, are given, the emotion is immediately evoked.

The second was *dissociation of sensibility*, first used by Eliot (in *The Times Literary Supplement* 20 October 1921, p. 669) to mean 'a separation of thought from feeling which Eliot held to be first manifested in poetry of the later 17th century' (*OEDS*).

For nearly seventy years students of English literature have cut their teeth on these two critical concepts, terms as important in their way as older critical expressions like *poetic diction* and the *pathetic fallacy*, gentler and friendlier by far than all the unappetizing vocabulary of Deconstruction.

II. 1924–49

The world keeps moving into new modes while discarding old ones. Guillaume Apollinaire had taken France into the realm of *surréalisme* in 1917, but it was not until the publication of André Breton's *Manifeste du Surréalisme* in 1924 that this new movement, characterized by its spectacular juxtapositioning of like and unlike, the rational with the irrational, really became established. This was an artistic breakthrough, not welcomed by everyone. More obviously beneficial was the discovery of penicillin in 1929, followed by the manufacturing of a great many healing antibiotics. By 1939 the concept of a 'sound barrier' had been established. The atomic bomb was dropped in 1945. The League of Nations was replaced by the United Nations, or *UNO* as it was called at first. All these fundamental changes brought crops of new vocabulary in their wake.

In the worlds of lexicography and linguistics the 1920s and 1930s were marked by several major milestones. The *OED* was completed in 1928, an achievement unmatched at that time in any other country. Sir William Craigie's plans[4] for the extension of the *OED* by the preparation of period and regional dictionaries got under way. A large Middle English Dictionary[5] was set in motion, and also two Scottish dictionaries on historical principles[6] and a large American one.[7] It began to look as if historical lexicography would be the most important linguistic activity of the twentieth century, as comparative linguistics had been in the nineteenth. A challenge to the dominance of historical linguistics had been set in motion by the Swiss scholar Ferdinand de Saussure, whose lecture notes had been published under the title *Cours de linguistique générale* in 1916. Two books by American scholars, *Language: an Introduction to the Study of Speech* (1921) by Edward Sapir, and *Language* (1933) by Leonard Bloomfield, like Saussure's, drew attention to the theoretical attractions of descriptive linguistics and also to the bias involved in concentrating on features displayed by the Indo-European languages. Sapir and Bloomfield were field anthropologists as well as linguists, and the tribes they studied were not Indo-European ones but North American Indian ones. The domestic philology of European scholars was thus under threat from two quarters: theoretical approaches on the one hand, especially a newly established Saussurean distinction between *langue* (the totality of a given language) and *parole* (that part of a given language actually used by particular groups or by individuals); and a new valuation of the linguistic particularities of languages outside the Indo-European group. The stage was set for the great linguistic battles of the 1950s and beyond.

Two important usage manuals were also published in this period: H. W. Fowler's *Modern English Usage* (1926), a book characterized by its idiosyncratic headings ('Out of the Frying-Pan', 'Battered Ornaments', and so on) and its exquisite judgements; and Eric Partridge's *Usage and Abusage* (1942), a shoulder-beating book of great severity.

The war of 1939–45

I shall not dwell long on describing the lexical fallout of the 1939–45 war. The vocabulary of the period is thoroughly treated in the *Supplement to the OED*. A simple listing of some of the new vocabulary will serve as a sufficient reminder of the way in which wars generate new words:

Anderson shelter (1939)	nylon stockings (1941)
Asdic (1939)	petrol ration (1939)
chinagraph pencil (1943)	Pluto (name of underwater pipeline
Chindit (1943)	to the troops in France, 1944)
Desert Rat (1944)	radar (1941)
G.I. bride (1945)	

These and hundreds of other words were some of the outward signs of war. And, as always in a time of war, the language was laced with elements of good humour, the *wizard prangs* (accidents) of P/O Prune, the downgrading of danger implied in the expression *tail-end Charlie*, the use of *scramble* as the verb describing the rapid take-off of Spitfires and Hurricanes to take on approaching enemy planes (*bandits*), and the proliferation of many kinds of slang to do with bossiness (*he tore me off a strip*), death (*he bought it over Dunkirk*), and weapons of war (*buzz bombs*).

I had the good fortune to combine cartography, trigonometry, and war, first by spending three years in the New Zealand army mapping unmapped areas of the North Island of New Zealand with the help of trig points, plane tables, and theodolites. And the last year of the war in Italy fixing the position of our own guns by certain trigonometrical procedures, and then establishing the exact location of German batteries by a technique called *flash-spotting*. One climbed to a high point, usually the top of a tall building or the spire of a church, and took a bearing on the flash of a German artillery gun as it fired. It was exciting to be able to combine spherical trigonometry, and in particular a process called 'phi minus 45', with the ordinary hazards of war. The lives of our comrades depended upon the accuracy and speed of our calculations.

The passage of the years from 1924 to 1949 can be recalled to some extent by the kind of words that came into the language and were not, initially at any rate, to do with the war. New dances were introduced: in the letters B and C alone there were the *Charleston* (1923), the *black bottom* (1926), the *carioca* (1934), the *beguine* (1935), the *conga* (1935), the *big apple* (1937), and *bumps and grinds* (1946). And, of course, there was the never-to-be-forgotten *Lambeth Walk*, the name of a street in Lambeth, used as the title of a Cockney song and dance first performed by Lupino Lane in the revue *Me and my Gal* in 1937.

The fecundity of American English continued and its new words trickled into this country, and then into the foreign languages of Europe, in ever-increasing numbers. A small list will give the flavour but will hardly account for the massiveness of the process of American lexical innovation:

freebie (1942)	pep pill (1937)
hijack (and derivatives, 1923)	pep talk (1926)
hillbilly (folk music, 1924)	schnozzle (Jimmy Durante, 1930)
hit-and-run driving (1924)	self-fulfilling prophecy (1949)
hitchhiking (1923)	soap opera (1939)

Meanwhile British English was not lying dormant. It is easy to draw up a similar list of words of UK origin in the period 1924 to 1949:

bright young thing (1927)	pink gin (1930)
heffalump (A. A. Milne, 1926)	pony club (1929)
hobbit (J. R. R. Tolkien, 1938)	squat (illegal occupation of a
Loch Ness monster (1933)	building, 1946)
loo (Nancy Mitford, 1940)	unperson (George Orwell, 1949)

The two-way traffic between the two countries, indeed the multi-way traffic throughout the English-speaking world, as the words and meanings cross and re-cross oceans, is now presenting lexicographers with unprecedented problems of labelling. It is, of course, very difficult to establish which of numerous synonyms is actually used in all the countries concerned.

An age of new suffixes

To judge from the formative elements that emerged in the period 1924 to 1949, it was an age of slickness and ingenuity. The neat ranks of traditional suffixes were joined by a rabble of elements monstrously plucked, mostly by the commercial world, from well-established words. One of the earliest of the new brash elements was -*teria*, taken from *cafeteria* by a 'logical' analysis of the word as *café* + *teria*. First recorded in 1923, it came to be used as the final element of names of many self-service retail or catering establishments, especially in America. Grotesque formations like *healthateria* (the reason for the internal -*a*- is not clear), *valeteria*, and *washeteria*. An Italian café-owner was reported in 1965 as switching his neon sign from *Pizzeria* to *Pie-teria*.

Another recycled element was -*(a)thon*. Extracted from *marathon*, it was first recorded in 1934 and soon spawned words like *moviethon*, *poolathon*, *talkathon*, *telethon*, and *walkathon*. The barbarism of the formative process is, no doubt, slightly alleviated by the fact that the words usually designate long-drawn-out performances of one kind or another for charitable purposes.

Another monument to the linguistic vulgarity of the age was the element -*burger*, sliced off the end of *hamburger*, and, from 1939 onward, extensively used as a terminal element in fast-food items like *beefburger*, *cheeseburger*, *lamburger*, *porkburger*, and *steakburger*. King George V was reported to have made two remarks on his deathbed in January 1936: 'How is the Empire?'[8] and, when his doctor promised him he would soon be well enough to visit Bognor Regis, 'Bugger Bognor'. I can just imagine that Dr C. T. Onions, the greatest English etymologist of the twentieth century, might have chosen to say 'How is the English language?' and 'Bugger -*burger*'.[9]

T. S. Eliot's later vocabulary

In 1925 Eliot left Lloyds Bank and became a director of Faber and Gwyer. In 1927 he became a British subject and a member of the Anglican church. His pilgrimage into High Anglicanism is doubtless clearly reflected in the poetry he wrote at that time. His linguistic Americanness had already been discarded by this time, but two words in 'The Dry Salvages', *dooryard* and *groaner* (a local Massachusetts term for a whistling buoy), show that there was still an archaeological American layer of words in his mind:

In the rank ailanthus of the April dooryard

and

>   the heaving groaner
> Rounded homewards

A computer search of the electronically coded version of the *OED* revealed that there are just over five hundred illustrative examples in the *OED* drawn from the works of Eliot. Of these, thirty-nine are from *The Cocktail Party* (1950), twenty-two from *Murder in the Cathedral* (1935), and forty-six from *The Waste Land* (1922, or earlier drafts). As it happens, the work most frequently quoted from – fifty-one examples – is *The Rock: a Pageant Play* (1934). The statistical evidence must, however, be treated with great caution. For example, the words *nervous breakdown*, *sanitorium*, and *transhumanised* occur in *The Cocktail Party*, and are central to the plot, but Eliot's use of the terms is not recorded in the Dictionary. The Victorian terms *sanitorium* and *transhumanized* were already sufficiently dealt with in the *OED*; and other writers, including Arnold Bennett and John Braine, are drawn on in the *OEDS* entry for *nervous breakdown*. Similarly, there is no record in *OEDS* of Eliot's famous use of the word *etherised* ('Like a patient etherised upon a table') in *The Love Song of J. Alfred Prufrock* because this nineteenth-century word was also covered by the *OED*, with illustrative examples beginning in 1800.

Eliot's work is frequently drawn on for routine illustrative examples. For example, from *The Cocktail Party*, *OEDS* took examples for the words *casting director*, *couchette*, *movie*, *moving picture*, and *scenario*, as well as for *cocktail party* itself. They all form part of the embroidery of the Dictionary.

I have already mentioned Eliot's use of the expression *loam feet* in 'East Coker', and my reason for including it in *OEDS* 1. Numerous other poetical compounds found only in Eliot's work are recorded in *OEDS*, including *bat-flight*, *dreamcrossed*, and *harefoot*. So are the words *inoperancy*, *rose-garden*, *smokefall*, and *un-being* from 'Burnt Norton', and *barbituric* and *unprayable* from 'The Dry Salvages'.

As in the period before 1923, Eliot continued to poach a few words from earlier centuries: the adjective *behovely* in 'Little Gidding' is a revival of a word not otherwise recorded after the fourteenth century.

Eliot almost certainly encountered it in Chaucer's *Parson's Tale*. And in *Ash-Wednesday* (1930) his use of *inconclusible* ('Conclusion of all that / Is inconclusible') is paralleled only by a solitary example of 1660 in the *OED*.

Obviously Eliot's work between 1924 and 1949 – and beyond – continued to be a valuable source of material for the largest dictionary in the English language.

III. 1950 to the present day

Lexicographically the period since 1950 has been one of high drama. Several major dictionaries on historical principles were undertaken and most of them were completed: in particular *A Supplement to the Oxford English Dictionary* (4 vols., 1972–86), and (published in March 1989) a 20-volume integrated text of the original *OED* and the four volumes of the Supplement. *The Australian National Dictionary*, a fine treatment of distinctively Australian vocabulary, *didgeridoo, kookaburra, whingeing Pom*, and all that, was published in 1988. Similar dictionaries on historical principles for Canada and Jamaica were published in 1969, and one for Newfoundland in 1982.

For dictionaries of current English, the period has been marked by scholarly and commercial battles of great significance. The publication of *Webster's Third New International Dictionary* in 1961 was greeted with immense pleasure by most academic reviewers and with implacable hostility by nearly every journalist who reviewed it. University teachers loved its inclusiveness and its up-to-dateness. Journalists spoke of 'sabotage at Springfield': they judged it to be a work of deplorable linguistic permissiveness. Nearly thirty years on, that battle is unresolved. It overlapped with another dictionary war – a fierce commercial war between publishers as they became aware of huge untapped markets for dictionaries. Go into any bookshop now and you will see the results. The shelves are lined with dictionaries at every level and price both for native speakers and for learners of English: usage guides, illustrated dictionaries, phrase books, dictionaries of English idioms, thesauruses, bilingual and multilingual dictionaries, subject dictionaries, etymological dictionaries, and so on.

Some universities have established centres for the study of lexicographical problems, notably the University of Exeter in this country and

Indiana State University at Terre Haute in the United States. The University of Waterloo in Ontario established a unit which greatly assisted the programming of the *New OED* project in Oxford. Lexicographical conferences have become a regular feature: lexicographers, grammarians, university teachers, and publishers make their way to Amsterdam, Berlin, Cambridge, New York, and many other cities, more or less in the manner satirized in David Lodge's novel *Small World* (1984). The titles of the papers read at such conferences are very diverse. For example, at the 1988 EURALEX conference in Budapest, there were papers entitled 'Computational Approaches to Alphabetization and Routing in Phrasal Dictionaries', 'Monosemy and the Dictionary', and 'Why Don't All Sleepers Sleep? A Study of the Treatment of -er Nominals in Dictionaries'.

The broad pattern emerging is that dictionary houses now throughout the English-speaking world are investing heavily in reference works of current English, and are turning away from great historical projects. The counting-house clerks of Oxford who fought James Murray for a quarter of a century are now making sure that their large investments give quicker returns than they did while the fascicles of the *OED* made their stately appearance between 1884 and 1928. The tide is slowly turning away almost everywhere from diachronic to synchronic scholarship in the whole realm of linguistics. It is a predictable cycle after a century and a half in which comparative and historical philology held sway.

The period since 1950 was marked at its beginning by the *beatniks* (1955) of the *beat generation* (1952), by *hippies* (1953), and by the lawless, leather-jacketed motor-cyclists called *Hell's Angels* (1957). It has ended with the spectre of *AIDS* (first noted in 1982). *Amphetamines* (1938) like *Benzedrine* (1933) and *cannabis* (1798) ceased to be drugs prescribed only under medical supervision and passed into the hands of the rebellious young, to be joined at a later stage by *heroin* (1898) and *crack* (1985). New vocabulary poured in from the wars (Korea and Vietnam), dissenting movements of various kinds, and from the world of computers. This is not a history lesson but just a reminder that great global events inevitably produce bucketsful of new vocabulary. A small list of new words since 1950 gives something of the flavour of the period:

ayatollah (1950, *fig.* 1979)	Ms. (1952)
baby boom (1967)	the pill (1957)
bananas, to go (1968)	Sloane Ranger (1975)
bar code (1963)	sputnik (1957)
beta-blocker (1970)	user-friendly (1977)
black economy (1969)	yomp (verb) (1982)
hi-fi (1950)	yuppie (1984)
monetarism (1969)	

According to Sir Ernest Gowers in 1965, some missionaries of moral uplift adopted as their slogan 'Prayerize, Picturize, Actualize'. He greatly doubted if this formula would help them very much in the practice of meditation. He meant, of course, that no good can come of any new word ending in -*ize*. Throughout the period since 1950, indeed throughout the century, new formations of the -*ize* type have continued to fall through this hated grille, among the latest being *condomize*, *entitize*, and *incentivize*. It is regarded by the general public as a kind of flagellation of the language.

A continuing source of new words in the period since 1950 is the slightly farcical world of blends and shortenings. The latest words of these kinds, all probably not used before the 1980s, include *bluesical* (a blend of *blues* and *musical*), *compunications* (*computer* + *communications*), *infotainment* (serious news presented as entertainment; also *docutainment* and *edutainment*), and *warnography* (gruesome films, from *war* + *pornography*).

One of the paradoxes of modern times is that while many of the concepts and practices of the last decade are extremely disagreeable – *battered wife*, *child abuse*, *nuclear winter*, *ozone hole*, for example – the expressions themselves are unexceptionable as words.

Conclusion

I have attempted to describe some of the ways in which professional scholars have sought out new means of documenting our fast-changing language, and have supplied us with rings of keys to unlock many of its mysteries. I have also described the work of some of the great lexicographers and philologists of past centuries. The English language is now at an uneasy stage of its development and expansion: the sheer voluminousness and complexity of the network of the language throughout the English-speaking world place almost insuperable obstacles in the path of those whose job it is to set down an accurate record of all of its varieties. I can but hope, as a historical lexicographer (retired) myself, that the process of sifting and resifting the English of past centuries will be allowed to continue, and that in this matter lexicographers and not counting-house clerks will prevail. To adapt the first two lines of 'Burnt Norton', let us hope that time past and time present will also be present in time future.

Notes

1. Mrs Valerie Eliot confirmed (in a conversation on 7 November 1988) that her husband possessed a copy of the *Shorter Oxford* but not of the *OED* itself.

2. Two of my father's sisters went ashore in Sydney and settled in Wollongong, New South Wales.

3. The word *defunctive* is recorded in the *OED* only from Shakespeare's *The Phoenix and the Turtle* (1601): Let the Priest in Surples white, / That defunctive Musicke can, / Be the death-devining Swan, / Lest the *Requiem* lacke his right.

4. First announced in a paper entitled 'New Dictionary Schemes Presented to the Philological Society, 4th April, 1919', later printed in *Transactions of the Philological Society, 1925–1930*, 1931, pp. 6–11.

5. *A – Sluggishnes* published by 1988.

6. *The Scottish National Dictionary*, 10 vols., 1931–76; *A Dictionary of the Older Scottish Tongue, A–P* published by 1988.

7. *A Dictionary of American English*, edited by W. A. Craigie and J. R. Hulbert, 4 vols., 1938–44. Later joined by *A Dictionary of Americanisms*, edited by M. M. Mathews, 1951.

8. In a private letter Mr Donald Morrison has informed me that other (doubtless apochryphal) versions of what King George V said were current at the time. One was 'What's on at the Empire?' and another 'What news of the vampire?' (meaning Queen Mary). Mr Morrison added, 'My apologies to the excellent Royals.'

9. In fact the word that did trouble Dr Onions shortly before he died was *beatnik*. 'Where can it possibly have come from?' he asked me several times in or round about 1965.

Part II: Eight Essays on
English Lexicography and Grammar

1 The Treatment of Controversial Vocabulary in the *Oxford English Dictionary*

The methodology of the *OED*

1. Here[1] I use the expression 'controversial vocabulary' to mean 'the vocabulary that lies on or near the admission/exclusion boundary in the *OED* and its 1933 ('Suppl.) and 1972 (²Suppl.) Supplements'. Sexual words and colloquial and coarse words referring to excretory functions were 'controversial' in the *OED*, and as a result not all of them were admitted, but they are no longer so, and these will not be discussed. On the other hand, in recent years, racial vocabulary has moved significantly from the uncontroversial area towards the admission/exclusion boundary and will be discussed. A number of peripheral classes of words that have nothing to do either with sex or race are also described. The admission or exclusion of highly complex technical and scientific terms, e.g. in Mathematical Logic and Physics, is no longer a matter of controversy and such classes will not be discussed here.

The best starting-point for any discussion of problems of admission and exclusion is the section of the *OED* entitled 'General Explanations'. It provides a classification of that portion of the *Lexicon totius Anglicitatis* that was included in the twelve volumes of the *OED*, with diagrammatic and verbal indications of some of the reasons for excluding the remainder.

> Practical utility has some bounds, and a Dictionary has definite limits: the lexicographer must, like the naturalist, 'draw the line somewhere', in each diverging direction. He must include all the 'Common Words' of literature and conversation, and such of the scientific, technical, slang, dialectal, and foreign words as are passing into common use, and approach the position or standing of 'common

words', well knowing that the line which he draws will not satisfy all his critics. (p. xxvii)

The natural model for any lexicographer wishing to treat new vocabulary is the *OED* itself. Unfortunately no detailed analysis of marginal word-classes in the *OED* exists. Consequently in Volume 1 of ²Suppl. I frequently had to base decisions about such vocabulary on instinct and general experience and on the likelihood that such-and-such a policy had been adopted. Occasionally it was possible to produce an *ad hoc* analysis of some of the smaller word-classes but the need to maintain steady progress precluded the possibility of attempting anything more elaborate.

It is important to understand the methodology of the *OED*. From the mass of alphabetized quotations submitted by the readers, numerous sub-editors, many of them outside Oxford and some even living abroad, by inspection arranged the material into parts of speech and into senses, added definitions, and returned them to the editorial staff. These *ébauches* were then converted into something approaching their final form by the editorial staff,[2] who then submitted them to Dr Murray and the other editors for completion. The editors were thus at several removes from the choice made by the readers, or 'contributors' as they were then called, but to a large extent the preparation of the final copy for press was governed by the choice first made by the contributors.

The same main consideration applies in ²Suppl. though the staffing arrangements are different and we have no outside sub-editors. I make the first choice of vocabulary myself from the collection of quotations in our files in 40 Walton Crescent, at present approaching two million in number. The criterion of choice for items at the boundaries of the core of common words is the expectation that such words are likely to prove to be editable by my staff and myself, with outside assistance in specialized fields when necessary. The composition of such a group of items selected for drafting is usually very diverse. For example on 8 May this year, the sorted *mi*-material yielded the following successive items, and these were given to a member of my editorial staff for investigation and drafting:

mithril	(word invented by J. R. R. Tolkien)
Mithuna	(= Gemini in Indian astrology)

miti   (only R. L. Stevenson: exotic food in the
                     Marquesas)
miticide   (chemical substance capable of killing mites)
mitigated, ppl.a. (of religious orders)
mitigatingly, adv.
mitin   (anti-moth substance)
mitla   (a small, black dog-like cat described by the
                     explorer Colonel Percy Fawcett in 1925)

At the moment of choice only *miticide* of these eight items seemed certain of inclusion. The fate of the others will be determined (I have not yet seen the results) basically by their editability, and one of the tests of editability for such marginal items is that, in general, matching entries should already exist in the *OED*. The problem is to recognize a matching entry if one exists.

A simple example will illustrate this problem of matchability. When the drafted material for the section *ib-* reached me recently I noticed that the word *Ibicencan*, 'a native or inhabitant of Ibiza', for which we had one or two examples, had been omitted. As it was impossible to know offhand whether words of the type 'a native or inhabitant of a small Mediterranean island' had been treated in the *OED* I made a search, with the following results:

Dict.:   *Gibraltarian, Minorcan, Rhodian* (Rhodes). Also *Gaditanian* (Cadiz) and *Lesbian* (of the island of Lesbos, but only as an adj.).
[2]Suppl. 1: *Corfiote* (Corfu), *Cretan*, *Cypriot(e)*, *Gozitan* (Maltese island of Gozo), and *Majorcan* (in [1]Suppl., 1933). Also *Carpathian* adj. and *Cycladic* adj.

Once the evidence had been assembled it was clear that *Ibicencan* should be included, and all the more so because of a dog called *Ibicencan hound* (or *Ibiza hound*). In the process of editing the word *Ibicencan*, the synonyms *Ibicenco/Ibizenco* and *Ivicene* were also resurrected and drafted.

If at any time in the future an item selected by our readers should belong to the type 'a native or inhabitant of a small island in the Indian Ocean', or some other area, e.g. the Pacific Ocean, the China Sea, and so on, more analyses will be needed, and also evidence for the existence of more hounds (or seals, field-mice, and so on). With *Gaditanian* 'a native or inhabitant of Cadiz' in mind it would be possible to start all over again with the names used of the inhabitants of all the cities in the world, past and present. I need not labour the point. When dealing with geographical names we are faced with the problem of the treatment of an unlimited class of words. In what follows it will become apparent that it is in dealing with such peripheral classes that the 'judicial and regulative authority'[3] of a lexicographer is put to the test most severely and operates most clearly.

Classes of words normally excluded from the *OED*

2. I shall begin with an examination of some classes of words that were normally excluded from the *OED*.[4] In the nature of things the treatment cannot be exhaustive.

Excluded classes were mostly names, and some of the more important are as follows:

• Names of countries, counties, provinces, and states (*France, Kent, Ontario, Idaho*), cities (*Paris, Tokyo*), or smaller urban units (*Abingdon, Le Lavandou, Lindos*), and other geographical names (*Ganges, Plymouth Sound*) unless they had acquired transferred senses used absolutely, as *Bedfordshire* (='bed'), *Bloomsbury, Everest, Jersey* (cow), or attributively, as *Aylesbury duckling, Chelsea bun, Eton jacket,* and *Oxford bags*.[5]

Some exceptions are made in the *OED*, apparently on grounds of antiquity and availability of the evidence (i.e. quotations had been submitted by readers). For example, of the names of countries there are no entries in the *OED* for *Africa, America, Australia, Crete, Finland, France, Germany, Greece, Ireland, Scotland, Switzerland,* and *Wales*. Only attributive uses are given under *Norway* and *Sweden* (though the history of the name *Sweden* is dealt with in some detail). But some names of countries are treated in straightforward denotative uses, among them *Britain* (first recorded *a* 855, latest example 1868), *England* (*c* 897–1702), *Holland* (*a* 1400–1655), *Iceland* (*c* 1205–1780), *India* (*c* 893–1818), *Portugal* (*c* 1386–1824), *Spain* (*c* 1205–1838), and *West Indies* (1555–1837).

● Street-names, field-names, district-names, house-names, and so on, unless a transferred use has developed, as in *Carnaby Street, Coronation Street, Downing Street, Grub-street,* and *Wardour-street.*

● Names of persons (*William Shakespeare, Queen Victoria, George Washington*) unless a transferred sense exists, as *Casanova, Garamond* (type-face). Such words sometimes lose their initial capital, pass into the general vocabulary (e.g. *boycott, mackintosh*), and thus qualify for inclusion. Though the names of persons as such are excluded, the *OED* freely admits adjectival forms of the type *Audenesque, Chaplinesque,* and adjectival and substantival words of the type *Baconian* and *Gilbertian.* Also includable, though not in any systematic way, are names of fictional and other characters. For example, the *OED* has entries for *Boniface* (Farquhar's *Beaux' Stratagem* 1707), *Bountiful* (ditto), *Braggadochio* (*Faerie Queene*), *Caliban, Dolly Varden* (Dickens's *Barnaby Rudge*), *Gamp,* and *Grundy.* In ¹Suppl. (1933) *Dandie Dinmont* (Scott's *Guy Mannering*) and *Gradgrind* are treated, while those in ²Suppl. (1972) include *Alice, Cassandra, Crusoe, Dracula, Electra, Fagin, Fauntleroy,* and *Galahad.*[6]

● Names of motor vehicles (*Austin, Puch-Maxi, Suzuki, Volkswagen*),[7] aeroplanes (*Boeing, Concorde, Dakota, Ilyushin*),[8] and ships (*Cutty Sark, Queen Mary, Victory*). Also normally excluded are the names of bicycles (*B.S.A.*), coaches (*Cobb*), and trains (*The Cheltenham Flyer, The Master Cutler*).[9]

● Names of places of business (*Foyles, Harrods, Gum* [Moscow], *Macy's* [New York]). It is worth pausing for a moment to note that a slightly more hospitable view was taken in the *OED* of the names of inns and public houses. It is true that many are excluded. For example, none of the following A and B names entered in the yellow pages of the Oxford Area telephone directory of 1973 is treated in *OED* or ²Suppl. 1:

> Abingdon *Arms, Admiral* Holland, *Albion* Public House, The *Anchor,* The *Angel,* The *Apollo,* The *Avon,* The *Bakers Arms,* The *Barley Corn, Barley Mow, Bat & Ball, Bear Inn, Bear & Ragged Staff,* The *Bee Hive, Beech Tree Inn,* The *Bell Inn,* The *Ben Jonson, Bird in Hand,* The *Black Boy,* The *Black Horse,* The *Black Lion,* The *Black Swan,* etc., etc.

But there are entries in the *OED* for such names under *chequer/checker sb.*¹ 4, *cross keys, crown* 6 c; *eagle* 2 c, *elephant* 3, *lion* 5, and *mitre* 5.

• Non-anglicized names of plants and animals above the generic level
(*Liliaceæ*). The inclusion of Latin generic names of plants or animals
depends on the quantity of evidence found for the use of such a word in
an English context as the name of an individual and not as the name of a
genus: thus *Aspergillus* was excluded, but *aspidistra* and *forsythia* were
admitted. The actual number of genus names in a given class of plants
and animals is also important. For example, *Acropora*, the name of a
genus of corals, was omitted from ²Suppl. when it was ascertained that
there were some 6,000 genus names of corals in all.

• Also normally omitted from the *OED* are words which appear in
technical and scientific dictionaries but are rarely encountered in the
literature of the subject. For example, in 1959 we drafted an entry for
the word *acroteric.* Its currency seemed satisfactory since it was listed in
G. M. Gould's *The Practitioner's Medical Dictionary* (ed. 3, 1924), in I. F.
and W. D. Henderson's *Dictionary of Scientific Terms* (ed. 3, 1939), and
in Dorland's *Medical Dictionary* (ed. 22, 1951). Moreover it seemed a
slightly better formation than *acrotic*, which was already in the Dictionary. We drafted an entry on the basis of these references and submitted
it to an Oxford physiologist for approval, asking her, *inter alia*, if she
would insert a quotation for the word taken from some source other
than a dictionary. But she recommended omission since, she said, she
had never encountered the word in print, and we omitted it.[10]

The previous two paragraphs illustrate two well-founded canons of
lexicography: first, that an English-language dictionary, even one as
large and as hospitable as the *OED*, cannot accommodate all the
members of certain classes of words and, conversely, must exclude all,
or all but a few, of other classes; and secondly, that once a specialized
dictionary has entered a word of small currency, the entry is often
carried forward in an uncritical way into other dictionaries. In this
respect Dr Murray's comments in his presidential address to the
Society on 21 May 1880 (*TPS*, 1880–1, p. 127) remain as valid as they
were then: 'I want proof of the word's use, not of its occurrence in a list.'
'It is marvellous, and to the inexperienced incredible, how Dictionaries
and Encyclopaedias simply copy each other, without an attempt either
to verify quotations or facts.'[11]

Classes admitted but with qualificatory labels

3. This third section will be concerned with words that were admitted to the *OED* but with labels like *rare*⁻⁰, *rare*⁻¹, and the paragraph sign ¶.

Hapax legomena and rare words were freely admitted to the *OED*. In this group as in others the pattern of admission was governed as much by the choice made by the readers as by any abstract principles adopted by the editors. If a reader made a slip for such an item it was likely to be included, with small regard for consistency in comparable words, or in words drawn from other writers, in other parts of the Dictionary. Conversely a word that was not copied by a reader had little chance of inclusion since the editorial staff would almost certainly be unaware of its existence.

Some of the main classes of rare words may be illustrated as follows:

rare⁻⁰ (i.e. a word known to exist which has not been traced in a non-dictionary context).[12]

  implank v. to enclose with planks. 1611 Florio.

  imprevalence unprevailing character. 1828 Webster.

  impoverishly adv. so as to impoverish. 1847 Craig.

Such words were frequently recorded as occurring in more than one dictionary:

  impotentness impotence. 1530 Palsgrave; 1727 Bailey.

  impigrity quickness. 1623 Cockeram; 1656 Blount; 1658 Phillips; 1721 Bailey.

  implumous adj. unfeathered. 1755 Johnson; 1818 Todd; hence in mod. Dicts.

  marinorama a panoramic representation of sea views. 1847 Webster. In mod. Dicts.

rare⁻¹ (used similarly when only one non-dictionary context was known to exist).

  grimcundleȝc grimness. *c* 1200 (Ormin).

  kikelot a tattling woman. *a* 1225 *Ancr. R.*

  marshly adj. marshy. *c* 1386 Chaucer.

  marrement trouble, affliction. 1390 Gower.

  seneke an 'elder'. *a* 1400 *Pistill of Susan.*

  senatoire a senate-house. 1474 Caxton.

seneschaunce a territory under the government of a seneschal. 1525 Berners.

martel v. to hammer. 1590 Spenser.

wealsman one devoted to the public weal. 1607 Shakespeare.

inadulterate adj. unadulterated. 1648 Herrick.

impoignant adj. not sharp or piquant. 1733 Cheyne.

sendaline sendal (a thin rich silken material). 1865 Swinburne.

sphairistic adj. tennis-playing. 1882 *World.*

manualism the action or process of teaching by means of the manual alphabet. 1883 *Amer. Ann. Deaf & Dumb.*

rare.

masuel a mace used in battle. 13.. *Cœr de L.*; 13.. *Sir Beues.*

senectute old age. 1481 Caxton; 1533 Elyot.

manuable adj. 1. that may be handled easily. 1594. 2. of money: ? of handy size. 1638.

inabrogable adj. not abrogable. 1617.

seneschally the territory under the government of a seneschal. 1700, 1708.

inaccentuated adj. accentuated, emphasized. 1716.

manuscriptural adj. of or pertaining to manuscripts. 1856, 1874.

Nonce-words are frequently entered:

jail-deliver v. to deliver from jail. 1631.

laugh-at-able (s.v. *Laughable* adj.). 1844.

manusculpt an inscription carved or engraved by hand. a 1859 (De Quincey).

manucapt v. to direct by a writ of manucaption. 1898.

In Volume 1 of [2]Suppl. these labels *rare, rare*[−0], and *rare*[−1] were used sparingly. In future volumes they will be used more frequently in order to bring our policy into line with that of the Dictionary. For example, among the 'I' words recently prepared for press:

imberb adj. Beardless. *rare* (only Aldous Huxley, 1923).

impotentizing ppl.a. *rare*[−1]. That renders one impotent. 1920 Joyce *Let.* (1957) I.149.

impressionize v. *rare.* 1894–1905 examples.

in-earnestness Seriousness, serious intention. *rare*[−1] (Hopkins).

inoperancy Failure to operate or function. *rare*[−1] (T. S. Eliot).

The use of ¶. In the *OED*, the small paragraph sign was used to indicate 'catachrestic and erroneous uses, confusions, and the like' (p. xxxi of Volume I of the *OED*).[13] This is by far the most important circumstance in which the *OED* was straightforwardly prescriptive. The sign was used freely in all volumes of the Dictionary with unabated sternness. There is space here to mention only a few of the main categories:

(a) Erroneous and confused uses: general.[14]

Euphuism. 2. ¶ Erroneously for euphemism. 1865 Mrs Gaskell *Wives & Dau.* in *Cornh. Mag.* Aug. 139 'If anything did – go wrong, you know,' said Cynthia, using an euphuism for death. 1866 Geo. Eliot *F. Holt* (1868) 63 Those are your roundabout euphuisms that dress up swindling till, etc.

prostitute. ¶ **4.** Misused for prostrate *v.* 1620 Shelton *Quix.* (1746) IV.ix.69 He flung himself from his Horse, and with great Humility, went to prostitute himself before the Lady Teresa. 1624 Darcie *Birth of Heresies* xv.61 Prostituting themselves before the Images. 1662 J. Chandler *Van Helmont's Oriat.* 94 Places wherein the Quellem is immediately prostituted beneath the Clay.

tarantula. ¶ **4.** Erroneously for tarantella, the dance. 1698 Fryer *Acc. E. India & P.* 111 They labour as much as a Lancashire Man does at Roger of Coverly, or the Tarantula of their Hornpipe. 1865 *Daily Tel.* 14 Dec. 7/3 All the dances of the civilised world, from the tarantula to the *trois temps*.

(b) Latinisms, Germanisms, Hebraicisms, etc.

ever, *adv.* ¶ **4.** Giving a distributive sense to numerals. (A mere Germanism.) 1535 (Coverdale).

proscribe, *v.* **3.** ¶. As a literalism of rendering in Rhemish N.T. 1582.

why, *adv.* **1.c.** ¶ *And why?* is used in some early biblical versions, and hence in the Prayer-book Psalter, to render Heb. *kī* because, since, for: app. in imitation of *forwhy* after this was apprehended as interrogative. 1535 (Coverdale).

woad-ashes. ¶. Forms representing the G. and LG. words [MLG. *wed(e)asche*, etc.] are illustrated in the following: 1705, 1708, 1780 examples cited.

wood, *a.* 2. ¶ 2. Used inaccurately to render L. *furialis.* 1387 Trevisa *Higden* (Rolls) I. 197 In þat lond is a lake wonderful and wood (L. *furialis*), for who þat drynkeþ þerof he schal brenne in woodnesse of leccherie.

(c) Used as a symbol introducing an *obiter dictum,* i.e. *not* indicating an erroneous or confused use.

good, *a.* ¶ 23. **Good old** (see old *a.*).

like, *a.* A.1.b. ¶ Some phrasal uses of the adj. in this construction have a special idiomatic force. 1684–1899 examples.

shall. B.7.a. ¶ (*c*) In ironical affirmative in exclamatory sentence, equivalent to the above interrogative use. (Cf. Ger. *soll.*) *rare.* 1741.

This symbol (i.e. ¶), which was used occasionally in ²Suppl. 1,[15] is now being used somewhat more frequently in Volume 2 as a convenient indicator of certain types of *evitanda* that occur even in educated writings. In material recently prepared for press, for example, it was used in the following instances:

ignorant, adj. 5. *dial.* Ill-mannered, uncouth. ¶ Sometimes written as *iggerant* in imitation of vulgar speech.

iligant, adj. ¶ Used, chiefly as an Irishism, for elegant *a.*

imprimatur. ¶ Used confusedly = imprint *sb.* 3. 1970 *Daily Tel.* 7 May 13/2 The agent, not the candidate, is the one liable to fines . . . if he . . . issues one word of election literature without his own and the printer's imprimatur on it.

Words admitted sparingly

4. Words that were admitted sparingly because unlimited in number or very numerous.

There are many classes of this kind but only three of the more important can be mentioned here in any detail.

(a) Obvious combinations

These are provided throughout the Dictionary as the first part of the '*attrib.* and *Comb.*' sections of the commoner nouns and adjectives. They are usually illustrated by one example and no systematic attempt was made to trace the earliest occurrence. The treatment of these became a matter of some concern in ²Suppl. partly because meanwhile they had received far more generous treatment in the period and regional dictionaries. In practice I decided to add further examples of these obvious combinations, illustrated more or less in the same way as in the *OED*. Thus, s.v. *elf* sb. 6:

	OED			²Suppl. (Volume 1)	
elf-castle	1884			elf-craft	1919
elf-child	1856			elf-flower	1921
elf-dance	1884			elf-folk	1922
elf-flame	1884	*were joined by*		elf-friend	1937
elf-girl	1871			elf-key	1924
elf-horn	1884			elf-kingdom	1954
elf-house	1884			elf-light	1913
elf-knight	1884			elf-speech	1955
elf-lady	1884			elf-wing	1929
elf-land	1483, 1847				
elf-like	1583, 1841				
elf-rod	1884				
elf-woman	1884				

The new examples were drawn from the works of Walter de la Mare, J. R. R. Tolkien, Robert Graves, and Edmund Blunden. The *OED* examples, as it happened, were mostly Victorian and almost all from Child's *Ballads* (1884). It was important to bear in mind that in both cases the examples were drawn from literary sources and that the list could have been greatly extended. Any such extension, however, would have made the *attrib.* and *Comb.* sections disproportionately long.[16]

(b) Nonsense and invented words

This is a large and important class and one where arbitrary factors are likely to govern the choice to a very large extent. In this connection it is interesting to observe the fate of the words that Lewis Carroll invented in the poem 'Jabberwocky' in *Through the Looking Glass* (1872). Of these words thirteen fall in the range A–G:

OED: beamish, chortle, galumph.
¹Suppl. (1933): frabjous.

[2]Suppl. (1972): bandersnatch, burble, frabjous, gyre.
Excluded: borogove, brillig, callay, callooh, frumious, gimble.

I now regret the omission of these six words from Volume I of [2]Suppl. and will include the H–Z 'Jabberwocky' words in later volumes.[17]

(c) Miscellaneous types of word-play

Typical examples in the *OED* and Supplements may be cited:

Dict.: **devilship. b.** *humorously.* As a title: cf. *lordship.* (Her devilship of a wife, 1760).
   foolocracy. a. Government by fools. **b.** A governing class or clique consisting of fools. 1832, 1861. Also **foolometer**, that which serves as a standard for the measurement of fools or of folly. 1837, 1851. And **foolosopher**, a foolish pretender to philosophy. 1549, *c* 1600, 1694. All three marked *humorous.*

[1]Suppl. (1933):
   highstrikes. *jocular colloq.* orig. *dial.* or *vulgar.* Perverted form of hysterics. 1834–1914.
   Ibsene, Ibsenity (*nonce-wds.*) (with play on *obscene, obscenity*). Entered s.v. Ibsenism.

[2]Suppl. (Volume 2, forthcoming):
   ickyboo *adj.* ill. ('Sapper' and later thriller writers.)
   ickylickysticky *adj.* (*nonce-wd.*) unpleasantly sticky. (James Joyce.)

These 'literary fungi', as Herbert Coleridge once termed them,[18] were not commonly admitted to the *OED*. At a meeting of the Philological Society on 8 November 1860[19] it was decided that word-puns, such as *hepistle* and *shepistle*, should be excluded, and the editors seem to have kept to this decision for the most part. Malapropisms, as such, were not admitted into the Dictionary. Sir Lucius O'Trigger may say of Mrs Malaprop that 'she's quite the queen of the dictionary!' (*Rivals* II.ii) but the Dictionary ignores her almost completely. Thus from one of the best-known contexts:

> Sure if I *reprehend* anything in this world, it is the use of my *oracular* tongue, and a nice *derangement* of *epitaphs*!   (*Rivals* III.iii)

only the erroneous use of the word *reprehend* is treated in the *OED* and then, curiously, with quotations from Shakespeare and John Gay but none from Sheridan. As if to emphasize the rejection of malapropisms, the only place where Mrs Malaprop seems to be quoted in the Dictionary is under *Impeachment* 4, 'I own the soft impeachment' which seems to be a genuine use, and not one of her customary ludicrous misuses.

Allusionary word-play that cannot be included in even large historical dictionaries like the *OED* can be illustrated by the following example:

> 1973 *Sunday Telegraph* 11 Mar. 19/3 In return for his efforts at the topping out [ceremony for Wolfson College, Oxford], Berlin was given an engraved goblet. Before one could say Poulson he had handed it over to the college as an heirloom.

Other large classes of words which received minimal or arbitrary treatment in the *OED* because of the necessity of 'drawing the line somewhere' included the following:

The technical terms of medieval and Renaissance rhetoric.

Counting-out rhymes of the type 'eeny, meeny, miney, mo' and other counting words, for example Celtic numerals of the type 'Yan, Tan, Tethera, Methera, Pip'.

Expressions of the type 'a Ben Jonson', 'a Dryden', 'a Churchill' (=a writer, etc., reminiscent of Ben Jonson, etc.).

Allusive uses of the following type: 1935 e. e. cummings *Let.* 2 Jan. (1969) 130 Of course if that tree hadn't been murdered, & murdered crosswise, that tree would have remained a *mute inglorious Milton.*[20]

Trade marks

5. Extralinguistic and sociolinguistic factors operate, or have operated, powerfully in the following three areas: sexual, proprietary, and racial terms.

In an article in *The Times Literary Supplement*[21] I gave a brief account of the stages leading to the reintroduction of the so-called four-letter words into twentieth-century dictionaries after an absence of something like 200 years. There is therefore no need to repeat the account here.

The treatment of proprietary terms[22] is attended by many difficulties, and I can do little more than present an outline of some of the problems. It is impressed upon the Dictionary readers that proprietary names are normally excluded from the *OED*: nevertheless they often encounter such words in literary contexts and make slips for them, e.g.:

> 1944 A. Christie *Towards Zero* 89 'It's raining, you know.' 'I know, I've got a Burberry.'[23]
>
> 1940 W. H. Auden *Another Time* 96 And had everything necessary to the Modern Man, A gramophone, a radio, a car and a frigidaire.[24]

Proprietary terms are of more than usual concern to lexicographers since such terms are often the subject of protracted and complicated correspondence or even of threatened litigation. Moreover dictionary entries are consulted by the Registrar of Trade Marks at the Patent Office in London, and by his analogues in other countries, and the registration of such terms is sometimes delayed or brought into question because, among other factors, dictionaries show a term without indication of its proprietary status.[25] The problems are made worse by the fact that few dictionary offices have the facilities to establish the latest credentials of the many terms involved.[26]

The preferred expression in *OED* work for the names of these marks is 'proprietary term'. It is used as a synonym of 'trade name', 'trade mark', and 'trade term',[27] notwithstanding the fact that the four expressions are not synonymous in legal and business language. Trade-mark lawyers, for example, usually employ the term 'trade mark' when speaking of the proprietary name of a product, e.g. 'Quaker' Oats; and use 'trade name' when referring to the name of a business, e.g. General Motors Corporation. When the expression 'proprietary term' is used in the *OED* it normally means that the editorial staff have verified that the term in question is the name of a product, etc., that has been registered either in the Patent Office in London,[28] or in Washington, or in both. It is usually impracticable, though of course not impossible, to seek information about the status of such marks in other countries. In ²Suppl. 1, for example, we simply assumed that the well-known brand-names of continental drinks like *Cinzano* and *Dubonnet* were registered in the appropriate manner in Italy and France. Trade names from

English-speaking regions other than Britain and the United States are usually omitted from the *OED* – hence the omission from ²Suppl. 1 of names like *Duco* (South Africa and elsewhere) and *Caliphont* (New Zealand), and the same applies to the proprietary terms of foreign countries outside Europe. In this respect our admission criteria are therefore more stringent than they are for other word-classes, since overseas words that are not trade marks are recorded on a generous scale.

Proprietary terms should properly be entered in dictionaries with a capital initial letter in the lemma (e.g. *Bovril*). If in literary works or other sources read for the *OED* such names are used with a lower-case initial letter the entry also contains the uncapitalized form (e.g. *Bovril* . . . Also *bovril*), at the risk of suggesting that the term is being used generically.

It is worth stating at this point that the generic use of a trade mark in a dictionary is probably not in itself actionable in this country at present, though since 1959 there has been an action in Denmark, Sweden, and Finland.²⁹ Naturally if erroneous information appears in an entry the editors and publishers of a dictionary would wish to make the necessary correction as soon as possible. But dictionary editors in Britain probably cannot be required to remove lower-case lemmata, or to delete literary examples showing a trade mark used more or less generically, provided that the entry accurately represents usage. An erroneous entry would not seem to amount to infringement under the Act, because the dictionary publisher will not normally be trading in the goods in question.³⁰ Nor will it be passing off for similar reasons.³¹ The only possibility of action would appear to be in the tort of injurious falsehood,³² but for a trade-mark proprietor to succeed he would have to show malice on the part of the publishers or editor of the dictionary. This would be unlikely if the entry did accurately represent literary use. Accurate recording of genuine use by the proprietor should, of course, never be actionable. None of us would be allowed to manufacture a toffee-lined chocolate sweetmeat shaped in bars, wrap the bars in shiny brown paper with the word 'Mars' on the outside, and put them on the market. But if we happen to be lexicographers we are free if we wish to enter this name as part of the general entry for the word *Mars*. Twenty-first-century readers will then know what it was that Toppy in C. Day ewis's *The Otterbury Incident*³³ gave to the errand boy,³⁴ and will be spared the long search that we had for 'Bengal lights' in *The Waste Land* (see p. 69).

It should not be assumed that such a term, once registered, remains a trade mark indefinitely. For example, *nylon* ceased to be a proprietary term in 1963 when the name *Bri-Nylon* was introduced for the same range of materials. In the United States the word *trampoline* ceased to be a trade mark and passed into the public domain on 5 April 1961 on the order of the Iowa District Court.[35] In 1962 the word *thermos* ceased to be a trade mark in the United States, and Canada followed suit in 1967, but it remains a trade mark in Great Britain at the time of writing (1973). The literary evidence for the use of the word *Thermos* outside advertising contexts – showing for example that Shackleton took Thermos flasks with him to the Antarctic in 1909[36] – is fascinating but must await treatment elsewhere, as must also a description of its word environment, that is, the rivalry of the general synonyms *vacuum flask/ Dewar flask*, etc., and of the brand names of similar articles, e.g. *Aladdin, Escort, Isovac, Nu-flask, Supervac*, etc.[37]

A perfect historical dictionary, it could be argued, would include the names of all proprietary terms found in literary works and in the newspapers (other than in advertisements) up to the present day, since future generations will not easily be able to ascertain the meaning of the names that do not survive, and all the more so because the Patent Offices do not preserve details of lapsed registrations. The truth of the matter, however, is that the number of such names at any one time in Britain alone probably equals or may even exceed the number of words in the whole of the *OED*. For example, the third edition of *U.K. Trade Names* (Kompas Publishers Ltd, 1970) contains more than 90,000 trade names drawn from a wide range of trades and businesses, but excluding, for example, industries engaged in the preparation of food, drink, tobacco, and pharmaceuticals, and also excluding all trade names and marks of which the registration had lapsed before 1970. In the light of these figures the inclusion of some 90 proprietary terms in ²Suppl. 1 is seen to amount to a policy of near exclusion of the whole word-class.

A classified list of the ²Suppl. 1 terms is provided in an appendix to this chapter. I do not know how many terms were treated in the *OED* but they were not numerous: perhaps the best-known entries are those for *Kodak, Tabloid*, and *Vaseline*.

It is interesting to observe that a comparatively small proportion of such terms generate adjectival, verbal, etc., terms, and even transferred senses. Thus in ²Suppl. 1: *biro* (verb), *biroed* (ppl.a.), *bovrilize* (verb), *caterpillar* (verb), *cellophaned* (adj.); sense 2 of *bovril* is defined as a 'facetious alteration of brothel sb. 3'; while *Coca-Cola* yields the pregnant forms *coca-colonization* and *coca-colonize*.

My preliminary investigation of this very large and largely unexplored field leads me to make the following observations:

(*a*) The entries in the *OED* for such words are valuable but antiquated, and should not be relied on as a guide to the proprietary status of the words at the present time.

(*b*) Because of the importance of the matter to the owners of the trade marks, it will be desirable to record in future volumes of ²Suppl. details of the later history and present status of all such words that are treated in the *OED*,[38] and to continue to record the registration details, in so far as these are establishable, in new entries for such words.

(*c*) In the absence of any clause in the Trade Marks Act about trade marks and dictionaries, it remains desirable to include in all dictionaries (as was done in ²Suppl. 1, p. xxiii) a statement that by the inclusion of such words no judgement concerning their legal status is made or implied.

(*d*) It is already difficult to establish the precise nature of many named commercial products that occur in literary works written before 1900. This loss of information will become progressively more serious, and points to the need for a dictionary on historical principles of commercial names occurring in literary works of the nineteenth and twentieth centuries.[39] Such a work would deal with all the elixirs, ointments, brands of blacking and stove-polish, commercial names of stockings, and so on, that occur in Dickens, Trollope, and other major writers of the period, as, for example, in chapter 11 of *David Copperfield* when David asks for a glass of Genuine Stunning ale, and in chapter 10 of *Pickwick Papers* 'a polish which would have struck envy to the soul of the amiable Mr. Warren (for they used Day and Martin at the White Hart)'.[40] As a further minor illustration of the need for such a work I noted that the *OED* entry for *chlorodyne*, 'a factitious formation from *chloroform* and *anodyne*', a common brand name of the time, leaves the status of the word obscure. At least two cases were heard, one in 1864 and the other in 1873 (Browne *v.* Freeman),[41] concerning the ownership of the name of this drug. Since it is said to have contained a tincture of Indian hemp among its ingredients, and since one of Ouida's characters 'could no more live without a crowd about her than she could sleep without chlorodyne', such a dictionary would presumably be of interest to medical historians as well as to students of language.

Racial and religious terms

6. Racial and religious terms required and received careful attention in the *OED* and its Supplements. Nevertheless the dictionary treatment of such terms has been brought into question in recent years. I have space merely to give a brief account of some recent developments and to set down some guidelines in these controversial matters. Most particularly I want to stress the importance of rejecting Guralnikism, the racial equivalent of Bowdlerism, as a solution as far as historical and 'unabridged' dictionaries are concerned. Dr David B. Guralnik, Editor in Chief of *Webster's New World Dictionary*, Second College Edition, 1970, excluded words like *dago*, *kike*, *wog*, and *wop* from his dictionary on the following grounds:

> It was decided in the selection process that this dictionary could easily dispense with those true obscenities, the terms of racial or ethnic opprobrium, that are, in any case, encountered with diminishing frequency these days. (Foreword, p. viii)

The definitions of the 'key' racial and religious terms in the *OED* are somewhat antiquated but are almost wholly inoffensive. A kind of old-fashioned charm can be observed in some definitions, e.g. that Quakers are 'distinguished by . . . plainness of dress and manners', and by the small-type note s.v. *Mormon* that polygamy 'is now understood to have been abandoned in obedience to the law of the United States'.

Similarly, the illustrative examples are mostly now only of historical interest since the *latest* examples are almost all of no later date than the last quarter of the nineteenth century. Thus (in each case the date stated is the date of the latest example in the *OED*):

Aboriginal	(1873)	Mormon	(1884)
Negro	(1864)	Quaker	(1876)
Red Indian	(1887)	Spiritualist	(1876)

Most of the examples are neutral in tone:

1864 C. Geikie *Life in Woods* xxii, 1874, 349 As he came near, I saw he was a negro.

or supportive:

1827 Ht Martineau *Soc. Amer.* II.120 No mean testimony to the intellectual and moral capabilities of Negroes

Exceptions like the following are rare (s.v. *Nigger*):

1818 H. B. Fearon *Sk. Amer.* 46 The bad conduct and inferior nature of niggars.

In the treatment of terms to do with subjects like spiritualism and clairvoyance the *OED*, in common with other dictionaries, makes frequent use of expressions like 'allegedly' and 'professedly'. No serious objection has been raised to this practice, and it is hard to see how else to define such words in the absence of objective verification of the data that is accepted as such by the whole community. For example:

Medium *sb.* **8.b.** *Spiritualism*, etc. A person *who is supposed to be* the organ of communications from departed spirits.
Spirit-rapping. 1. *pl.* Rappings *alleged to be made* by spirits in answer to questions addressed to them.

In Vol. 1 of ²Suppl. the same method of defining was adopted, e.g.:

ectoplasm. 2. A viscous substance *which is supposed* to emanate from the body of a spiritualistic medium, and to develop into a human form or face.

From the earliest times, unpleasant attitudes and practices based upon the supposed inferiority or beastliness of specified ethnic or provincial groups have produced a large number of terms of vulgar abuse, and the more important of these are recorded in the *OED*. Thus, for example, and it is a potent example, supported by illustrative examples from 1620 to 1887, s.v. *Yorkshire* sense 2:

Used allusively, esp. in reference to the † boorishness, cunning, sharpness, or trickery attributed to Yorkshire people. *To come* (or *put*) *Yorkshire on one*, to cheat, dupe, overreach him. *Yorkshire bite*, a sharp overreaching action or person. †Also in prov. phr. *a pair of Yorkshire sleeves in a goldsmith's shop*, said of anything worthless.

This use appears now to be obsolete but the *OED* entry ensures that its currency in the seventeenth, eighteenth, and nineteenth centuries is permanently recorded.

As far as I know this use of *Yorkshire* was never the subject of hostile correspondence to the editors of the *OED* and no adverse comments on its inclusion in the Dictionary have been received since 1957 when I began work on the new Supplement. But some other dictionary entries have had considerable attention. For example, the Negroes of the United States have been campaigning for at least half a century against the use of *nigger* and for the capitalization of *Negro*. They have succeeded only in the second of these. Since the capitalized forms *Negro* and *Negress* were first adopted by the *New York Times* on 7 March 1930,[42] all major publications in the United States and elsewhere have gradually fallen into line. Similarly it is usual for the words *Aborigine*, *Aboriginal*, and their derivatives to be printed with a capital letter in Australian publications. Further examples of general changes that have been made in editions of dictionaries and reference books issued since about 1930 are the replacement of the word *Asiatic* by *Asian*[43] and of *Muhammadan* by *Muslim*. Many publications in the United States have abandoned the word *Negro* in favour of *black*, and collocations of *black* (e.g. *Black English, Black Studies*) are now common in written work. Others again favour *Afro-American* instead of either *Negro* or *black*.

For the future treatment of racial and religious terms certain conclusions seem inescapable:

(*a*) The entries in the *OED* for such words are valuable as a record of their currency and application down to the end of the nineteenth century but are in many respects antiquated and misleading now because of changes in social, religious, and ethnic attitudes and opinions.

(*b*) New terms of this kind should be admitted to the Dictionary, however opprobrious they may seem to those to whom they are applied, or however controversial the set of beliefs professed by the members of minority sects (e.g. *dianetics, scientology*), and should receive parity of treatment with non-religious and non-ethnic terms.

(*c*) To avoid misunderstanding and hostility it is desirable that the historical record of words like *Jew, Mormon, Negro, nigger,* and others already entered in the *OED* should be brought up to date in ²Suppl. Such modifications will not need to be restricted to the ethnic and religious terms themselves. For example, since it is now wholly inaccurate to describe the Indians of North America as 'savages' the following *OED* definition will need to be revised:

> *Waugh.* An exclamation indicating grief, indignation or the like. Now chiefly as attributed to N. American Indians *and other savages*.

In such a case it will be a simple matter to add a note: 'For last three words of def. read "and other indigenous peoples".' In other cases the updating process will be more complicated.

Our forthcoming entry for the word *Jew* will serve as an example of a word needing more complicated updating. *OED*'s sense 2 of *Jew* read as follows:

> *transf.* As a name of opprobrium or reprobation; *spec.* applied to a grasping or extortionate money-lender or usurer, or a trader who drives hard bargains or deals craftily. (Illustrative examples 1606–1844.)

Similarly *Jew* (verb) is defined as follows:

> *colloq. trans.* To cheat or overreach, in the way attributed to Jewish traders or usurers. (Illustrative examples *a* 1845–91.)

Sense 2 of the noun will be brought up to date in the following manner:

> (Further Examples.) In medieval England, Jews, though engaged in many pursuits, were particularly familiar as money-lenders, their activities being publicly regulated for them by the Crown, whose protégés they were. In private, Christians also practised money-lending, though forbidden to do so by Canon Law. Thus the name of Jew came to be associated in the popular mind with usury and any extortionate practices that might be supposed to accompany it, and gained an opprobrious sense.

Illustrative examples will follow, ranging in date from 1846 to the present day and including the following:

> 1906 J. M. Synge *Let.* 29 Sept., 1971, 31 What have I done that you should write to me as if I was a dunning Jew? 1920 T. S. Eliot *Ara Vos Prec* 14 The jew is underneath the lot. Money in furs. 1952 G. Bone *Came to Oxford* xi.34 There is a curious fallacy, rather wide-spread,

that a borrower of money is an innocent and hapless person, while a lender is a shark, a harpy, a 'Jew'.

The expression *Jew boy* (sense 3 a of *Jew*) is still current and further examples stand in the drafted entry, starting with one of 1796 and including the following more recent examples:

> 1929 D. H. Lawrence *Let.* 10 Oct., 1962, II. 1208 Spring doesn't only come for the moral Jew-boys. 1959 N. Mailer *Advts. for Myself*, 1961, 50 Jewboy, blond Jewboy Wexler perched by the cellar window, tackling Japs with machine-gun bullets. 1972 *Observer* 7 May, Mrs Lane Fox dismisses what she calls the country set, who call their children 'the brats', talk about 'thrashing them into shape', support Enoch Powell and still refer to 'jew boys'.

The expression *to jew down* will be added under *Jew, jew* (verb), and the examples in the drafted entry include the following:

> 1939 A. Powell *What's become of Waring* v.140 Then we can meet again and jew each other down. 1969 R. Lowell *Notebook 1967–1968* 69 This embankment, jewed – No, yankeed – by the highways down to a grassy lip. 1972 *New Society* 11 May 201/1, I got jewed down in [name of store] over the cheap offer.

The essential point is that such expressions, however deplorable their use may be taken to be, are not difficult to find in print and must therefore by the usual standards of the *OED* be regarded as 'current' and so recordable.

Conclusion

7. Throughout this chapter I have endeavoured to place emphasis upon the need for constant decision-making at the boundaries of many word-classes. The 'judicial and regulative authority' of the editor must be applied with firmness and consistency to avoid the inclusion of more than a reasonable number of items from some very large classes of words that straddle the border, leaving the remainder to be treated in separate period, regional, and subject dictionaries. 'Offensiveness' to a particular group or faction is unacceptable as a ground for the exclusion of any word or class of words. 'Sensitive' terms, i.e. those to do with

race, religion, and sex, as well as proprietary terms, will need to be kept under constant review in the remaining volumes of the Supplement to the *OED* since it is unlikely that any further opportunity will present itself in the twentieth century to complete the historical record of such words. But in the end I return to a purely practical point: the main governing factor in the choice of words to be treated is the editability of a given item in the time available and with the resources at my disposal. A dictionary that is delayed indefinitely is of no value to anybody.

Appendix

Classification of Proprietary Terms in Volume 1 (A–G) of *A Supplement to the OED* (1972).

Aircraft and vehicles: autogiro, Caterpillar, clipper *sb.*¹, Ford, Gyro-dyne.

Business equipment, including stationery: addressograph, Biro, Comptometer, Dictaphone, Dictograph, Flexowriter.

Chemical (other than pharmaceutical): Decalin, Freon, Gammexan(e).

Clothing and fabrics: Acrilan, Burberry, Celanese, Crombie, Duvetyn, Dynel, Fibro, Fibrolane, Grenfell Cloth.

Devices, apparatus (other than business): Brownie *sb.*³, Cordtex, Dome of Silence, Editola, Elsan, Fade-Ometer, Frigidaire, Frisbee.

Electrical and electronic: Amplidyne, audion, Dekatron, Digitron.

Food, drink, and tobacco: Bass, Bovril, Bristol cream, Carpano, Cinzano, Coca-Cola, cointreau, Coke, Corona, Cracker Jack, Drambuie, Dubonnet, Dundee marmalade, Gauloise, Gentleman's Relish, Gervais, Gitane, Guinness.

Pharmaceutical: Amytal, atebrin/atabrine, Avertin, Benzedrine, chinosol, Coramine, Dexedrine, Dial, Dicumarol, Dramamine, Drinamyl, Evipan, Fucidine.

Paper and plastics: bakelite, Cellon, Cellophane, Duxeen, Formica, Galalith.

Substances (non-chemical): alundum, Armour-plate, Bitumastic, blanco, Calor, Carborundum, Ciment Fondu, Coalite, Cocoon, Duralumin, Ess Bouquet, Eureka, Fiberglas, glyptal, Gunk.

Unclassified: CinemaScope, Cinerama, En-Tout-Cas.

Notes

1. The original place of publication of this and of the essays that follow is given in Acknowledgements on p. xv.

2. '[In the Scriptorium in Banbury Road] the copy lay on the shelves having been prepared into senses and provided with definitions, by so-called sub-editors (see *OED* Introd.). Some of these were excellent, as Rev. C. B. Mount, and the sisters Toulmin-Smith; many were indifferent. In addition there were loose slips of 'new material' which had to be run in . . . I don't think any of us three [*sc.* Maling, Yockney, G.W.S.F.] made much use of the sub-editors' work; we usually dissembled all the sections, arranged the slips in chronological order, and started *de novo*, perhaps glancing at the definitions to see whether there were any good ideas.' – G. W. S. Friedrichsen in a private letter to me of 27 May 1971, describing his work on the *OED* between 1909 and 1912.

3. The Revd. Derwent Coleridge in *TPS*, 1860–1, p. 154.

4. I do not know of any class of words that was *totally* excluded though I cannot say that I have investigated every possibility.

5. The examples are drawn from the *OED* itself or from the 1933 or 1972 Supplements without distinction.

6. It is easy to demonstrate how unsystematically the choice was made from the absence of such names as *Ariel, Arthur* (King), *Banquo, Barkis, Bottom, Bumble, Christopher Robin, Faustus, Gulliver,* and so on.

7. The only exception in ²Suppl. was *Ford*.

8. But *clipper*¹ and *Gyrodyne*, both in ²Suppl., are minor exceptions.

9. But *Flying Scotchman*, the nineteenth-century name of the *Flying Scotsman*, is dealt with in the *OED* s.v. *Scotchman* 1 b. Cf. also *OED Irishman* b (Wild Irishman). *Blue Train* was included in ²Suppl. 1.

10. We could have made an entry like that in the *OED* for *Genesiology*: The science of generation. 1882 in Ogilvie; and in later dictionaries. But in an age of proliferating technical and scientific terminology, omission of such unsupported items is the better policy.

11. Nevertheless the *OED* editors included some entries 'cannibalized' from other dictionaries: see below.

12. The examples are placed in chronological order. It will be noted that all centuries from the thirteenth to the nineteenth are represented.

13. It is defined in the *OED* s.v. *Paragraph* sb. 1 as 'sometimes introducing an editorial *obiter dictum* or protest'.

14. Curiously it is not used in many places where it would be expected, e.g.:

> **comprehend,** *v.* 1.b. As an illiterate blunder for apprehend. 1599 Shaks. *Much Ado* III.iii.25 You shall comprehend all vagrom men.
> **exion.** Blunder of Mrs Quickly for 'action'. 1597 Shaks. *2 Hen. IV,* II.i.32, I pra' ye, since my Exion is enter'd . . . let him be brought in to his answer.
> **expressivo,** bad form of Espressivo. 1823 in Crabb *Technol. Dict.*; and in mod. Dicts.
> **vagrom,** *a.* [Illiterate alteration of vagrant *a.* . . . . In mod. use only after Shakspere.] 1599 (Shaks. *Much Ado* [Dogberry] and four nineteenth-century examples.

15. E.g. *aspidistra* (¶ Illiterate forms were formerly frequent); *culture* (¶ with distortion of spelling to indicate affected or vulgar pronunciation); *datum* (¶ used in pl. form with sing. construction); *employee* (¶ in US often written *employe*).

16. The absence from ²Suppl. (Volume 1) of *car-stung, dreg-boozed, electric-eyed* and *gun-blue* (Christopher Ball's review in *TES*, 22 Dec. 1972) does not imply that 'the coverage of the literary vocabulary is rather more limited than that of the core vocabulary of English'. Many more obvious combinations from *all* areas of vocabulary could have been included had we wished to. In practice the great majority that are admitted are in fact from literary sources.

17. I have not analysed our treatment of the vocabulary of Edward Lear, James Joyce, Ogden Nash, and others, in ²Suppl. 1, but I would expect to find that the pattern was similar to that for the 'Jabberwocky' words.

18. *TPS*, 1860–1, p. 40.

19. *Ibid.*, p. 43.

20. But note ²Suppl. (Volume 1) s.v. *bang* sb.¹ 2, with allusion to T. S. Eliot's line 'Not with a bang but a whimper'.

21. 'Four-letter words and the *O.E.D.*', *TLS*, 13 Oct 1972, p. 1233.

22. In this section I am grateful to Mr Peter Hayward, St Peter's College, Oxford, Editor of *Reports of Patents, Design and Trade Marks Cases* (published annually by the Patent Office, London), and Mr Harvey W. Mortimer, a New York trade-mark attorney and formerly a member of the Dictionary Listing Committee of the United States Trademark Association, for expert advice and assistance.

23. The registered trade mark is in fact *Burberrys*. See ²Suppl. *Burberry*.

24. In the original paper I dealt here with T. S. Eliot's expression 'Bengal lights' (see p. 69 above).

25. '[Under US law] the route by which a trademark is adjudged to have passed into the public domain is via adversary litigation. For example, a registrant may sue for infringement and the defense will be that the mark has become generic of the goods. Proofs are adduced by the defense on this point. They include (most damaging) generic use of the trademark by the owner himself wherein he refers to the product in such a way as to lead the public to believe that the trademark is the generic name for the product, rather than an indication of a particular brand of the product. Other proofs are convincing: common use by the public of the trademark as a generic term, the same type of use by periodicals, trade journals, dictionaries (e.g. lower case initial letters, instead of capitals). Thus the fate of *aspirin, mimeograph, nylon, linoleum* (a British case), *dry ice, escalator, shredded wheat, trampoline, yo-yo,* and *raisin bran*.' Private letter dated 1 May 1973 from Mr Harvey W. Mortimer to R. W. B. For the UK law as to registered marks which have become generic, see section 15 of the Trade Marks Act, 1938.

26. Indispensable reference works on trade marks include I. B Sebastian, *A Digest of Cases of Trade Mark, Trade Names, Trade Secret, Goodwill, &c. decided in the courts of the United Kingdom, India, the Colonies and the United States of America,* London, 1879; *Digest of the Patent, Design, Trade Mark & Other Cases* (relating to Patents, Designs, and Trade Marks from 1883 to 1949), 3 vol., Patent Office, London, 1959; Frank I. Schechter, *The Historical Foundations of the Law relating to Trade-Marks,* New York, 1925; and *Kerly's Law of Trade Marks and Trade Names,* 10th edition, ed. T. A. Blanco White and Robin Jacob, London, 1972. A useful concise treatment of the subject is provided in T. A. Blanco White and Robin Jacob, *Patents, Trade Marks, Copyright and Industrial Designs,* London, 1970. But a search must still be made in the Patent Offices to establish the present status of a given mark.

27. All these terms are also used in the *OED* and Supplements.

28. The Register of Trade Marks kept by the Patent Office under section 1(i) of the

Trade Marks Act, 1938. A trade mark may also be protected, irrespective of registration, by an action for passing off (see below).

29. 'Misuse of Trademarks in Dictionaries: the Remedy in Denmark', *Trade Mark Reporter* LXI (1971), pp. 468–9. Protection for trade-mark owners was enacted in Section 11 of Denmark's Trade Mark Act in 1959 which reads as follows: 'In publishing encyclopaedias, handbooks, textbooks or similar literature of nonfictional nature the author, editor and publisher are liable at the request of the proprietor of a registered trademark to ensure that the mark is not reproduced without indicating that it is a registered trademark.

'If any person neglects the provisions of paragraph 1 of this section he will be liable to pay the costs of publishing in a suitable manner a rectifying notice.'

30. See the case of Ravok (Weatherwear) *v.* National Trade Press (1955) 1 Q.B. 554 in which the publishers of a directory of trade marks were held not liable in an infringement action under the Act for an erroneous statement as to the proprietorship of a mark, but where the possibility of other remedy was left open.

31. Passing off is an action whereby, even without registration, a trade-mark proprietor may prevent a competitor using the same or a similar mark. The proprietor has to show that the mark has *by use* become distinctive of his goods or business, and it is of particular help in those areas when registration is not possible, e.g. the names of hotels or in other service industries. See Kerly, *op. cit.*, chapter 16.

32. This is an action available to A where B maliciously publishes a false statement to C which is likely to cause damage to A. What amounts to malice in this tort is a matter of some difficulty and dispute. For general discussion of the tort see e.g. Kerly, *op. cit.*, chapter 18. See also J. D. Heydon, *Economic Torts*, Sweet & Maxwell, London, 1973, chapter 4.

33. Chapter 6, p. 112.

34. The word occurs commonly in fiction, e.g. in Len Deighton, *Horse under Water* (1963), ix, p. 45 and M. Waddell, *Otley Pursued*, 1967, xii, p. 105.

35. American Trampoline Co., Jefferson, Iowa *v.* Nissen Trampoline Co., Cedar Rapids, Iowa.

36. The *OED* entry includes the following quotation: '1909 *Westm. Gaz.* 16 Sept. 5/2 Lieutenant Shackleton testified to the fact that the Thermos flask helped him to perform his wonderful feats in the Antarctic.'

37. Thirty-six brand names of vacuum flasks are given in an article in the consumer magazine *Which?*, July 1967.

38. Volume 1 of ²Suppl. contains an entry for *Angustura/Angostura* to set the record straight but, as far as I recall, no other proprietary term listed in the *OED* was revised in this volume.

39. Perhaps 1800–1950 would satisfactorily delimit the range of sources to be covered but more research is needed before the most suitable beginning and terminal dates could be established with any certainty.

40. Examples kindly supplied by Professor G. L. Brook.

41. Cited by Sebastian, *op. cit.*, pp. 134, 253.

42. See H. L. Mencken, *The American Language*, abridged by Raven I. McDavid Jr, 1963, p. 379.

43. See ²Suppl. s.v. *Asian*, a. and sb.

2 The Turn of the Screw: Ethnic Vocabulary and Dictionaries

At the beginning of *Macbeth*, a bleeding sergeant describes how brave Macbeth killed the 'merciless' rebel, Macdonwald: 'he unseamed him from the nave to th' chaps', that is, from the navel to the jaws, 'And fixed his head upon our battlements.' It may seem a far cry from the rebellious 'kerns and gallow-glasses' of Macdonwald to the persevering scholarship involved in dictionary editing, but the connection will be made clear as I go on.

The head some want to display on the battlements is that of a dictionary, or of its publishers, and, especially, any dictionary that records a meaning that is unacceptable or at best unwelcome to the person or group on the warpath. The ferocity of such assaults is almost unbelievable except as a by-product of what Professor Trevor-Roper calls the twentieth-century 'epidemic fury of ideological belief'. Key words are *Jew, Palestinian, Arab, Pakistan, Turk, Asiatic, Muhammadan*, and *Negro*, and there are others.

It is impossible to discover exactly when the battle-cry was first heard, but certainly by the 1920s a pattern of protest existed. In the *Jewish Chronicle* of 24 October 1924, a leading article expressed 'no small gratification' that, in deference to complaints that had been published in the *Jewish Chronicle*, the Delegates of the Clarendon Press had decided that the 'sinister meaning' attached to the word 'Jew' (that is, the meaning 'unscrupulous usurer or bargainer', and the corresponding verb meaning 'to cheat, overreach') should be labelled to make it clear that this was a derogatory use. The *Jewish Chronicle* had maintained that users of the *Pocket Oxford Dictionary* would conclude that 'every Jew is essentially the sort of person thus described'. Mr R. W. Chapman, who at that time was the head of the section of OUP which publishes dictionaries, replied that 'it is no part of the duty of a lexicographer to pass judgement on the justice or propriety of current usage'. The editor of the *Pocket Oxford Dictionary*, the legendary H. W. Fowler, in a letter to Chapman declared:

> The dictionary-maker has to record what people say, not what he thinks they can politely say: how will you draw the line between this insult to a nation and such others as 'Dutch courage', 'French leave', 'Punic faith', 'the Huns', 'a nation of shopkeepers', and hundreds more? The real question is not whether a phrase is rude, but whether it is current.

The *Pocket Oxford* and other Oxford dictionaries, and dictionaries elsewhere, labelled the 'sinister meaning' of the word *Jew* 'derogatory', 'opprobrious', or the like, and an uneasy peace was established. But not for long. Some other sinister meanings in the *Pocket Oxford* were pointed out. 'Turk: Member of the Ottoman race; unmanageable child.' 'Tartar: native of Tartary (etc); intractable person or awkward customer.' 'Jesuit: member of Society of Jesus (etc); deceitful person.' Fowler felt that he was being incited, as he said, 'to assume an autocratic control of the language and put to death all the words and phrases that do not enjoy our approval'. He maintained that the *POD* was not keeping the incriminated senses alive but that, unfortunately, they were not in danger of dying. In a letter to Kenneth Sisam in September 1924, he insisted: 'I should like to repeat that I have neither religious, political, nor social antipathy to Jews' – nor, by implication, to Turks, Tartars, or Jesuits. The episode passed, but was not forgotten. The *Jewish Chronicle* at that time appeared to be satisfied by an assurance that the unfavourable senses would be labelled as such. They did not ask for, far less demand, the exclusion of the disapproved meanings.

In the United States in the 1920s, a parallel protest movement, aimed at the compulsory capitalization of the initial letter of the word *Negro* and the abandonment, except among black inhabitants of the United States, of the word *nigger*. Again, dictionaries were among the main targets, and here, too, the lexicographers replied that if writers, including the editors of newspapers, used a capital initial for *Negro*, they would themselves be happy to include this form in their dictionaries, and to give it priority if it became the dominant form in print.

A half-century later, it is easy to see that the lexicographers had 'scotch'd the snake, not killed it'. Resentment smouldered away in certain quarters, and the issues were brought out into the open again after the 1939–45 war. But, this time, there was a difference. Dictionaries remained a prime target, but the protesters brought new assault techniques to bear, especially the threat of sanctions if the lexicographers did not come to heel. Now, dictionary editors, judged by the standards of the broad world, are a soft target. With little personal experience of the broil that forms the daily experience of, for example, politicians, newspaper editors, and psychiatrists, editors of dictionaries tend to be too unworldly and too disdainfully scholarly to recognize the severity of an assault made on them. What is this assault and what form does it take? Quite simply, it is a concerted attempt by various pressure-groups to force dictionary editors to give up recording the factual unpleasantnesses of our times, and to abandon the tradition of setting down the language as it is actually used, however disagreeable, regrettable, or uncongenial the use.

Two definitions in the *Concise Oxford Dictionary*, one in the early Fifties and the other in 1976, exacerbated things. One concerned the word *Pakistan*, and the other, the word *Palestinian*. The editor of the *Concise Oxford Dictionary* unwisely entered the word *Pakistan* in his dictionary in 1951 – unwisely, because names of countries as such do not normally qualify for an entry in Oxford dictionaries – and defined it as: 'A separate Moslem State in India, Moslem autonomy; (from 1947) the independent Moslem Dominion in India.'

It lay apparently unnoticed until 1959, when somebody must have pointed it out. The Pakistanis, understandably, were outraged, and called for a ban on the *COD* in Pakistan and for all unsold copies in Pakistan to be confiscated. The OUP admitted that the definition was 'tactless' and 'locally irritating', but pointed out that the intention had been to show that Pakistan was in the familiar, triangular section of territory which had always been called India on maps and in geography books. No political motive was in question. The Karachi police raided bookstalls in the city and seized 215 copies of the fourth edition of the *COD*. They also raided the Karachi office of the OUP, and seized the only copy of the dictionary on the premises, which was, in fact, the typist's copy. Copies in government offices were commandeered by the police, and apparently hundreds of copies were collected from public offices, schools, and colleges.

After high-level discussion, the Pakistan government decided to lift its ban on the *COD* in November 1959, after an undertaking by the OUP to issue a correction slip for insertion in all copies of *COD* sold in Pakistan, and to enter a new definition in the next impression of the dictionary. Later, a more permanent solution was found when the word *Pakistan* was dropped from the main-line Oxford dictionaries altogether, as a proper name with no other meanings. It remains in the semi-encyclopaedic *Oxford Illustrated Dictionary*, where it is defined as: 'Muslim State in SE Asia, formed in 1947 from regions where Muslims predominated.'

This was a striking example of the serious consequences arising from a simple error of judgement by a lexicographer. There were other minor skirmishes, for example, when it was noticed that the definition of the word *American*, in some of the Oxford dictionaries, failed to allow for the existence of black Americans and of Latin Americans. The dictionary editors gladly revised the definitions and brought them up to date with a minimum of fuss and with no heat generated on either side.

However, the problem of the word *Jew* kept returning in an increasingly dramatic way. Some correspondents contrasted the derogatory definitions of *Jew* with the colloquial senses of the word *Christian*. *Christian* is defined as 'a human being, as distinguished from a brute', for example, in Shaftesbury (1714): 'The very word Christian is, in common language, us'd for Man, in opposition to Brute-beast.' It is also recorded with the colloquial sense, 'a decent, respectable, or presentable person', as in Dickens (1844): 'You must take your passage like a Christian; at least as like a Christian as a fore-cabin passenger can.'

One correspondent, in 1956, said that she was concerned with the way in which stereotypes about groups of people become formulated, and she argued that the preservation of derogatory definitions in dictionaries did nothing to prevent the persistence of such stereotypes. Others drew attention to the cultural and scholarly achievements of Jews, for example, that thirty-eight Nobel prizes had been awarded to Jews by 1960. A representative of the American Conference of Businessmen crossed the Atlantic in March 1966, and we discussed the problem amicably. 'Men of good will,' he said, 'should unite to do everything possible not to give any appearance of acceptance to unfavourable applications of the word *Jew*, if they exist.' If they exist? But we knew from our quotation files that unfavourable applications of the word *Jew did* and *do* exist, both in speech and in print, deplorable though they are. All I could do was to repeat the familiar lexicographical arguments. It is the duty of lexicographers to record actual usage, as shown by collected examples, not to express moral approval or disapproval of usage; dictionaries cannot be regulative in matters of social, political, and religious attitudes; there is no question of any animus on the part of lexicographers against the Jews, or the Arabs, or anyone else.

In 1969, a Jewish businessman from Salford came on the scene and claimed that the definitions of *Jew* were 'abusive and insulting and reflected a deplorable attitude towards Jewry'. He turned the screw more forcibly by releasing the text of his letters to the national newspapers, who by now realized that the matter was an issue of public controversy. He also wrote to politicians, church leaders, including the chief rabbi and the archbishop of Canterbury, to the commissioner of police, and to other instruments of the Church and state.

In 1972, this Salford businessman brought an action against the Clarendon Press and acted for himself, claiming that the secondary definitions of the word *Jew* were 'derogatory, defamatory, and deplorable'. He lost the case in the High Court in July 1973. Mr Justice Goff held that, in law, the plaintiff had no maintainable cause of action because he could not, as required by English law, show that the offending words in the dictionary entries 'referred to him personally or were capable of being understood by others as referring to him'.

The next episode occurred on the other side of the world. Towards the end of 1976, Mr Al Grassby, Australia's commissioner for community relations, called for the withdrawal of the *Australian Pocket Oxford Dictionary* from circulation because it contained a number of words applied in a derogatory way to ethnic or religious groups: words like *wog*, *wop*, and *dago*.

Knowing very little, if anything, about lexicographical policy, he thought it deplorable that there was no entry for *Italy* but one for *dago*, none for Brazil as a country but one for *Brazil nut*, and so on. This wholly simplistic notion was rejected with humour and scorn by the Australian press. A cartoon in the *Australian* showed two European migrants looking very unhappy, and the caption read: 'Did you hear what those ignorant Aussie dingoes called us?' And a headline in the *Melbourne Sunday Press* made its point quite simply: 'You are on a loser, pal Grassby.'

The most recent example of hostility towards dictionary definitions occurred a short time ago. On this occasion, as with *Pakistan*, the criticized definition *was* inadequate, and, curiously, the concession of its inadequacy merely transferred the attack from one quarter to another. In the sixth edition of the *Concise Oxford Dictionary*, published in July 1976, the word *Palestinian* was defined as: '(Native or inhabitant) of Palestine; (person) seeking to displace Israelis from Palestine.' Early in 1977, the definition provoked angry editorial comment in newspapers in the Middle East, and threats were made that if the Oxford University Press did not agree to amend it at once, the matter would be brought to the attention of the Arab League, with a proposal to place the OUP on the Arab boycott list.

Each day's post brought fresh evidence of what appeared to be a severe reaction throughout Arabic-speaking countries, if the newspapers were anything to go by. The sales records for the *Concise Oxford Dictionary* in Egypt showed that all of eleven copies had been sold there in the financial year 1976–7! But, sales apart, what was clear was that the Arabs considered the definition to be partisan, and that, in my opinion, would have been the attitude of the man on the Clapham omnibus, too.

In two lines of the *COD* – because that was all the space available in such a small dictionary – we concluded that it was not possible to arrive at other than a formulaic definition of *Palestinian*. Any form of words ascribing motives to Palestinians simply failed by one test or another when the space available was so limited. We therefore decided to adopt another type of definition, one of the type that is used in every desk dictionary in the world, and the new definition reads as follows: '*n.* Native or inhabitant of Palestine. *a* Of, pertaining to, or connected with Palestine.'

The Arabs were satisfied ('it represents a victory for truth and objectivity', declared the *Egyptian Gazette* of 3 May 1977) and, had the matter rested there, without further publicity, that would probably have been the end of it. Not content with severing the head, however, the Arabs wished to fix it upon the battlements. A press statement was issued to British national newspapers by a London-based Arab organization, and even though this statement was factually and unemotionally expressed, it brought an instant reaction from the other side.

Letters of protest began to arrive from various Jewish organizations, and the gentle lexicographers of the OUP had to endure the kind of concerted campaign with which politicians have always been familiar. The letters expressed 'profound distress' and declared that the lexicographers 'had departed from their usual standards of scholarly objectivity in yielding to pro-Arab pressure groups'. The 'selfsame tune and words' came from several directions. 'We consider this an encroachment on traditional British integrity and on British values', 'political appeasement for commercial considerations', 'I wish to register the strongest protest against such abject and cowardly behaviour on the part of your organization', and so on. It dawned on us, as the letters arrived, that we were dealing with an organized petition. The individuals and groups writing to us had been urged to write to us by some central body. The same phrases occurred in several of the letters, for example: 'In describing a Palestinian as a native or inhabitant of Palestine, you impliedly deny the existence of the State of Israel.' That 'impliedly' rather gave the game away.

This Palestinian affair is for all practical purposes over, though not without bruises on all sides. Dictionary editors are now at last aware that they must give maximum attention to sensitive words, like *Palestinian*, *Moluccan*, and so on. Politically sensitive words like *Palestine* and *Kashmir* can be entered only as geographical and not as political entities, unless there is adequate space to describe the claims and counter-claims and there are facilities for the frequent updating of the entries. Dictionary editors should not quail when they receive large numbers of letters asking for the removal of unwanted senses; they need only reflect that they have joined those groups that have long since received thinly disguised circular letters of this kind.

In the end, in their function as 'marshallers of words', lexicographers must set them all down as objectively as possible to form a permanent record of the language of our time, the useful and the neutral, those that are decorous and well-formed, beside those that are controversial, tasteless, or worse. And to this list I would add those that are explosive and dangerous, as well.

3 The Point of Severance: British and American English

Recently I visited 78 Banbury Road in Oxford, until 1915 the home of Sir James Murray, the founding editor of the *Oxford English Dictionary*, and stood on the sacred spot of the 'Scriptorium', now gone for ever – the damp, ill-ventilated shed in which Sir James and his immediate colleagues edited the *OED* until Murray's death. The present owner of the house, Dr Desmond Morris, well known as the author of *The Naked Ape* and *Manwatching*, showed me his own fine collection of dictionaries, including a first edition of Johnson's Dictionary, and numerous other treasures, among them a set of the *OED* with the original prefaces still in place. When he bought the house, Dr Morris noticed a mound at the end of the garden: he decided to excavate it because North Oxford was once a dwelling-place of the prehistoric mound-building Beaker people. In fact he found no beakers but he did find a child's iron hoop, a little rusty but otherwise in good condition. It was identified by Dr Murray's granddaughter, Miss Elisabeth Murray, the author of the successful biography *Caught in the Web of Words*, as probably the actual hoop that Dr Murray bought for his children about a century ago. I exchanged the hoop for a copy of the *Concise Oxford Dictionary* and this trivial item of industrial archaeology now forms part of the archives of the *OED* Department in Oxford.

The child's hoop takes us back to the last quarter of the nineteenth century when English was still thought of as the language of Great Britain, with variants of it, pronounced in strange and not necessarily unpleasing ways, and with its syntax and vocabulary modified or amplified in certain respects, in various other parts of the globe. The vocabulary being collected and analysed in that improbable and ill-lit Scriptorium was mainly the English of Great Britain from Anglo-Saxon times onward, together with such additional items from abroad as could conveniently be gathered from the sources available to the editors.

Go back another century, to the last quarter of the eighteenth century, and in particular to the year 1776, a year that can be regarded as a point of linguistic, as well as of political, severance.

In England George III had reigned for sixteen years and Lord North was the first minister of the Tory government of the time. Other leading politicians included William Pitt the Elder, who had been the first minister in 1766 and 1767 but was now too ill to spend much time in Parliament; Edmund Burke, a great Irish-born orator and writer; the controversial radical John Wilkes; and Charles James Fox, one of the best known debaters in the House. William Pitt the Younger had just taken his MA at Pembroke Hall, Cambridge, and was not yet a force in politics. Many of the major literary figures of the eighteenth century were already dead, Pope in the 1740s, Henry Fielding in 1754, Laurence Sterne in 1768, Smollett in 1771, and Oliver Goldsmith in 1774. Jane Austen and Charles Lamb were babies of one year old, as was the painter J. M. W. Turner; Samuel Taylor Coleridge was four, Walter Scott five, and William Wordsworth six. William Blake was a young man of nineteen and Fanny Burney a young woman of twenty-four. Samuel Johnson was sixty-seven and his friend Mrs Thrale thirty-five. The language of Johnson and Mrs Thrale, and that of their adult contemporaries, was the stately language of the time, polished, stylish, unordinary, even in the intimate pages of their diaries, and the regime of instruction was severe and practical. Here is what Hester Thrale wrote in her diary on 20 January 1775, describing the education of her sixth child Susanna, then five years old:

> Her Improvements more than equal my hopes, my Wishes, nay my very Fancies. She reads even elegantly & with an Emphasis, says her Catechism both in French & English: is got into Joyn hand [i.e. cursive script] with her pen, & works at her Needle so neatly, that She has made her Sister a Shift all herself. She knows the Map of Europe as well as I do, with the Capital Cities, Forms of Govt. &c the Lines Circles & general Geography of the Globe She is Mistress of; & has a Knowledge of the Parts of Speech that She cannot be ensnared by any Question.[1]

I will not go into detail here, but what emerges from the books and dictionaries of the time is an orderly language. Almost everyone had absolutist views of linguistic correctness, and their views were buttressed by contemporary grammarians like Robert Lowth and Lindley Murray.

From the early eighteenth century, and especially in Swift's *Proposal for Correcting, Improving and Ascertaining the English Tongue* (1712), the rallying cry was for a linguistic standard. The main outlines of the argument are well documented and are well known. Inherent in Swift's *Proposal* is the cyclical nature of language – that, however language first descended to Man, whether as a gift from God, or as a spontaneous creation of a group of men at a particular point in time, or for whatever reason, a given language slowly made its way to a fine point of perfection, as it had in ancient Greece and Rome, from which it would gradually become subject to debilitating influences and become weakened. Swift was hopeful that the cyclical movement of English might be arrested at the point of perfection:

> The English Tongue is not arrived to such a degree of perfection, as to make us apprehend any Thoughts of its Decay; and if it were once refined to a certain Standard, perhaps there might be Ways found to fix it forever.

The debilitating influences, he thought, as others also did, were far more potentially dangerous in the *spoken* language than in the *written* form, and were present especially in regional and provincial forms of English. In the coffee houses and picture galleries of London the language of the literary elite, that is, of Johnson and his companions, was proclaimed to be the form of English to which others should aspire. Out there in the provinces, and in the colonies, the death-watch beetles of language lurked.

Dr Johnson learned many things through the actual practice of lexicography that escaped the theorizing minds of the unlexicographical Swifts and Defoes – lexicography is a chastening as well as an illuminating and fascinating art. For example (and this is pure entertainment, and not relevant to my main argument), he discovered from his dealings with the brewing business of the Thrales that his routine treatment of brewing terms in the first edition of his dictionary (almost all the terms being drawn from current manuals on the subject) was capable of subtle and substantial improvement in the fourth edition of 1773, by which time he had personal acquaintance with the terminology of the subject. But he did not visit America, and his well-known comments on America, and on the English used in North America, fall far short of the subtlety with which he applied his mind to subjects like brewing that he knew from personal experience. That other great lexicographer of the eighteenth century, Nathan Bailey, in his *Universal Etymological English Dictionary* (1721) gave scant space to words like *spider* and *butterfly*, both of which are defined simply as 'an insect well known'. But he tried harder with many American words: for example, the to him exotic *loon* is defined as

> A bird, in New-England, like a Cormorant, that can scarce go, much less fly; and makes a noise like a Sowgelder's Horn.

In passing, it is interesting to compare the definition of *loon* in the current edition of Webster's Collegiate:

> Any of several large fish-eating diving birds (genus *Gavia*) of the northern part of the northern hemisphere that have the legs placed far back under the body and as a result have a clumsy floundering gait on land.

Dr Johnson would have none of this: there is no entry for *loon* in his Dictionary, nor entries for any of the Indian words like *skunk*, *squaw*, and *moccasin*, that we know now were well established in American written English long before 1755. In his review of Lewis Evans's *Map and Account of the Middle Colonies in America* (1756) Johnson remarked: 'This treatise [is] written with such elegance as the subject admits tho' not without some mixture of the American dialect, a tract of corruption to which every language widely diffused must always be exposed.'

In 1776, at the point of severance, except for an infusion of words from East Coast Indian languages, the English language of North America was not in any radical way dissimilar from that of what the American settlers called the mother country. Some regional English words and senses had already made their way to America, but not to London: for example, the word *body*, to mean 'a person', as in 'a body should be very cautious in admitting a stranger to her family', was taken to North

America by regional speakers of English, and was not a home-grown Americanism. And English reviewers of about this time were already complaining about the presence of distinctive American words and senses in publications emanating from North America: for example, a reviewer in the *Critical Review*, writing of Charles Chauncy's *The Benevolence of the Deity* (1784):

> The style of this treatise is, in general, clear and unaffected, though not elegant. We meet with some uncouth words; such as *bestowment*, *exertment*, *lengthy*, *enlargedness*, *preparedness*; which we cannot account for on any other supposition than that of their being current in America.

The same reviewers made very similar remarks about works written outside the literary groups of London. For example, the *Monthly Review* reviewer of a book by 'Peter Pennyless' called *Sentimental Lucubrations* (1770), believing that 'Peter Pennyless' was either a Scotsman, or a Scotsman living in America, objected to such 'unspiritual and carnal words' as *perlimanory*, *facilitously*, *positiviously*, and *concentricated*. It was the start of a long period of assuming that unfamiliar words were very likely either of provincial origin, or, much more disastrously, of American origin. In 1776, however, the cloud was no larger than a man's hand. There were only three million people in the American colonies, that is, as many people as there are at present in New Zealand, and no one sees any threat to current English from New Zealand.

Great changes came about. The pound turned into the dollar, and the population of the USA increased at a phenomenal rate. The heady and healthy nationalism of the period brought political and linguistic imperatives in its wake. From 1806 onward Noah Webster made at first a tentative and then a more permanent record of the vocabulary he found in the works of his fellow countrymen. He observed that certain spellings were more frequently used in American publications than in their analogues in Britain, and he built them into his dictionaries. American English, no longer in his eyes a mere dialect of English, was on a separation course from any variety of English spoken or written in Great Britain, and the outline differences are clearly observable in successive versions of his dictionary.

This is not the occasion to give a formal account of the attitudes of scholars and men of letters to the evolution of the English language in the nineteenth century. Suffice it to say that the two forms of English slowly drifted apart, as languages tend to, when most of the speakers of one branch of a language never actually meet or talk to most of the speakers of a geographically separated branch. Even by 1926, however, one writer who knew both countries well – T. S. Eliot – did not judge that American English had any particular independent power:

America is not likely to develop a new language until its civilisation becomes more complicated and more refined than that of Britain; and there are no indications that this will ever happen. Meanwhile, America will continue to provide a small number of new words which can usefully be digested by the parent language.

I was recently asked by the editor of a student journal in Oxford if the English language was an endangered species. Clearly he, and many other people, felt that our precious English language is suffering from a sort of creeping fungus. *Time* Magazine had claimed that the air is 'saturated with recent coinages, "reverse discrimination", "mainstreaming", "ten-four", "good buddy" ', and so on. Books and articles appear all the time, pushing out a boat of prescriptivism, complaining of new applications of words like *charisma, consensus, fruition, scenario,* and so on.

My reaction was roughly as follows. Notwithstanding the fundamental changes to the language over the centuries, structural as well as lexical – for example, the sense of anxiety some gifted Anglo-Saxons must have felt when they realized that the progressive simplification of their language, especially the loss of grammatical gender, was leading them away from Europe and into an unpredictable grammatical isolation – no abstract sense of past suffering has been transmitted to us genetically, or by word of mouth, or by the formalization of any transmissible rules or laws.

Our present century stands out from all that precedes it as one in which educated people, or at any rate some sections of them, suffer more grievously than in the past from the way in which language appears to be being wounded *now* by those who use it. And it is Americans who are being blamed for much of the wounding. But prolonged study of the English language leaves me with a conviction that nearly all the linguistic tendencies of the present day have been displayed in earlier centuries, and it is self-evident that the language has not bled to death through change. Vulgarity finds its antidote; old crudities become softened with time. Distinctions, both those that are useful and those that are burdensome, flourish and die, reflourish and die again.

I am convinced that the structure of the English language is not seriously at risk. I am equally sure that the two main forms of English, American English and British English, separated geographically from the beginning and severed politically since 1776, are continuing to move apart, and that existing elements of linguistic dissimilarity between them will intensify as time goes on, notwithstanding the power of the cinema, TV, *Time* magazine, and other two-way gluing and fuelling devices.[2] In Britain the standard form of southern English remains unthreatened by the captive and contained regional forms of English within the British Isles, and it is this Received Standard that is learnt by foreigners. It may be true that there is a form of Standard American to which all Americans ultimately aspire. If there is I have not yet encountered it, though the several approximations to one standard spoken form tend to merge into one in the written form of the language when the copy editors of newspapers, and of books and journals, have done their work. What one finds in America is a series of freeranging, self-assertive, unrestrained regional forms of English. In the UK it seems unlikely that Scottish English, in any of its numerous regional varieties, will supplant Received Standard southern English, as the 'best' and 'most admired' form of English. Similarly, it seems unlikely that any of the varieties of English used in speech or writing by the Chicanos, Indians, blacks, or Anglos of Arizona, for example, would be chosen in a nation-wide referendum as the 'best' or 'most admired' form of American English, however admirable they may be in their own right. At present it seems unlikely too that educated white Americans will decide to adopt any of the apparently ungrammatical linguistic features commonly found in the written work of black college students in many parts of the United States, for example, uninflected plurals ('all my black brother'), the reduction of final consonants ('a novel base on'), the absence of the verb 'to be' in utterances like 'he a black bitch', or double negation ('God didn't make no two people alike').[3]

At present our knowledge of eighteenth-century English vocabulary is inadequate. The editors of the *OED* only dimly realized the linguistic significance of the events of 1776 and beyond, and gave routine treatment to the vocabulary they collected from English sources of the century, and quite inadequate treatment to the vocabulary of North America. Professors Craigie, Hulbert, Mitford Mathews, and others have set the American record straight in those two noble works, the *Dictionary of American English* and the *Dictionary of Americanisms*.

But a new dictionary is required in which the vocabulary of all forms of eighteenth-century English is recorded in one work – that of Great Britain, North America, the West Indies, South Africa, and Australasia. With such a dictionary all of us could see the language that our great-great-grandfathers actually wrote, whether they lived in Boston or in Bristol or had strayed to more distant parts of the globe. Present-day vocabulary is being collected on a massive scale and the reference works needed for the purpose are reasonably adequate if one knows how to use them.

I hope that this dreamed-of eighteenth-century dictionary will be embarked on one day, so that English vocabulary at the point of severance will receive parity of treatment with that of the 1970s.

Notes

1. Mary Hyde, *The Thrales of Streatham Park*, 1977, p. 112.
2. Dr Conor Cruise O'Brien (*Observer*, 2 July 1978), commenting on reports of my remarks in Chicago, maintained that 'barring disasters of the order of thermonuclear war, the indicators surely are that the rate of divergence is much more likely to slow down than to speed up'. In reply (*Observer*, 30 July) I pointed to powerful models of the severance of a language into two or more constituent parts, especially the emergence of the great Germanic languages of Western Europe – English, German, Dutch, Norwegian, Swedish, and so on – from the mutually intelligible Germanic dialects of the fifth century AD. East German and West German are already demonstrably dissimilar after a period of just over thirty years of political severance: West German, for example, has a seemingly limitless capacity to absorb English and American loanwords, while East Germans seem reluctant to absorb any – even Russian – loanwords. Moreover such East German words as *Reisekader* (staff who undertake most of the official visits abroad) and *Solispenden* (solidarity donations or contributions) have no equivalent in West German and could not have in any German-speaking capitalistic country. Dr Cruise O'Brien, in pointing out that 'in so far as there is a world language today, that language is English', overlooks the fact that English, as the *second* language of many speakers in countries throughout the world, is no more likely to survive the inevitable political changes of the future than

did Latin, once the second language of the governing classes of regions within the Roman Empire.

3. Examples cited in a paper by David L. Shores in *Papers in Language Variation*, edited by David L. Shores and Carole P. Hines, University of Alabama Press, 1977, pp. 181–3.

4 The Fowlers: Their Achievements in Lexicography and Grammar

The Revd Robert Fowler, a 'Military Tutor' at Tonbridge School in Kent in the middle of the nineteenth century, and the son of a master carpenter at either Ashburton or Buckfastleigh in Devon, and his wife Caroline Fowler (*née* Watson) had seven sons and one daughter. In what follows I shall be concerned almost entirely with the life and achievements of their eldest son, Henry Watson Fowler, and with two of his brothers, Francis George Fowler and Arthur John Fowler. For all I know the other Fowlers, including the daughter, led useful lives and made their mark in the circles in which they moved. I have not gone into this. My account is one of scholarly endeavour in spartan circumstances, of two men who enriched English scholarship, especially in that part of it concerned with lexicography and grammar, in a most remarkable manner, and of a third, potentially as brilliant as the other two, who settled for a minor role as a contributor to the *OED*.

Fowler senior gave his whole family an excellent education. *Henry Watson Fowler*, born on 10 March 1858 at Tonbridge in Kent, was educated at Rugby School and went up to Balliol College, Oxford, with a scholarship in 1877. His contemporaries at Balliol included several who later became distinguished scholars, men of letters, politicians, and so on, including R. L. Poole, T. F. Tout, Arnold Toynbee, J. W. Mackail, and Lord Curzon, but HWF himself was apparently at that stage best known for 'his reserve and his refinement'. His class, a second in Moderations and also in Literae Humaniores (that is, the study of Greek and Roman classical literature, philosophy, and ancient history), disappointed his friends, and doubtless left its mark on HWF himself. Dr Jowett, the famous Master of Balliol, gave him a routinely worded testimonial:

I have a very high opinion of Mr H. W. Fowler. While at Balliol College he has made himself respected. He is quite a gentleman in manner and feeling and has good sense and good taste. He is a very fair scholar and has, I think, a natural aptitude for the profession of Schoolmaster.[1]

HWF later revealed that of his contemporaries at Balliol he especially envied J. W. Mackail, 'watching how he emerged for lunch from the College library with the attractive pallor of a true student, and wishing that he himself could rise to the same intense expenditure of tissue over his books'. His final examinations over, he left his College in the Broad and taught briefly at Fettes School in Scotland before moving to Sedbergh School in north-west Yorkshire (now Cumbria) in 1882, where he remained as a master for seventeen years until 1899. G. G. Coulton remarks:

At the time with which we are concerned in Fowler's life, the average Public Schoolmaster would have borne comparison with the members of any other learned profession under the combined test of intellect, culture, and character.[2]

The years as schoolmaster at Sedbergh School were HWF's great formative period. Spurred on by the school's motto *Dura Virum Nutrix* ('Hardy Nurse of Men'), he applied himself diligently to the teaching of classics and of English literature. One of his pupils (Sir Alexander Lawrence) later recalled that he found Fowler 'a cold mechanical machine' but said that the boys 'developed a great regard for "Joey Stinker", as he was called, mainly because his room and he always smelt of tobacco. I am sure he found the form discouragingly stupid and unreceptive, except one term when he tried us with the "Shilling Browning" and found us surprisingly interested . . . I don't think I or any one else in the form ever got through his shell to know him as a human being. I for one respected him immensely, but in those days I should have said he lacked humanity.'[3] Sir Alexander also recalled how HWF introduced him to Lamb and Pope and reinterpreted *Hamlet*, but that most of the form, when HWF read out pieces of English prose or verse, only welcomed it 'as meaning that much less Latin or Greek'. His view of HWF as a schoolmaster was that 'his defects as a schoolmaster all arose from shyness, coupled with his great fastidiousness (moral and intellectual) and something in the Sedbergh atmosphere that kept a barrier between boys and masters'.[4]

His diligence was exceptional. He told Coulton more than once that, during his seventeen years at Sedbergh, he worked for an average of ten hours a day in term-time, Sundays included. In the vacations he worked at his Greek, Latin, and English texts, and also read a little French and German. The obituarist in the school magazine, the *Sedberghian* (March 1934), throws further light on his activities in these formative years:

> Fowler loved the fells and the curlew's note: he was a first-rate swimmer, skater, and climber: though light of build he was a marvellous first-line forward (in Rugby football). Never did he miss the plunge before each morning's 'early prep' in Strait Bridge pool, or during holiday time in some river or glacier stream at a corresponding hour.

A colleague of Fowler's at Sedbergh, the Revd A. J. K. Martyn, recalled that Fowler 'was always a stickler for etiquette. In his Sedbergh days he usually took Sunday afternoon tea with the French master and his wife: it was always said that he never failed to don the top-hat and tail-coat for this occasion.'[5]

HWF's decision to leave Sedbergh in 1899 arose from a point of principle. It became clear that if he was to be offered a housemastership at the school he would be required to undertake the training of the boys for Confirmation in the Church of England. He told the headmaster that 'a religious test – and that is what your decision amounts to – ought not to be imposed on house masters here . . . The choice is between acquiescence and resigning my post, and the latter is what I now feel compelled to do.'[6]

He left Yorkshire and found lodgings in Chelsea in London where he set up as a freelance writer and journalist. He had just enough money to live on: to the £120 a year that he had inherited from his father he added £30 a year from his journalistic work.

His way of life was a replica of Sedbergh except for the absence of pupils. His routine included a morning bathe in the Serpentine, summer and winter alike, preceded by a run to and from the water's edge 'at nine or ten miles an hour',[7] in other words at a jogging pace.

Coulton recalls his coming home from the Christmas Day race in the Serpentine. 'He had won, I think; but there was a thin crust of ice which had cut even his shaggy chest to pieces as he ploughed through it. On another occasion there was a fog; he lost his direction altogther, and had already been swimming at haphazard far too long in the icy water before the boatman heard him and picked him up in a state of exhaustion.'[8] It was at this time that he is reported as having a curious recurrent dream: he found himself at tea with Queen Victoria, and saying to himself, 'Here I am in reality, and I had always thought it was a mere dream!' After the Queen's death, she was gradually replaced in his dreams by Edward VII! What Freud would have made of this I cannot imagine. His published work in this brief London period bore such titles as 'Books we think we have read' and 'More Popular Fallacies' (for this he used the pseudonym 'Quillet' – a word meaning 'a subtle distinction, a quibble'), the latter title suggested, of course, by Charles Lamb. Coulton reports that most of them fell flat, 'being neither good enough nor bad enough for popular success'.

In 1903 he left London to join his brother Frank in Guernsey.

Francis George Fowler was born on 3 September 1870 at Tunbridge Wells, Kent. He went to St Paul's School, London, and Peterhouse, Cambridge, which he entered as a Classical Scholar in 1889. He was placed in the first class in the Classical Tripos in 1892, but did less well in his Part II. He remained at Cambridge until 1899, living on his patrimony (like his brother he had inherited £120 a year from his father) and on the fees of a few private pupils. In 1899 he moved to Guernsey where he 'joined a tomato-growing friend, Wilson, probably only as sleeping partner'.[9] There is no evidence of the kind of dedication shown at Sedbergh and in London by his more famous brother. FGF bought a small piece of land and built on it a three-roomed granite cottage in 1902. When HWF arrived in 1903 he built a second granite cottage, fifty yards from that of his brother on a sloping meadow. Henry's cottage resembled Frank's in outward appearance but internally it was arranged as a single room, divided only by a long, standing bookcase which acted as a screen.

In these two cottages in the little parish of St Peter-in-the-Wood, with the sea about a mile away, the two brothers did all their work until the 1914–18 war. The routine never varied in any important respect.

The early-morning run to the beach, the swim, and then breakfast. After breakfast, the translation of Lucian and work on a grammatical treatise which, to begin with, they thought of calling 'The New Solecist'. If the weather was tolerable the work was done in football jersey and shorts. The well-known photograph of HWF shows him thus garbed, not in a swimming costume as some have thought, though I have not been able to establish from which team or club the football jersey came. The present headmaster of Sedbergh, Mr P. J. Attenborough (in a private communication of 15 March 1978), says that he wonders if it could be a Lancashire (Red or White) jersey: apparently it is not a Sedbergh shirt. Lord Wakefield of Kendal, the President of the Rugby Football Union, was unable to improve on Mr Attenborough's suggestion. The brothers lunched together, taking turns to do the cooking. They walked or cycled the ten miles to St Peter Port, the capital of the island, and back as often as was necessary for shopping and business. The rest of the day followed the same pattern: work, with frugal meals at the usual intervals.

One personal matter should be mentioned. On 10 March 1908, on his fiftieth birthday, Henry married Miss Jessie Marian Wills, aged forty-six, a lady superintendent in a nursing home in St Peter Port. Their way of life changed only slightly. Mrs Fowler started a nursing home of her own and to this Henry cycled home in the evenings from his work in the cottage, except for weekends, when she came over to him. In 1912 they moved into the house of Frank's tomato-growing partner, and they remained there until the war.

The first important work that the two brothers embarked on was a translation of the works of the Greek writer Lucian of Samosata, published in August 1905. This formed part of the Oxford Library of Translations; other works in the series were translations of *Beowulf*, Dante, Machiavelli, and Heine.[10] The successful translator of Lucian needs ideally to be as clever and ingenious as Lucian himself. Of the few existing English translations those of the Fowlers are highly competent and often distinguished as well as entertaining. Lucian's work falls into three main categories: rhetorical essays and speeches, sophistic and philosophical problems, and satirical sketches. In the last of these *genres* the Fowlers' translations stand the test of time least well and are in parts now noticeably old-fashioned.

'Mother, you could not expect me to desert Chaereas and let that nasty working-man (faugh!) come near me. Poor Chaereas! he is a pet and a duck.' (IV.61)

'Well, but, Chrysis, I don't call a man in love at all, if he doesn't get jealous, and storm, and slap one, and clip one's hair, and tear one's clothes to pieces.' (IV.62)

As was to be expected they expurgated pieces 'of doubtful authenticity or less than doubtful decency' (letter of 22 April 1902 to Charles Cannan)[11]; for example, in the *Vera Historia* (I.22), the story of an imaginary Odyssey, which includes a description of the reproductive system of the inhabitants of Selene: children are produced from males alone, in the calf of the leg, instead of a womb. There is also a description of Dendrites ('tree-people'), who reproduce by having their right testicle cut off and planted in the ground, producing a large phallus-like tree. Men are produced from the acorns. These passages were left out. Rather more prudish by modern standards are the omissions from the *Dialogue of the Gods*, such as the pieces (iv) in which Zeus tries to persuade Ganymede to sleep with him, and a dialogue (xvii) in which Hephaestus catches Aphrodite and Ares in the act of making love, and sundry other passages concerned with the ritual selling of women, with orgiastic mysteries, and with phallic offerings made to Dionysus.

The expurgations were defended by HWF in a letter (31 January 1905) to Charles Cannan: 'As to stopping the mouths of Puritans, there really is nothing, I think, for them to open them over now. At any rate there is nothing left to satisfy any undesirable curiosity, even if there is anything to excite it.'[12]

The question arose of what they might translate next and HWF wrote to the Clarendon Press on 29 November 1904 asking if 'there would be room, or any demand, either for a Terence (in blank verse), for a Seneca's Letters, or for a Don Quixote', but nothing came of these suggestions.

The translation of Lucian linked them to the Clarendon Press and it was not long before Charles Cannan was sent a description of their next work (19 December 1904):

We have just begun to collect materials for a little book which we think might serve a useful purpose, but which would perhaps not be in your line. This is a sort of English composition manual, from the negative point of view, for journalists & amateur writers. There is a vast number of writers nowadays who have something to say & know how to make it lively or picturesque, but being uneducated cannot write a page without a blunder or cacophony or piece of verbiage or false pathos or clumsiness or avoidable dulness. The book we are thinking of would consist chiefly of classified examples displayed in terrorem, with a few rules on common solecisms. The examples would not be artificial, but taken partly from standard authors, & partly from papers like the Times and the Spectator. It might possibly, we think, be mildly entertaining as well as serviceable.

Charles Cannan replied favourably: 'We in the office would welcome an antibarbarus' (22 December 1904), and said that there would be two publics, the schools and the journalists.

Much correspondence followed in the process of which the Clarendon Press sent the Fowlers copies of Henry Sweet's Grammar, Hart's hints for compositors, and Henry Bradley's *The Making of English*. The choice of title proved difficult. The Fowlers themselves suggested 'The New Solecist for literary tiros' (after Lucian's title 'The Solecist') or 'The (or the Clarendon Press) Book of Solecisms for journalists, novelists, & schoolboys'. They offered to put out the book anonymously but Cannan said that 'the Delegates do not care much about anonymous books' (10 January 1905). HWF said (16 January 1905) that he was afraid that the Solecisms would 'prove more serious reading than we had hoped. We try to throw in a little elegant flippancy here & there, but grammar is a very solemn theme, & our hands are subdued to what they work in.'

Cannan sent the brothers some material on his own behalf (31 January 1905):

I enclose a heap of filth of various degrees of abomination – from the American 'just how much' (it was all over the Times advts. of the Encyclopaedia Britannica) to a Leather Trade report.

The Fowlers cast aside fears about criticisms from scholars (10 July 1905):

As to the expert, we have done our best to keep out of his danger; that is, we have practically based no arguments on historical grounds, have made no pretensions whatever to technical knowledge, & have occasionally implied that our authority is only that of the halfhour's start.

Henry Bradley saw the typescript and praised it as an 'admirably acute and solid piece of work'. He suggested the title 'Bad and Good English: Chapters on Common Faults in Composition'.

By 9 February 1906 the Fowlers had several more possible titles in mind:

Solecism & Journalism
Solecisms & minor literary faults
Solecisms and literary blemishes
The Unmaking of English
The English of the times

But they still preferred 'The New Solecist: for sixth form boys & journalists'. They even thought of dedicating it to *The Times*, unless this would be thought of as being 'a 400-page joke'!

At the last moment, it is not clear from what quarter, came the title *The King's English*, and the book was published in 1906. Another publisher, Jarrold and Sons, had published a book with the same title in 1903 (by John Bygott and A. J. Lawford Jones), but Henry Frowde of OUP rejected their complaint, and said that OUP was 'not proposing to change its title'.

The reviews did not please the Fowlers. 'We are much annoyed by the way they *will* make us out to have said much ruder things than we have, & to have drawn distinctions that we have not drawn between different authors, & generally read themselves into us. This is inevitable; I fear we have sailed too near scurrility.'

The Fowlers then thought of adding a 'controversial appendix' to a second edition, to contain *inter alia*, 'further discussion of the preposition at end; another is the tendency of books like ours to encourage a dull uniformity of style, or again to make writers self-conscious; another is the idea that we have impudently undertaken to teach George Meredith his business' (3 July 1906).

Other suggested notes were to be on *serviette* and *napkin*, fashionable terminations, suburban words, and so on. Neither Charles Cannan nor Henry Bradley liked the idea and it was dropped. The drafts have not survived as far as I know, though some of the material made its way in due course into *Modern English Usage* under the heading Genteelism, and elsewhere.

Peter Sutcliffe (p. 152) provided an interesting account of the book itself and of its reception by reviewers:

> On old problems like ending sentences with a preposition, the distinction between 'which' and 'that' and 'will' and 'shall', 'different from' and 'different to', the permissible uses of a split infinitive, the Fowlers had something tantalizing and original to say . . . The only reassuring aspect of the book was the abundant evidence that it provided that everybody made mistakes . . . The Fowlers were criticized for deepening the division between colloquial and written English, for being precisionists at heart and inflexible grammarians, for imposing rules which if followed would actually mar a writer's style.

In practice it introduced a new national pastime – the hunting of solecisms. The Delegates and their Secretary led the hunt and England, a nation of schoolteachers as well as of shopkeepers, eagerly followed. H. W. Fowler, *crème de la crème* of schoolmasters, had placed the nation in a schoolroom, and with all proper Edwardian obedience, the nation's pupils tried, though in vain, to mend their ways.

The two brothers, among the tomatoes of Guernsey, then addressed themselves to an even sterner task, the compilation of a 'short dictionary'.

The Concise Oxford Dictionary. When the two hermits started this formidable piece of work in 1906 the parent work, the *OED* itself, had reached the letter *M* (down to *misbirth*). By 1911, five years later, the OUP advertisement bound into copies of the first edition of the *COD* as an end-paper could claim that 'Seven Volumes (of the Oxford Dictionary) have now been published, and the Dictionary is complete from *A* to *Sc*'. Because of their isolation the Fowlers had no access whatever to the materials in the range *S* to *Z* that Dr Murray and his colleagues were working on in Oxford. The Fowlers did not visit Oxford and no one from Oxford went to Guernsey. To some extent therefore the vocabulary of *S* to *Z* was out of key with the rest of the dictionary. Examples which point to the Fowlers' dependence on other dictionaries, or at any rate to the absence of the corresponding sections of the *OED*, are easily findable, e.g. under *salve*[1], *COD* 1/e has the sense 'account for, dispose of' as if from OE. *sealfian* 'to salve', but *OED* shows this to be a meaning of *salve* v.[2], an obsolete English word from L. *salvāre*, 'to save'. There are entries for the words *scrinium*, 'cylindrical or other box for rolled MSS', and *scrutin*, a term used in French voting systems, whereas neither of these qualified for inclusion in the *OED*. Also included in *COD* 1/e is the world *sexillion*, '6th power of a million, 1 with 36 cyphers'; *OED* merely lists it without supporting evidence except an indication of its inclusion in Ogilvie's dictionary. All these items and numerous other weaknesses in the first edition survived in the *COD* until the publication of the sixth edition in 1976!

From the beginning the Fowlers followed certain principles which may now seem to be commonplace but which have played an important part in the way in which the smaller English dictionaries in Oxford are prepared. I quote from the Fowlers' Preface:

> In its own province and on its own scale [the *COD*] uses the materials and follows the methods by which the Oxford editors [of the *OED*] have revolutionized lexicography. The book is designed as a dictionary, and not as an encyclopaedia; that is, the uses of words and phrases as such are its subject matter, and it is concerned with giving information about the things for which those words and phrases stand only so far as correct use of the words depends upon knowledge of the things . . . It is to the endeavour to discern and keep to this line that we attribute whatever peculiarities we are conscious of in this dictionary as compared with others of the same size. One of these peculiarities is the large amount of space given to the common words that no one goes through the day without using scores or hundreds of times . . . ; chief among such words are the prepositions, the conjunctions, the pronouns, and such 'simple' nouns and verbs as *hand* and *way*, *go* and *put*. Another peculiarity is the use, copious for so small a dictionary, of illustrative sentences as a necessary supplement to definition when a word has different senses between which the distinction is fine, or when a definition is obscure and unconvincing until exemplified.

They saw the *OED* as 'the first dictionary . . . in which quotations have served not merely to adorn or convince, but as the indispensable raw material'. The articles of the *OED* they saw 'rather as quarries to be drawn upon than as structures to be reproduced in little'. For *S* to *Z* they drew quotations from 'the best modern dictionaries (the *Imperial*, the *Century*, the *Standard*, Cassell's *Encyclopaedia*, Webster, &c.)' or 'from other external sources or from our own heads'. But they emphasized in their Preface that the process was never one of simple reduction from the *OED* itself, or from other large dictionaries, but of restructuring, and, as the world soon recognized, this restructuring process produced a small dictionary – it contained 1,054 pages and was issued at 3s.6d. – of majestic power, one that, despite gradually increasing competition, remained not seriously challenged in the decades that followed as the most authoritative concise dictionary in Britain. The first printing was one of 25,000. Since then it has been re-edited five times and millions of copies have been issued, but the hands of the original shapers are still to be seen in the proportion of the articles, in the style of the illustrative examples, and in the avoidance of any undue encyclopaedic quality.

The *COD* was not launched into a vacuum. Other publishers, Chambers, Collins, Macmillan, Cassells, and so on, had already seen the marketing possibilities of what are now commonly called desk dictionaries. This is not the occasion for a consumer guide to all the dictionaries of 1911 but it is perhaps worth mentioning that the nearest rival was *Chambers' 20th Century Dictionary*, first issued in 1901, priced like *COD* at 3s.6d., larger by 200 pages than *COD*, and having some illustrations. Then, as now, both dictionaries owed a great deal to the *OED*, as an examination of long entries for verbs like *get* and *run* quickly shows. Already the Chambers dictionary had a tendency to admit obscure words and, in particular, words seldom heard outside Scotland, as if some instinct was guiding them already to the mysteries of the crossword puzzle, not yet in existence.[13] The Fowlers, on the other hand, placed much greater emphasis on the commoner words of the language, and were more rigorously 'English' in every respect. All the dictionaries were vying with one another to keep up with the new words of the Edwardian period – e.g. *aeroplane, carburettor, motorist, radioactive, radium, rag-time, wireless,* and *Zionism*.

When the Fowlers started out on the *COD* they were entirely untrained in lexicography, or, as Henry Fowler expressed it in his Preface to the second edition of 1929, using a familiar kind of image,

> When we began, more than twenty years ago, the work that took shape as *The Concise Oxford Dictionary*, we were plunging into the sea of lexicography without having been first taught to swim.

Now, alphabet-hardened,[14] they turned to the preparation of a new dictionary. At first it was known as the Shilling Dictionary for convenience of reference. In 1911 most dictionaries were priced at either 3s.6d. or 1s. and the latter kind were designed to slip conveniently into the pocket for quick reference. The dictionary had to be physically smaller than *COD*, of course, and some items had to be omitted. But scholarly smaller dictionaries are not produced simply by omitting some of the words of a larger dictionary ('the larger book was found not to be easily squeezable', as HWF puts it) but by 'changes in method unconnected with mere reduction of quantity'.[15] The *Pocket Oxford Dictionary* retains the principle that 'a dictionary is a book of diction, concerned primarily with words or phrases as such, and not, except so far as is needed to ensure their right treatment in speech, with the things those words and phrases stand for'. In other words *POD*, like *COD*, is a dictionary not an encyclopaedia, and emphasis was again particularly placed on the use of illustrative sentences (*his eye fell on me; accent falls on the end; expense falls on me; Easter fell late; fall into a rage*). One change made was the introduction of a system of diacritical marks giving an indication of the pronunciation *of every word*: 'the C.O.D. assumption that pronunciation might be dispensed with for most words has been abandoned' (Preface). Active service in France, a strange and pathetic experience for the two brothers, delayed the appearance of the new dictionary, but of course made them personally acquainted with many army words which might otherwise have been slightly out of focus. The *COD* definition of *parapet* – 'defence of earth or stone to conceal & protect troops' – referred to nineteenth-century warfare; in this new dictionary, not issued until 1924, a *parapet* is a 'mound along front of trench'. In *COD* 1/e *trench* had been defined as a 'ditch about 3 ft deep with earth thrown up to form parapet'; in the new post-war dictionary *trench* is defined as a 'deep ditch esp. one dug by troops to stand &c. in sheltered from enemy's fire'. In 1911 *barbed wire* was 'for fences, with wire prickles at intervals'; from their own observations in

1915–16 it became in *POD* 'with wire prickles at intervals; used in fencing, & esp. *as obstruction in war*'.

One important innovation in the new pocket-sized dictionary was what the Fowlers called 'an experiment in collecting words that form a series and letting the reader know where to find them'. Thus, for example, the entry for *ox*, after its definition ('kind of large usually horned cloven-footed ruminant quadruped used for draught, for supplying milk, & as meat'), continues:

(sex &c.: *bull, cow, bullock, calf, steer, heifer, calve, stall, byre, pasture, graze, browse, chew the cud, bellow, low, moo, charge, gore, butt, toss, moo-cow, bovine*).

In such cases a separate definition is provided for each word in the correct alphabetical place.

Under *officer* the *POD* (1924) gave lists in descending order of seniority of ranks in the Navy (Admiral of the Fleet, Admiral, Vice-Admiral, etc., down to Midshipman), Army (Field Marshal down to Second-Lieutenant), and Air Force (Marshal of the Air down to Pilot-Officer), and these are not all separately defined in their alphabetical place.

Similar lists were provided under *accelerando* (all the main musical directions, *crescendo, diminuendo, pianissimo, sforzando*, etc.); *paper* (sizes of paper, *royal octavo, crown quarto, demy, elephant, imperial*, etc.); *reference*, marks used for various purposes like asterisk (*), obelisk (†), double obelisk (‡), section mark (§), parallel mark (‖), and paragraph mark (¶); and numerous others. These engaging segments were dismantled in stages in succeeding editions, and are not to be found in the sixth edition (1978). Their absence will doubtless be regretted by many.

Any account of the Fowlers would be signally incomplete if their experiences in the army were left unrecorded. Both Henry and Frank joined up. Henry was fifty-seven but gave his age as forty-four, and enlisted in the 'Sportsmen's Battalion'. Frank was only forty-five but was less robust. These two fastidious scholars were drafted to France in December 1915, and began their fairly brief encounter with cattle-trucks, route marches, and trenches behind the fighting line. They were told that 'no man over 40 . . . is in future to go into the trenches'. The RSM said to HWF one day in January 1916, just before a bout of physical drill, 'I shouldn't go out, Fowler, if you don't like it', which means (says Fowler in a letter to his wife) 'that he regards me as a poor old gentleman who must be let off easily. I did the drill, of course, but I have an uneasy suspicion that I shan't get to the trenches.' In February 1916 the brothers, both private soldiers thirsting for action, but denied the opportunity, wrote to their Commanding Officer in memorable terms:

> Pte H. W. Fowler (M.A. Oxon., late scholar of Balliol; age 58) and Pte F. G. Fowler (M.A. Cantab., late scholar of Peterhouse; age 46) have been engaged for some years in Guernsey on literary work of definite public utility for the Oxford University Press . . . They enlisted in April 1915 at great inconvenience and with pecuniary loss in the belief that soldiers were needed for active service, being officially encouraged to mis-state their ages as a patriotic act . . . They are now held at the base at Étaples, performing only such menial or unmilitary duties as dishwashing, coal-heaving, and porterage, for which they are unfitted by habits and age. They suggest . . . that such ungenerous treatment must, when it becomes generally known at the end of the war, bring grave discredit on those responsible for it.
>
> (Signed) H. W. Fowler, M.A.
> F. G. Fowler, M.A.
> authors of *Translation of Lucian*, 4 vols.; *The King's English*; *The Concise Oxf. Dict.*

Henry was discharged in June 1916, but Frank, whose health had broken down, returned to England, still in the armed forces, and died of tuberculosis in May 1918, aged forty-seven, while still a soldier.

Henry returned to Guernsey and his beloved Jessie, and went on alone with the preparation of the *POD*. They obtained an ideal house for the purpose, a converted mill called 'Moulin de Haut', about a mile from Vazon bay on the west side of Guernsey, and here, among the rooks and kestrels, he did much of his best work.[16]

The Idiom Dictionary (= *Modern English Usage*). Since at least 1909, when work on the *COD* was nearly finished, the Fowler brothers had cherished the notion of what they envisaged as an 'Idiom Dictionary'.

Another scheme that has attractions is that of an idiom dictionary – that is, one that would give only such words as are in sufficiently general use to have acquired numerous senses or constructions & consequently to be liable to misuse; being able to omit three-quarters of the words, we should be able to give adequate treatment & illustration to the remaining quarter. A dictionary of this sort would give in detail the information about constructions, synonyms, &c., that in the King's English can only be hinted at with a scanty selection of examples. *We should assume a cheerful attitude of infallibility* [my italics], & confine ourselves to present-day usage; for instance, we should give no quarter to *masterful* in the sense of *masterly*, as the OED is obliged to do because there is antiquated authority for it, & generally speaking should try to give a shove behind to the process of differentiation.[17]

The twists and turnings of misconstrued syntax and faulty usage had been partly recorded in *The King's English* (1906), but they saw some value in rearranging the material in alphabetical order, in the manner of a dictionary, with an index and copious cross-references to guide the reader to any matter in which he was particularly interested; and there were many freaks of idiom, patchings of the unpatchable, and so on, not dealt with in *The King's English* to which they wished to draw attention.

R. W. Chapman said of the plan in its original form 'a Utopian dictionary would sell very well – in Utopia'. Much correspondence ensued in the course of which Charles Cannan, R. W. Chapman, and Kenneth Sisam in turn, each drawing readily offered support from Henry Bradley and C. T. Onions, persuaded the Fowlers to reduce an over-ambitious scheme to the correct proportions. HWF declared (5 April 1911) that they had their eyes 'not on the foreigners, but on the half-educated Englishman of literary proclivities who wants to know Can I say so-and-so? What does this familiar phrase or word mean? Is this use English? . . . the kind of Englishman who has idioms floating in his head in a jumbled state, & knows it.'

R. W. Chapman, in particular, sent the Fowlers a great many notes on points of detail (which he called his 'favourite vices'), e.g. on uses of the word *last* (as in 'the two last lines') and *other* (as in 'the other two railways'). Henry Bradley and HWF quarrelled about the spelling of *align/aline* (HWF wanted to condemn *align*) and each of them remained impenitent and unconvinced by the other's case. Sisam and HWF could not agree about the best way to indicate the pronunciation of the word *fortune*. Dr Onions and HWF quarrelled about the definition of *nem.con.* (Dr Onions said it meant 'with no one dissenting' but Fowler insisted on keeping 'unanimously').[18] HWF decided to 'nail *alright* and *all-right* to the counter' (5 October 1911). Even as late as 1919 HWF wanted the dictionary to contain lists of synonyms, including, for example, the fifty or so synonyms that he had collected for *courage* (e.g. *bravery*, *fortitude*, *resolution*, *valour*), and there was to have been one long alphabetical article called 'Generic Names'. Dr Chapman and Dr Onions insisted on their omission because they would not be *ejusdem generis* with the main book or with each other. HWF (8 November 1924) submitted a draft Preface which he called 'Oxford Pedantics'. Sisam commented 'Terrible' and made Fowler rewrite it. Almost at the last moment, Sisam came up with the title *A Dictionary of English Usage*, and HWF persuaded him to insert the word *Modern*.

When the book was published in 1926 with the title *A Dictionary of Modern English Usage* Henry Fowler dedicated it to the memory of his brother Francis George Fowler 'who shared with me the planning of this book, but did not live to share the writing'. The dedication goes on: 'I think of it as it should have been, with its prolixities docked, its dullnesses enlivened, its fads eliminated, its truths multiplied. He had a nimbler wit, a better sense of proportion, and a more open mind, than his twelve-year-older partner.'

This quite extraordinary book, the Bible of prescriptivists, is the product of a scarifyingly diligent search for fastidious distinctions in English, for example how *apocope* (cinema/cinematograph) differed from *syncope* (pacifist/pacificist) and from *aphaeresis* (special/especial). Fowler observed the delicate complexities of the written language, assumed, with all due Edwardian arrogance, that the central system needed no description, but that educated people everywhere had need of a handbook in which every major hazard or pitfall was plainly marked with a 'Keep Off' sign. He believed that writers, even famous ones, in some respects acted like golfers who were content to go round in 120. Even Shakespeare is taken to task for an instance of *nominativus pendens*: '*They* who brought me in my master's hate/I live to look upon their tragedy' (*Richard III*). The book is gravid with evidence of the existence of what might be called an eighth deadly sin – that of linguistic misuse – and the Great Schoolmaster set himself to identify and analyse its main aspects. In his Presidential Address to the English Association in 1957, the late Sir Ernest Gowers said that there were 'five themes with variations that form the texture of Fowler's teaching . . . first the careful choice of precise words, second the avoidance of all affectations, third the orderly and coherent arrangement of words, fourth the strict observance of what is for the time being established idiom, and fifth the systemization of spelling and pronunciation.'[19]

Fowler chastised himself as well as others. In a letter of 29 September 1926 to Kenneth Sisam he declared: 'I have been caught accenting *crème* wrong for twelve years, in three books, & in six places. Would you put on record, for corrections to be made when possible, the three slips enclosed herewith.'

Modern English Usage entered a world already riven by fundamental disputes about attitudes towards linguistic correctness and incorrectness. Henry Fowler, however, in what he called his 'lotusland', whether it was Guernsey or Hinton St George in Somerset to which he later moved, remained essentially unaware of the linguistic controversies sweeping through the universities of Europe and the New World. He did not read journals like *Englische Studien* and the *Modern Language Journal* where continental scholars like de Saussure and American scholars like Leonard Bloomfield and Edward Sapir were propounding the new doctrine of descriptive linguistics. His model was one hallowed by time, that of the ancients he knew so well, the world of Honour Moderations and of Literae Humaniores. He himself was the twentieth-century equivalent of the eighteenth-century prescriptivist and universal grammarian.

At a Foyle's Literary Luncheon in London in 1978, celebrating the 500th anniversary of printing at Oxford, the historian A. J. P. Taylor singled out *Modern English Usage* as perhaps the greatest work ever published by the Oxford University Press. He declared that he read it through at least once a year. In 1958,[20] on the other hand, Professor Randolph Quirk, perhaps the most distinguished of modern English grammarians, said that Henry Fowler 'was no great grammarian, still less a linguist in the modern scientific sense, and many of the articles in *Modern English Usage*, as well as its title, invited judgement of him as a grammarian. Any of a score of his major articles on grammar shows clearly his deficiencies in this field.' A. J. P. Taylor, speaking as it were for all scholars who have not been exposed to the gales and storms of modern linguistics, turns to *MEU* for guidance in the differences between *peninsula* and *peninsular*, in the use of the fused participle, and for many other features. Randolph Quirk dwells on Fowler's deficiencies: the article 'on cases, for instance, draws attention to the inadequacy of his analysis ("me and my mates likes ends" is supposed to show that the speaker had no use for the subject form "I"), and it exemplifies his reliance – as in this example – on literary evidence for spoken English, and his belief that it was feasible to change pronoun usage by some kind of intellectual agreement arrived at between the speakers of English . . . While he deprecates on one page the *s* genitive in usages like "the narrative's charm", he falls into the practice himself elsewhere with "the termination's possibilities" and "the sentence's structure". He recommends us to say "Could you tell me what the time is?" while in the same breath saying that nevertheless it would be "strictly correct" to say "Could you tell me what the time *was*" – another example . . . of the inadequacy of his analysis in reckoning "could" as a past tense in this function.'

The question 'Who is in lotusland, Fowler or the descriptive grammarians?' is one that can only be posed, not answered. It is clear, however, that scholars in every discipline but that of modern linguistics and linguistic philosophy, not to go further out into the world of ordinary BAs or beyond, suffer from a strange inability to put aside their Fowler, and take up Quirk or Chomsky instead. It is as if most people see written English as a kind of long-established lawn with a delicious herbaceous border, and that instruction is needed only about weed-killers, fertilizers, lawn mowers, and the best ordering of shrubs and plants. The nettles and brambles in the lanes outside, and the manner in which the turf grew to its level seemliness, are deemed to fall outside the realm of necessary inquiry.

The Quarto Oxford Dictionary. The last years of Henry Fowler's life were spent on an unfinished and unpublished dictionary, which was to have been called *The Quarto Oxford Dictionary*. Its beginnings are fairly obscure. The earliest letter in the correspondence files is one of 17 December 1925 written by Humphrey Milford, the London publisher of OUP:

Of course we will try waiting for the Fowlers. I am glad that there is another brother; I had never heard of him before.

This was a reference to Arthur John Fowler. He was ten years younger than Henry, and with a similar track record. He had been educated at Rugby School and at Sedbergh. He emerged from Oxford with a somewhat better result than Henry's in classical studies, and was also awarded a Blue for long-distance running. From 1891 to 1920 he taught at Sedbergh – one wonders how the school continues without a Fowler or two about! – and in 1920 retired to Swanage where he became a lowly-paid reader of sources (or 'contributor' as such readers were called) for the first Supplement to the *OED*. His slips, all typed with a purple ribbon, are among those that have survived to this day in the *OED* files – they include numerous quotations from daily newspapers of the late 1920s, from the poems of Thomas Hardy, and from a work by one C. F. S. Gamble, entitled *The Story of a North Sea Air Station* (1928).

The Quarto Oxford Dictionary was to be a dictionary of current English in one volume, quarto-size, of about 1,500 pages. It was often informally called the 'Unconcise 4to'. At first HWF wanted a divided page. In a letter to the Oxford office of OUP he described the idea:

> What do you think of this plan: A double dictionary, with a line across each page as in Webster, but with a different dichotomy, into words requiring literary treatment above the line, &, below it, all words for which mere definition suffices? I to be responsible for the upper part, & you to find experts fit to select & define the items of the lower.

He enlarged on this idea (21 February 1930) by saying that he 'thought of sending downstairs everything that required no literary treatment, whether important or not in itself, e.g. *okapi, zinc, Wellingtonia, grate* n., *equilateral,* would be below the line, whereas *hyena, iron, oak, window, symmetrical,* would be above it'. Kenneth Sisam, the Delegates' Secretary, was uneasy about this, and he was also worried about another matter. 'We shall never sell a dictionary (in America) without a liberal sprinkling of Americanisms. Do you feel that it would be a sin to admit them, even with an asterisk or an obelus or some other sign of disapprobation?' (Letter to Fowler, 21 June 1928). To which Fowler replied (3 July 1928): 'QOD is still quite in the clouds; but I have no horror of Americanisms; on the other hand I know nothing about them, except the small proportion that are current here, & don't like dealing with material that I have to take at second hand.'

Fowler decided to use the swung dash (~) in the *QOD* – the tilde-like symbol used in derivatives to avoid repetition of the headword, and first introduced, in the Oxford family of dictionaries, in the *Little Oxford Dictionary* in 1930.

He also wanted 'status letters' – what we now call 'usage labels'. They were to be represented by almost every letter in the alphabet:

A archaic	I illiterate	Q (vacant)
B borrowed	J jocular	R rare
C colloquial	K (vacant)	S slang
D dialect	L literary	T technical
E erroneous	M (vacant)	U unseemly
F fustian	N natural history	V vernacular
G general	O obsolete	WXYZ (vacant)
H historical	P poetical	

Of the letters marked vacant Sisam later suggested 'modern Latin scientific word' for M, and 'word not certainly naturalized' for Q.

Specimen pages were printed, and OUP contracted to pay Henry Fowler £200 a year for ten years, to which he replied 'All right; if you insist on making a millionaire of me, do so.' But privately he determined to pay both his brother Arthur and a new colleague, Col. Le Mesurier, out of the £200. In 1931 (28 September) C. T. Onions scotched the idea of dividing the page: 'I have no hesitation in saying that the horizontal division of the page would be a fundamental blunder. We have found nothing so exasperating here as this division of Webster's page.' Fowler immediately conceded the point (30 September 1931): 'Clearly the two-deck plan must be abandoned.'

He went on with the work but the end was not far off. On 20 September 1932 Fowler reported that his doctor had found high blood-pressure, albuminuria, &c. and had 'cut off my running, cold bath, lawn-mowing, all weight-lifting or other exertion, & any food more meaty than chicken'.

A year later R. W. Chapman invited Fowler, or either of his collaborators, to attend the Goldsmiths' lunch on 21 November 1933 to celebrate the reissuing of the *Oxford English Dictionary* in twelve volumes and the publication of its first Supplement. There is no record of any reply. The last letter of Fowler's in the files is one to R. W. Chapman, dated 4 November 1933:

> I told you at a guess before beginning that QOD would take *me* about ten years . . . Our present calculation, now that we [*sc.* HWF, AJF, & Le Mesurier] are settling down after preliminaries and hold-ups into something like a consistent pace, is that (barring deaths & other such inconveniences) six years from now – the end of 1939 – ought to see the work done. On that point of death &c., I don't want to draw any statement of intention from you; but I should like, now that I have been working for some months in close communication with A.J.F., to state that I believe him to be just as competent as myself to carry on the work, & to be by this time in full possession of any notions of mine that might make for a readable dictionary.

Henry Fowler died eight weeks later, on Boxing Day 1933. Three weeks later, on 19 January 1934, the Delegates of the Press printed and promulgated a tribute that reads as follows:

> The Delegates record their sense of loss in the death of Henry Watson Fowler who for nearly thirty years had placed his time and talents at their service. Though Mr. Fowler's work consisted largely of compilation, it exhibited not only great learning and sound judgement, but also a rare originality. His skill in the presentation of linguistic facts and his felicity in their illustration won the affectionate regard of all discerning students, and gave fresh lustre to the great Dictionary which he was content to abridge.
>
> But his labours were not merely those of a recorder. *The King's English* and his other critical books placed him in the first rank of grammarians. *Modern English Usage*, a model of sound learning, good taste and good feeling, has done more than any other book of our time to maintain the purity of the English language.

Notes

1. G. G. Coulton, *H. W. Fowler*, S.P.E. Tract XLIII, 1935, p. 101.
2. Coulton, p. 102.
3. Coulton, p. 104.

4. Coulton, p. 105.
5. Coulton, p. 108.
6. Coulton, p. 111.
7. Coulton, p. 118.
8. Coulton, p. 120.
9. Coulton, p. 121.
10. Peter Sutcliffe, *The Oxford University Press: an Informal History*, 1978, p. 151.
11. This letter and others quoted from *infra* are in the files of the Oxford University Press in Oxford.
12. I am grateful to my *OED* colleague, Dr R. E. Allen, for considerable help with this section on Lucian.
13. H. W. Fowler in a letter to R. W. Chapman, 27 December 1925: 'As to puzzles, I thank goodness the MS of POD was sent in before the cross-word was ever heard of.'
14. 'It is of course true that we have acquired a modicum of expertry at the job, & natural that it should be thought foolish to waste this.' (Letter by HWF to OUP, 6 January 1911)
15. 'Reflection, & the casting of a business eye over a few pages, does not convince us that the abridging of an abridgment is attractive work, but on the contrary that it would be like nothing so much as pulling out the hairs of one's own head one by one.' (Letter by HWF to OUP, 6 January 1911)
16. Coulton, p. 145.
17. Letter by HWF to OUP, 20 June 1909.
18. Dr Onions was still talking of this conflict in the late 1950s, and still maintaining that Fowler was wrong. Perhaps the old quarrel accounted for his glee on hearing that Fowler's definition of *adultery* in *COD* ('Voluntary sexual intercourse of married person with one of opposite sex') did not appear to exclude the sexual intercourse of married couples. The definition has since been amended.
19. E. A. Gowers, *H. W. Fowler: the Man and his Teaching*, English Association, 1957, p. 14.
20. *Listener*, 13 March 1958, pp. 449–51.

5 The Genealogy of Dictionaries

Precise texts and eclectic results

Genealogy is defined in the *Oxford English Dictionary* as 'an account of one's descent from an ancestor or ancestors, by enumeration of the intermediate persons: a pedigree.' As with most abstract nouns, figurative extensions are permissible and the *OED* itself gives an example of 1793 in which Thomas Beddoes speaks of 'the genealogy of significations' of words. I am here concerned with the ways in which English dictionaries are related to one another, with particular attention to Dr Johnson's *Dictionary of the English Language*, the dictionaries connected with the name of Noah Webster, and the Oxford dictionaries. Indebtedness and cross-linkage will form part of the theme, and also the need for the emergence of a new sub-group of bibliographical scholars to turn my outline account into a much more professional form.

Genealogical tables – that is, 'family trees' – exhibit startling and unpredictable directional changes of pattern because of unforeseeable deaths or marriages. New hereditary lines needed to be drawn, for example, when Prince Charles married Lady Diana Spencer, and, similarly, when Princess Margaret married Anthony Armstrong-Jones (Lord Snowdon) and, later, when their marriage was dissolved. The ordinary dislocations and joinings of life provide endless opportunities for genealogists to display their skills.

For lexicographers, one of the more startling discoveries of genealogy – 'the climax of genealogical ingenuity', A. L. Reade called it – is that Samuel Johnson and Lord Chesterfield, the 'poor scholar' and the 'aristocratic patron', separated by the formidable social barrier of patronage, were linked by marriage and kinship through the peer's brother, Sir William Stanhope, to the Reverend Cornelius Ford (died 1731), first cousin of Johnson.[1]

The genealogical chart of a particular dictionary is in a sense less complicated than that of a member of the Royal Family, or even, for that matter, of an ordinary citizen. Obviously there are more people, all with individual names, than there are dictionaries. Nevertheless the lineage of a given dictionary is normally less obvious than might appear to be the case. Prefaces of dictionaries seldom give an accurate account of the way in which the work that follows has been compiled, and promotional handouts or blurbs even less so.

One of the traditional assumptions of textual criticism was that if an ancient work existed in several manuscripts, and the autograph manuscript of the author had not survived, it was reasonable to believe that the remaining manuscripts were descended from a single archetypal ancestor. By a process known as 'recension', the archetypal readings were deduced (or, at any rate, approximately deduced) by systematically rooting out readings that, for one reason or another, could not have formed part of the original text. The resulting text, 'the residue' as it were, represented the nearest that one could rescue, or reconstruct, of the author's original work.

Later scholars – the French medievalist E. Vinaver and the English Renaissance scholar W. W. Greg among them – came to see that the genealogy of manuscripts of works surviving in many versions was much more complex than had once been assumed. They treated variant readings on their merits and arrived at what might be called eclectic texts.[2] At first sight it would appear that the connection between the ramification of the manuscripts of *Piers Plowman* and of other medieval works on the one hand, and that of families of dictionaries on the other, might be difficult to demonstrate. But I am not so sure.

Lineal descent is not a common feature of dictionaries, however much the works of a given dictionary house are plastered with words like *Concise, Collegiate, Pocket,* etc. Conflation, reduction, and adaptation occur on such a scale in the members of a family of dictionaries that one can normally detect only a general similarity between one such dictionary and another. But my concern is not so much with the relationships of the dictionaries within one family as with those between the products of different publishing houses.

The key dictionaries in any study of the genealogy of dictionaries are those of Dr Johnson, Noah Webster, and Dr J. A. H. Murray. If we knew no more about the editors of all subsequent English dictionaries, and the way in which they were prepared, than we know about the authors or scribes of the seventeen surviving manuscripts of the A-text of *Piers Plowman*, and had only the text of the dictionaries themselves to go by, it would be possible to build family trees showing the complex genealogical relationships of these dictionaries and of the way in which they themselves are related.

The nature of the relationships would, of course, be revealed more quickly if publishing houses would open up their correspondence files, and if lexicographers would set down accounts of their actual sources and their week-by-week working methods. But as neither of these processes seems likely to occur, lexicographical genealogists must needs employ the techniques of textual criticism and of genealogy to establish the kinship of dictionaries.

Let me start with a trifling question. Which dictionary do you think lacks the words *anus, irritable,* and *euphemism*, though the words were well-established at the time?

Anus is first recorded in 1658, *irritable* in 1662 (in the work of the seventeenth-century philosopher Henry More), and *euphemism* is listed in several dictionaries in the seventeenth and eighteenth centuries, leading off with Thomas Blount's *Glossographia* (1651–81). The absence of these reasonably ordinary words from Samuel Johnson's dictionary in 1755 demonstrates a principle of lexicographical genealogy – that the mere existence of words at a given moment and even the use of them by a lexicographer in his own work (since Johnson certainly used *irritable*, for example) do not guarantee the inclusion of such words in dictionaries. In 1755 dictionaries were much more like herbaceous borders in a private garden, filled with well-cultivated flowers that had been planted with reasonable deliberation. Numerous classes of words that are now admitted 'on principle' were then excluded on principle. And a certain haphazardry was also more obviously at work then than at the present time.

Of course there are differences between the genealogy of medieval manuscripts and the genealogy of dictionaries, but I am focusing on the similarities. The date of composition of many medieval works needs to be deducted from the script itself, by other palaeographic means, or by looking for external evidence. Thus, for example, from the work of Professor E. J. Dobson on the *Ancrene Wisse:*

> We know that the 'Corpus revision' must have been made after 1224, when the Franciscans came to England, and was probably a little later than 1227, the approximate date of the establishment of their house in Hereford.

Such external evidence is less apposite for the dating of modern dictionaries though it is not entirely inappropriate. The date of publication of new dictionaries and of new editions is not usually in doubt, even if by skilful use of the copyright device © a dictionary can be made to seem more up-to-date than it actually is. External evidence, however, is occasionally useful in the dating of new *impressions*, the sort described as 'reprinted with corrections'. Date-determinable items like *ayatollah*, *yomping*, and *zero option* establish dates before which particular impressions could not have been published. The habits of medieval scribes, as Professor Dobson says, can also be paralleled in minor ways:

> Scribe D did not use *wynn*, or *yogh*, or *eth*, and apparently did not understand the last when he saw it.[3]

By the same token the conventionally printed versions of modern dictionaries will shortly be distinguishable from the print-outs of electronic word-processed packages by the abandonment in the latter of such ordinary conventions as ligatured letters (e.g. *fi*, *œ*, *æ*), old-style Arabic numerals, and a range of diacritical marks that are awkward for microcomputers to reproduce. Other orthographical devices of the first 500 years of printing – for example, the ligatured *we* and *wo* and some other sets of letters in Caxton's type 2*, the long *s*, the use of the apostrophe, the employment of final *-t* instead of *-ed* in words like *wished* and *kissed* (thus *wisht*, *kist*) – have come and gone, and can be used as useful orthographical watermarks of particular periods. A 2-shaped *r* is a useful guide for the dating of medieval manuscripts. The spellings *authentick* and *critick* usually point to a date between 1700 and 1800.

Our own period is characterized by similar date-determining conventions. For example, all Oxford dictionaries before the 37th edition (1967) of *Hart's Rules for Compositors and Readers at the University Press,*

Oxford used the spelling *connexion*, with an *x* – thereafter *connection*, with medial *-ct-*. The programming of microcomputerized dictionaries of the future is bound to lead to normalization of many matters of spelling and punctuation. Modern equivalents of the 2-shaped *r* are bound to disappear – among them, I suspect, the freedom to use *-ise* or *-ize* according to taste, and the more important spelling differences between American and British English, the types *center/centre*, *color/colour*, *marvelous/marvellous*, and *esthetic/aesthetic*. And the development of even more sophisticated Optical Character Recognition machines will lead to pressure on people to make the shapes of their handwritten letters of the alphabet more uniform, and also to reduce the variety of founts of type available for any given letter of the alphabet.

I turn now to the heart of the matter.

The *American College Dictionary* and its derivatives

Let me follow a path of descent. In 1947 a new American collegiate dictionary was published – the *American College Dictionary*, edited by Clarence L. Barnhart. The introduction reported that it was 'a record of the English language prepared by more than 350 scholars, specialists, and editors . . .'. It was 'The first abridged dictionary to be prepared by a staff larger than is usually assembled for an unabridged dictionary . . .'. It also claimed to be based on significant advances in the study of language by linguists and psychologists; and, in general, this claim was justified. Some of the more dazzling names of the period were listed as advisers for general areas or special fields (Leonard Bloomfield, Charles C. Fries, Kemp Malone, Zellig S. Harris, Allen Walker Read, Sir William A. Craigie, George L. Trager, and numerous others), as well as scores of authorities in subjects like anatomy, plant physiology, insurance, medieval history, textiles, typography, etc. It was an exceedingly good dictionary. Its policy about inclusion and exclusion was based upon the frequency of appearance of words and meanings in print, and upon certain principles of phonetics, and so on, that seemed acceptable at the time. As far as one could tell it was a 'fresh start', and not an abridgement of any other dictionary.

Under the careful eye of Clarence Barnhart the dictionary went through various editions and in the normal manner absorbed new words and meanings and abandoned others to make room for the new items. It became established as an ideal dictionary for use at college or university in the United States.

In one of the introductory sections, Irving Lorge, a member of the Editorial Advisory Committee, drew attention to the words *aorist*, *enclose*, and *stupefacient*; and to the names *Pohai* (a place-name) and *Marie Antoinette*. Let me set out the definition of *aorist*:

> **n. Gram.** 1. a tense of the Greek verb expressing action (in the indicative, past action) without further limitation or implication. – *adj.* 2. of or in the aorist.

Now move on twenty-four years to *Hamlyn's Encyclopedic World Dictionary* (1971), edited in London by Patrick Hanks. Under *aorist* what do we find?

> **n. Gram.** 1. a tense of the Greek verb expressing action (in the indicative, past action) without further limitation or implication. – *adj.* 2. of or in the aorist.

Move on ten more years to the *Macquarie Dictionary* (1981), edited in Australia by A. Delbridge and others, and we find:

> **n.** 1. a tense of the Greek verb expressing action (in the indicative, past action) without further limitation or implication *as to completion, continuation, etc.* – *adj.* 2. of or in the aorist.

Admittedly the phrase (my italics) 'as to completion, continuation, etc.' is new, but by then this phrase had also crept into Barnhart's *American College Dictionary*.

In Barnhart's *ACD* and Hanks's *EWD* the definition of *enclose* is identical, except that Hanks inserted '*Law* or *Archaic*' before the spelling *inclose*; and he also spelt the word *cheque* in a British way in place of the American *check*. *Macquarie* repeats *EWD* except for the pronunciation (which is shown in the IPA system instead of *EWD*'s and *ACD*'s respelling system).

By now you will not be surprised to learn that the entry for *stupefacient* is identical in all three dictionaries[4] except that *ACD* allows for the probability that any Americans encountering the word might be inclined to pronounce it as /stu:p-/ not /stju:p-/.

Exactness ends at that point. Barnhart's *ACD* entry for *Pohai*, 'a NW arm of the Yellow Sea, forming a gulf on the NE coast of China', survives intact in Hanks's *EWD*. But the observant Australians have dropped it to make room for the New Zealand word *pohutukawa* (which they seem to have picked up from the *EWD*). Similarly the *ACD* entry for *Marie Antoinette* survives intact in the *EWD* but was dropped from the *Macquarie*.

Let me apply another test. On one opening, *ACD* has accompanying illustrations of *Malta, Mammillary structure of malachite, Columbian mammoth, Florida manatee, Manchuria, Mandalay*, and *Mandible* (of a bee).

EWD has *Malta* (identical), *Woolly mammoth* (i.e. a different genus), *Florida manatee* (identical, except for a slight variation in the size of this aquatic herbivore), *Manchuria* (identical except that the illustrator seems to place Peking in Manchuria), *Mandalay* (identical), and *Mandible* (redrawn, with a different caption). The illustration for *Mammillary structure of malachite* does not appear because in British English the word *mamillary*, spelt with only one medial *m*, is a column of type away.

In the *Macquarie* a policy decision removed all maps or parts of maps. Accordingly *Malta, Manchuria*, and *Mandalay* were excised. Of the original seven illustrations only the *Woolly mammoth* and (yes) the *Florida manatee* survive. The definition of *mandible* is still that of 1947 – but the illustration shows the mandibles of a human jaw instead of the mandibles of a bee.

The comparisons made are based on editions of the three dictionaries that happen conveniently to lie at hand. For all I know – but it lies outside my brief – Barnhart's *ACD* had also dropped maps and changed their mandibles by the time the *Macquarie Dictionary* was prepared.

What emerges with the utmost clarity is that the exact wording and ordering of senses has been carried over, and deemed appropriate, from an American dictionary of 1947 to a British one of 1971 and then to an Australian one of 1981.

I tested the three dictionaries in another way in order to see what relationships emerged for typical local expressions from each country – what might be called the 'nationality test'.

Typically American items

ACD (USA)	EWD (GB)	Macquarie (Australia)
chowder	(identical)	(identical)
coyote	(identical)	(2 of 3 senses identical, 1 dropped)[5]
kibitzer	(identical)	(identical)
lagniappe	(identical)	(no entry)

To judge from this sample the editors of *Hamlyn's Encyclopedic World Dictionary* were prepared to accept the text of their exemplar as it stood. The Australians were willing to exclude items deemed to be too exotically American, but not to adapt the other definitions for Australian consumption. Exclusion, not adaptation, was the test applied; the axe, not the plane.

Typically British items

ACD (USA)	EWD (GB)	Macquarie (Australia)
boot (in motor vehicle)	(slightly revised)	(same as *EWD*)
pram (cross-referred to *perambulator)*	(main definition at *pram*)	(same as *EWD*)
(no entry)	*prang* (n. & v.)	(same as *EWD*)

The same general picture emerges. Some Briticization occurred in *EWD*, and this was carried straight over to the *Macquarie*.

Typically Australian items

ACD (USA)	EWD (GB)	Macquarie (Australia)
corroboree	(identical)	(identical)[6]
(no entry)	(less elaborate entry)→	*didgeridoo* (elaborate entry)
dingo	←(identical)	(elaborated definitions)
no entry	(identical)→	*jumbuck*

Again some local adaptation has occurred but, surprisingly, a 1947 American definition of one of the most Australian of all words, *corroboree*, was still judged to be suitable for Australian users in 1981.

The editors of *EWD* admitted their indebtedness to the *American College Dictionary*. By the time the package had moved on to Australia, the connections were set in much less explicit terms:

Naturally, we could not prepare a book of this size without having access to another good dictionary for use as a base. We were fortunate in having access to the *Encyclopedic World Dictionary*, published by Hamlyn in England in 1971. This dictionary was itself based on the well-known *American College Dictionary*, first published in 1969. (Preface, p. 12)

The primary derivativeness of the dictionary was fudged, not by the blurb-writers, but by the editor in chief, Professor A. Delbridge himself. I estimated that the amount of material shared by all three dictionaries was of the order of 93 per cent of the whole. The distinctive American vocabulary that was removed by the Hamlyn dictionary and replaced by British vocabulary was about 7 per cent of the original. The unshared 7 per cent constituted the 'Britishness' of *EWD*, and a different unshared 7 per cent made up the Australian distinctiveness of the *Macquarie Dictionary*.

And the derivativeness, as I have suggested, is not restricted to the text. The same illustrations, not even redrawn – of *bald eagle, capybara, raccoon*; and (of Australian subjects) *boomerang, dingo, kangaroo, koala*, etc.; as well as general English subjects like *davit, eclipse, halberd*, and *kettledrum* – were carried over from the *ACD* to the *EWD*. And all of them have made their remorseless way, along with hundreds of others, into the *Macquarie Dictionary*.

My comment in a review of the *Macquarie* was, I admit, uncharitable: 'one can only say "Thank you England and America." ' I also said, however, that the taking on board of material from other dictionaries was not necessarily in itself reprehensible. But the amount of the indebtedness should have been made clear; and it could even have been turned into a virtue.

Webster's Third and the *OED*

Perhaps the most surprising example of indebtedness, that became clear as my investigation continued, was that of *Webster's Third New International* to the *OED*. I should make it clear at once, though, that it is a restricted and, as you will see in a moment, an unavoidable indebtedness, given that the Merriam-Webster quotation files, magnificent as they are, have been built up on the assumption that dictionaries prepared from the evidence contained in the files would be dictionaries of 'current English', not of the English of former centuries.

Webster's Third set the year 1755 as its backward terminal limit. In general terms – Shakespeare and the Authorized Version of the Bible apart – their exclusion zone included the whole of the period before 1755. But their quotation files are extraordinarily rich from the period since 1900, and progressively thinner as one works backwards from 1900 to 1755. In other words, for classes of words that flourished and possibly died in the period 1755 to 1900 they had very little confirmatory or disconfirmatory evidence of their own, and had to resort to the great historical dictionaries, the *OED* itself and the historical dictionaries of special periods and special regions.

It is not easy to demonstrate the indebtedness in the way that I have done above for the *American College Dictionary* and its derivatives; but it is not impossible.

The arrangement of senses in *Webster's Third* for most words is strikingly and admirably fresh. The editor and his staff systematically reconsidered the facts, no doubt with a weather eye on the *OED*, but mostly with a view to arranging them in a way that reflected their quotational material. Their filed-away citations – some thirteen million of them – are numerically richer than those held by any other dictionary house.

One important area in which the genealogical relationship of the *OED* and *Webster's Third* can be tested is in the treatment of phrasal verbs: that is, in expressions of the type *to make out, to put off*, and *to put over*.

The synchronic rules of *Webster's Third* prevented it from taking such expressions back to their beginnings. For example, the phrasal verb *to put over* is subdivided into eight senses in the *OED*, beginning with a specialized sense in Falconry from the *Book of St Albans* (1486). By proper application of the synchronic rules, these eight senses were reduced to just one in *Webster's Third*, this one sense surviving only because it was revived in the United States in the sense 'to delay, to postpone' from about the time of Mark Twain.

> If you can without fail issue the book on the 15th of May – putting the Sketch book over till another time.
>
> (Mark Twain, 1871)

The only thing to do is to put it over for a week.

(H. Kemelman, 1978)

Naturally, the rather thin entry in *Webster's Third* for this phrasal verb only very poorly illustrates the historical development of the expression in its various old senses. And it baldly illustrates the two common present-day meanings by short examples from writers (not known to me) called Alzada Comstock and Rosamund Frost. Such synchronic treatment of words inevitably resembles attempts to reconstruct the true shape of ancient hominids from fossilized remains found by chance in scattered caves and gorges.

In a great many other entries the deletion rules have been applied with skill – the old discarded senses have been left like so many tombstones in the *OED* and only the living senses are left in *Webster's Third*. Close analysis of some other phrasal verbs, however, bring out the transatlantic dependence.

Thus, for example, the fifteen senses and sub-senses of the phrasal verb *to make out* in the *OED* (senses 91a to n) correspond closely in their ordering and in their wording to the fifteen senses and sub-senses in *Webster's Third*. Some of them could only be drawn from the *OED*, especially those marked *dial.*, *chiefly dial.*, *dial. Brit.*, or *obs.* Thus the *Webster's Third* sense 3 of 'to make out' – '*obs.*: to count as or complete (a total)' – corresponds to sense †91e in the *OED*: 'Of an item in a series: To complete (a certain total). *Obs.*' The snag is that this sense existed only in the sixteenth century and should have been deleted under the 1755 cut-off rule of *Webster's Third*.

A detailed study of the phrasal verbs, and of other complicated items with many senses, would bring out the extent of the direct dependence of *Webster's Third* on the *OED*. It is substantial and it is not acknowledged. The date of publication of Dr Johnson's dictionary, 1755, had been chosen as the cut-off date because the editors dared not venture into territory where their own citation files were sparse or nonexistent. It is rather like an aeroplane that can do dazzling manoeuvres and stunts as long as the fuel holds out, but then becomes merely a glider, a pretend-aeroplane, kept buoyant only by thermals and its aerodynamic shape.

The Random House and Collins connection

Let me turn to a branch of another family tree. In 1979, with much swashbuckling publicity, Collins, one of the largest publishing houses in Britain, put out *Collins Dictionary of the English Language*. It was a dictionary of collegiate size, mid-way in size between the *Concise Oxford Dictionary* and the *Shorter Oxford English Dictionary*. The publishers' foreword described it as 'a completely new and original English dictionary'. The editorial director was Laurence Urdang; the editor was Patrick Hanks; and the managing editor was Thomas Hill Long. The chief defining editor was Paul Procter and the deputy defining editor Della Summers. I set to wondering how such an ambitious project as 'a completely new and original dictionary' could have been compiled, as nothing in the prefatory matter gave any clue to the way in which the evidence had been assembled and the editorial work done. There was no mention of extensive quotation files and of the kind of classified scholarly information that we have permanently available in the *OED* Department in Oxford and that Merriam-Webster's have in Springfield, Massachusetts.

The names of the main editors set me on the trail. The trail led first to Longmans (*Longman Dictionary of English Idioms*, 1979, editorial director, Thomas Hill Long, and managing editor, Della Summers). And then to *The Random House Dictionary of the English Language* College Edition (*RHDC*), 1968 (and later impressions): editor in chief, Laurence Urdang, and senior editor (with seven others), Thomas Hill Long. The *Longman Dictionary of English Idioms* proved to be a false scent. But the Random House connection was quite another story. In the Collins promotional matter released with their dictionary it was said that they began by feeding into a computer data-bank the headwords of five different (unspecified) existing dictionaries. It soon became evident that the *Random House Dictionary* (College Edition) was one of them – and not only the headwords. Compare the following definitions:

green manure
Random: 1. A crop of growing plants plowed under to enrich the soil.
Collins: 1. A growing crop that is ploughed under to enrich the soil.
Random: 2. Manure which has not undergone decay.
Collins: 2. Manure that has not yet decomposed.

Green Mountain Boys
Random: The soldiers from Vermont in the American Revolution, originally organized by Ethan Allen in 1775 to oppose the territorial claims of New York.
Collins: The members of the armed bands of Vermont organized in the 1770s to oppose New York's territorial claims. Under Ethan Allen they won fame in the War of American Independence.

It was at once apparent, however, that the genealogical relationship of the two dictionaries was much more complicated than that of Barnhart (*ACD*), Hanks (*EWD*), and *Macquarie. Collins English Dictionary* had no illustrations, whereas *Random House* had an average of two or three per opening. *Collins* had a high proportion of proper names; by comparison *Random House* had relatively few, and some of these were not in *Collins*.

Collins	Random House
Hoad, Lew A.	Hoangho (China)
Hobart	Hoare, Sir Samuel
Hobbema, Meindert	Hobart
Hobbes, Thomas	Hobbema, Meindert
Hobbs, Sir John Berry	Hobbes, Thomas
Hoboken (Belgium)	Hobbs (New Mexico)
Hochhuth, Rolf	Hoboken (New Jersey)
Ho Chi Minh	Hobson, Richmond Pearson
Ho Chi Minh City	Hoccleve, Thomas
Hockney, David	Ho Chi Minh

The sharing of names is not such as to suggest any kind of direct indebtedness except in so far as any such list is useful in establishing and carrying out a policy for a particular class of lexical items.

The collation of medieval manuscripts is often assisted by seeking out shared errors. An error found in two of a number of manuscripts of the same text helps to establish the line of descent. But this stemmatological method does not help in the present case. I found a recurring error in *Collins*, namely the repetition of phrases like *to bury the hatchet* and *to burn one's fingers*, once under the first main word in the phrase and then under the other main word, differently defined in each case. Thus:

bury the hatchet, to cease hostilities and become reconciled.

bury the *hatchet*, to make peace.

burn one's fingers (*informal*), to suffer from having meddled or interfered.

burn one's *fingers*, to suffer as a result of incautious or meddlesome action.

Such duplication, with diverging definitions in the same book, occurs repeatedly in *Collins: beat* about the *bush*, *toe* the *line*, a fine *kettle* of *fish*, *flog* a dead *horse*, etc. But there is nothing of the kind in *Random House*. Some other stemmatological explanation of this fault needs to be found.

I have shown one stemma (Barnhart's *ACD*/Hanks' *EWD*/*Macquarie*) where the relationship of the dictionaries is crudely direct – a second (*Random House*/*Collins*) in which a relationship exists but is much more of a cross-cousin sort than anything more direct – and a third (*Webster's Third*/*OED*) where the smaller of the two dictionaries is entirely independent until it reaches the limits of its citational evidence.

Webster's Ninth Collegiate

My final piece of circumstantial evidence from modern times comes from *Webster's Ninth Collegiate* (1983). I quote from the preface: 'Before the first entered sense of each entry for a generic word, the user of this Collegiate will find a date that indicates when the earliest example known to us of the use of that sense was written or printed.'

It is instructive to see the thousands of signposted dates throughout the dictionary. They form one of the two main new features of *Webster's Ninth* as compared with *Webster's Eighth* (1973). Our old friends *anus*, *euphemism*, and *irritable* are unchanged between 1973 and 1983 in all main respects – pronunciation, part of speech, etymology, and the wording of the definitions.[7] But the definition of *anus* is preceded by the date (15c); that of *euphemism* by the date (*c.* 1656); and that of *irritable* by the date (1662) – in other words by the date of the first quotation for each of these words in the *OED*.

I tested *Webster's Ninth* in the range *Kikuyu* to *kiwi fruit*, and the pattern was the same. In every case for words that existed before 1900 the date provided was taken from the *OED*. Thus:

	OED or OEDS 2 (1976)	Webster's Ninth (1983)
Kikuyu	1894	1894
Kilim (carpet)	1881	1881
kill, v.	c1330	14c
kill sb.²	1669	1669
kill-joy	1776	1776
kindle, v.	c1200	13c

For words of our own century the earliest examples in their own files normally coincided in date with those of the *OED* and supplementary volumes:

	OEDS 2 (1976)	Webster's Ninth (1983)
kilobyte	1970	1970
kilocurie	1946	1946
kilohertz	1929	1929
kiss of life	1961	1961

But in a few cases *Webster's Ninth's* dates were earlier than ours. In other words they had on file quotations of an earlier date than the earliest in our files:

	OEDS 2 (1976)	Webster's Ninth (1983)
kilobar	1928	1926
kiss of death	1948	1943
kitchen sink (of drama)	1954	1941

These minor discrepancies apart, a main and impressive feature of a new edition of a famous American dictionary is heavily dependent on another dictionary, specifically the dates provided in the volumes of the *OED*.

Precedents

Such direct dependence of one dictionary on another is not restricted to the present century, and it is not part of my argument that it is reprehensible, except in so far as the dependence is euphemistically concealed by publishing houses by the use of phrases like 'having access to' or concealed by a failure to mention the existence of any antecedents at all. Let me turn back to the eighteenth century. Plagiarism – *'the wrongful appropriation or purloining and publication as one's own, of the ideas, or the expression of the ideas (literary, artistic, musical, mechanical, etc.) of another'* (*OED*) – is a relatively modern concept. Medieval European authors took it as axiomatic that their main purpose was to 'translate' or adapt the great works of their predecessors. The word *plagiarism* itself is first recorded in 1621, but the association of *plagiarism* with guilt and furtiveness came rather later. In lexicographical terms, lists of 'hard words' steadily increased in size throughout the medieval and Early Modern period as glossators took over earlier lists and amplified them. The first English dictionaries in the seventeenth century had a direct relationship to these lists of hard words (as Jürgen Schäfer has largely demonstrated)[8]. Adoption signified acceptance of and approval of earlier work. Each new dictionary was better than the one that preceded it because the undoubted riches of the exemplar were being added to by the new compiler. The lexicographers were rather like the beneficiaries of a will – 'Look', they seemed to say, 'I have inherited all these gems from my predecessors . . . I have kept them all and here are some more.'

Let me illustrate the point from some eighteenth-century dictionaries. Compare the definitions of *Elysian Fields* in the dictionaries of John Kersey (*Dictionarium Anglo-Britannicum*, 1708) and Nathan Bailey (*A Universal Etymological English Dictionary*, 1721) – I have italicized the trivial differences:

> **Kersey** (*1708*). *Elysian Fields*, a certain Paradise of delightful Meadows, into which the Heathens held that the Souls of Just Men pass'd after Death.

> **Bailey** (*1721*). *Elysian Fields*, a certain Paradice of delightful *Groves and* Meadows, into which the Heathens held that the Souls of *good* Men passed after Death.

Comparison of John Ray's *Collection of English Proverbs* (1670) with the same dictionary of Bailey's produces the same broad result, a more than coincidental likeness of phraseology:

Ray (*1670*). As wise as a Man of Gotham (*Nottinghamshire*). It passeth for the Periphrasis of a fool, and an hundred fopperies are feigned on the Towns folk of Gotham, a village in this County.

Bailey (*1721*). As wise as a Man of Gotham. This proverb passes for the Periphrasis of a Fool, and an hundred Fopperies are feigned and father'd on the Townfolk of Gotham, a Village in Nottinghamshire.

These examples are taken from the standard book on the subject, *The English Dictionary from Cawdrey to Johnson 1604–1755* (by D. T. Starnes and G. E. Noyes, 1946). But any comparison of eighteenth-century dictionaries, one with another, shows at once that direct adoption of material from an earlier source was *not* considered a matter for reproach. Dr Johnson's definition of a technical meaning of the word *counter* –

of a *Horse*, is that part of the horse's forehand that lies between the shoulder and under the neck

– is for all practical purposes the same as that in Nathan Bailey's *Dictionarium Britannicum* (1730) –

[of a *Horse*] is that part of the fore-hand of a horse, that lies between the shoulder and under the neck.

This definition and also that of *fetlock* are taken in all essentials from a slightly earlier *Farrier's Dictionary*. It would be easy to multiply cases of more or less exact carrying-over of definitions.

But my hypothetical lexicographical genealogist would not always find the going so easy. Other considerations took Samuel Johnson far from Nathan Bailey when it suited him. For example, Bailey took an extremely encyclopaedic view of the word *fever*, and gave it the kind of treatment one would expect to find in a large medical dictionary. He dealt with twenty-one specified kinds of fever (*continual fever, intermitting fever, a hectic fever, putrid fever, a quotidian fever,* and so on) with each one fully defined. Johnson merely defined *fever* as

a disease in which the body is violently heated, and the pulse quickened, or in which heat and cold prevail by turns. It is sometimes continual, sometimes intermittent.

Similarly, under *God*, Bailey (1730) gives the names of all the Roman gods (Juno, Jupiter, etc.), and then deals with 'deities' of other kinds (*Mens*, the mind; *Honor*, honour; *Pietas*, piety; etc.) with full definitions, the whole entry running to a column-and-a-half of large folio size. Johnson's treatment is much more restrained:

> 1. The Supreme Being. 2. A false god; an Idol. 3. Any person or thing deified or too much honoured.

Exact resemblance of definition is commonplace and seems to have been not regarded as objectionable. But perhaps the more frequent procedure of the time was a recognizable kind of adaptation. A rather vivid example of this is shown by comparing the definitions of the word *Ascarides* in Nathan Bailey (1730), Ephraim Chambers's *Cyclopaedia* (1751), and Samuel Johnson (1755). For those with a tender stomach, the definitions that follow are not very suitable!

> **Bailey** (*1730*). Arse-Worms, a kind of little Worms sometimes found in the Rectum, which tickle it, and are troublesome.

> **Chambers** (*1751*). In medicine, a slender sort of worms, found in the intestinum rectum, chiefly of children, and frequently voided with their fæces; sometimes also adhering to the fundament, or even pendent from it. [Followed by two more sentences of encyclopaedic detail.]

Johnson, with these and other definitions before him, chose as usual the shorter style:

> Little worms in the rectum, so called from their continual troublesome motion, causing an intolerable itching.

In such cases the resemblances are oblique and the precise sources need to be ascertained.

In this computerized age a new bibliographical game can now be played. The rules are those of genealogy and very similar to those so laboriously carried out by the 'recensionists' and the 'eclecticists' when considering the relationship of medieval manuscripts. The genealogical relationship of dictionaries – a subject not hitherto easy to approach because copies of *all* the relevant works are seldom to be found in the library that one happens to work in, even those as great as the Bodleian Library in Oxford, the British Library in London, or the Library of Congress in Washington – can shortly be attempted as a brand-new branch of the humanities.

The relevant dictionaries, including the *OED*, are making their way into microcomputers; and the information within them needs only to be captured in the proper way for it to be possible to demonstrate the relationship of one dictionary to another in a manner that up till now could only be done with great difficulty. If analysis of a much more sophisticated and systematic kind is undertaken than I have attempted here, it will be of interest to discover what effect the results will have on modern dictionary houses as the more intimate relationships – everything that has been furtively copied or covertly concealed – are brought to the surface and shown to us all.

Computer science can achieve some miraculous things. Here is a small area of scholarship that might bring some ancient habits into question; or, alternatively, it might take the word *plagiarism* right out of the subject as an unnecessarily delicate consideration in the provision of information for mankind.

Notes

1. A. L. Reade, *Johnson's Early Life*, 1946, p. 157. The evidence is set out in tabulated form by A. R. Wagner in his *English Genealogy* (1960), Table III.
2. A well-known anti-recensionist scholar in the Vinaver/Greg tradition is a Canadian, Professor George Kane, and his edition of the A-Text of *Piers Plowman*, 1960, is a classic of its kind.
3. *The English Text of the Ancrene Riwle*, edited from B. M. Cotton MS. Cleopatra C. VI. pp. ix, xii.
4. '*adj*. 1. Stupefying: producing stupor – *n*. 2. a drug or agent that produces stupor. [L *stupefaciens*, ppr., stupefying].'
5. The omission is evidently due to the Australian lack of interest in '*Amer. Ind. Legend*, the culture hero and trickster of the American Indians of the West (sometimes human, sometimes animal).'
6. Identical except for the substitution of 'Aboriginal' for 'native Australian'.
7. With the minor exception that *Webster's Ninth* inserts 'perh.' in the etymology of *anus*. *Webster's Eighth* said 'akin to OI *äinne* anus', and *Webster's Ninth* 'perh. akin to OIr *äinne* anus'.
8. See his several articles in learned journals, for example 'Chaucer in Shakespeare's Dictionaries: The Beginning' (*The Chaucer Review*, Vol. 17, No. 2).

6 The *Oxford English Dictionary* and Its Historical Principles

On 6 June 1928 the Prime Minister, the Rt Hon. Stanley Baldwin, at a banquet in the Goldsmiths' Hall to celebrate the completion of the *Oxford English Dictionary*, proposed the health of the editors and staff of the *Oxford English Dictionary*. His central point was put in question-and-answer form:

> What was the genesis of this great work? It was this: it was the desire to record and to safeguard and to establish for all time the manifold riches of the English tongue.

In the same month the Delegates of the Oxford University Press, in the customary manner of the time, issued a statement about the nature of the book they had just published:

> It is perhaps less generally appreciated that what makes the Dictionary unique is its historical method; it is a Dictionary not of our English, but of all English: the English of Chaucer, of the Bible, and of Shakespeare is unfolded in it with the same wealth of illustration as is devoted to the most modern authors.[1]

Both statements have the forcefulness, but also the weaknesses, of a manifesto.

Apparently Edward Elgar once said, 'the people yearn for things that can stir them'. I believe this to be profoundly true, and I believe too that, in the right hands, the *Oxford English Dictionary* is a work that can satisfy this yearning.

In 1972, on the day in which Volume 1 (A–G) of the *Supplement to the OED* was published, Miss Marghanita Laski prophetically declared:

The *OED* is still – just – a working tool that is deservedly a world-famous glory of English culture. Soon now it will be a magnificent fossil.[2]

What is the true nature of this great work set in train by Archbishop Trench and brought into being by James Augustus Henry Murray and his colleagues and associates? Is it – should it be – simply a record of the language? Has its presence in any way safeguarded the language? Has it established the manifold riches of the English tongue? Is it now a magnificent fossil?

I cannot hope in a short space to answer these questions. But the questions themselves point the way towards the nature of this book, which is, without doubt, the greatest dictionary of modern times, and the most influential.

Before James Murray set to work in the 1870s English lexicography had been marked by the publication of numerous pleasing works of undoubted usefulness but of unpleasing insufficiency. From Robert Cawdrey's *A Table Alphabeticall of English Wordes* in 1604 to Charles Richardson's *A New Dictionary of the English Language* in 1836–7 English vocabulary was presented in handsome volumes of various sizes, with greater prominence given to 'hard' words than to 'easy' ones, and with fluctuating and often meagre attention given to matters now seen to be of central importance. The least satisfactory dictionary of the period was, not surprisingly, the first, Cawdrey's *Table Alphabeticall*. But the name of its compiler, Robert Cawdrey, the Rutland schoolmaster, will stand for ever in reference books as a pioneer figure, his fame secure, as the first Englishman to place English words in alphabetical order, with explanatory definitions, usually just near-synonyms, written in the same language. In the decade in which William Shakespeare was writing the most brilliant plays of all time, English lexicography was moving and stumbling on infant legs, tentative and directionless, and with no power to illuminate or assist anyone but foreigners, and, it would appear, ladies from whom the more demanding aspects of education had been withheld.

The slow expansion of the art of lexicography has been set down in various places, and in particular by Sir James Murray himself in his Romanes lecture *The Evolution of English Lexicography* (1900), and by the American scholars Starnes and Noyes in their book *The English*

Dictionary from Cawdrey to Johnson (1946). It need not be repeated here except to characterize it as a period when, step by step, the essential ingredients of a satisfactory dictionary were gradually identified and then brought into being. These ingredients have turned out to be:

(a) Head words, or lemmata, placed for the most part in strict alphabetical order.

(b) Pronunciation(s) in some agreed system, normally now a version of the IPA.

(c) The etymology or derivation of each word, that is, taking back the current shape or spelling of each word to its earliest form in English, and the establishment of its cognates in other Germanic languages, or, if it is a loan-word, of its form in the borrowed-from language.

(d) A definition or definitions of each word and of each meaning of words that have more than one, with a structured lineal plan of the meanings, set out either in chronological order, or in logical order, or in a combination of both.

(e) Illustration of the definitions by quotations which support and confirm the definitions while adding contextual dimensions of their own. The illustrative quotations also have the secondary function of demonstrating to discriminating users that senses of words are never totally isolable or exclusive, but are conveniently arranged segments drawn from a merged and continuous chain of meanings and applications.

(f) An array of labels of convenience – *archaic, dialectal, slang, temporary*, and so on – as reinforcing agents and helpful signposts.

Very few dictionaries have all six features. And the only dictionary which has aimed to present them all for all English-speaking areas is the *Oxford English Dictionary*.

Sir James Murray and his colleagues established a model for all time. Whenever I have cause to examine the competing models, the great historical dictionaries of Germany, Sweden, Holland, and France, the only countries so far to have embarked on and completed or nearly completed multi-volume dictionaries of this kind, the superiority of Murray's techniques and of the layout of his page is clear. By one practical test or another the *OED* emerges as the most ambitious and the most successful treatment of a national language ever undertaken.

I should like to place emphasis on the value of the *OED* as a permanent record of the central vocabulary of the language from the

Anglo-Saxon period until the present day. Its limitations are well known and are often tiresomely and sometimes unfairly set down by scholars unaccustomed to the historical method of lexicography, or unpersuaded of its virtues. For example, the *OED* excluded some well-defined areas of vocabulary, among them Anglo-Saxon words that were not attested after 1150 – words like *dædfruma*, 'doer of deeds', *dæitu*, 'gentleness', and *dwildman*, 'heretic'. This particular exclusion left perhaps three-quarters of all surviving Old English words unrecorded in the dictionary. The shortcomings of the *OED* record for words of particular periods and from particular regions are also well known. For example, the vocabulary of the Middle English period, 1066 to about 1475, is being recorded in a much more ambitious way in the *Middle English Dictionary*, edited by H. Kurath, S. Kuhn, and later scholars at Ann Arbor. Similarly the distinctive elements of the vernacular English preserved in Scottish records from about 1475 until the present day turn out to be much more extensive than one could judge from the pages of the *OED*. *The Dictionary of the Older Scottish Tongue* and the *Scottish National Dictionary*, the latter already completed and the former with A–O completed and P begun, bear witness to the relative incompleteness of the *OED*. It has also been demonstrated, especially by Jürgen Schäfer in his *Documentation in the OED* (Oxford, 1980), that the works of some authors, for example Shakespeare, were more thoroughly excerpted by the contributors (quotation-gatherers) than the works of some others, for example, Thomas Nashe. All this is true. But it remains the case that the compilation of the *OED* made it possible for everyone to have before them the historical shape and configuration of the language, both its core and myriads of specialized peripheral components, from the eighth century AD to the present day.

Theodora Bynon[3] remarks that 'the speakers for whom a particular language serves as a means of communication are in general quite unaware of its historical dimension'. In broad terms this is inevitably true and always has been true. But those who are interested in the vocabulary of a particular period are now immeasurably better informed than they were before the *OED* and its supplementary volumes were prepared. Blurred beliefs and assumptions about the past meanings and history of words can now be corrected or qualified by reference to the disciplined and informative pages of the Dictionary. You may remember the 1950s, and you would probably be able to recall the main events of that decade if given a little time to do so. Without the supplementary volumes to the *OED* it would be harder for you to recall or verify the date of first use of particular expressions. It was a decade marked by a new quest for personal freedom from authority and a casting aside of authority. The *beat generation* emerged (1952), *do-it-yourself* (1952), *angry young man* (1956), *consenting adult* (1957), *the pill* (1957), and *beatnik* (1958). The same search for freedom of expression was observable in the arts with the emergence of *action painting* and *abstract expressionism* in 1952 and *pop art* in 1957; also in music with the arrival of *rock and roll* in 1954, shortened to *rock* by 1957.

Space travel became a reality when the first sputnik was propelled into space in 1957. It was the period in which words like *blast-off* (1951), *countdown* (1953), *aerospace* (1958), *moon-shot* (1958), and *cosmonaut* (1959) entered the language and became as familiar as the language of the 1939–45 war had been. New inventions made their mark: the *adventure playground* (1953), *Ernie* (1956), the *geodesic dome* (1959) of Buckminster Fuller, *hovercraft* (1959), and *shrink-wrapping* (1959).

Computers began to make a significant impact: *hardware* is first recorded in 1953 – though curiously *software* has not been found before 1960 – and *data processing* in 1954.

It was the decade when we began to link up with Europe; thus *Eurovision* (1951), *Common Market* (1954), and *EEC* (1958). And it was the beginning of nuclear brinkmanship and of widespread opposition to the proliferation of nuclear weapons. The first record of the following words underlines these events: *Nato* (1950), *anti-missile missile* (1956), *brinkmanship* (1956), *Aldermaston marcher* (1958), *CND* (1958), *overkill* (1958), and *nuke* (1959).

Transformational grammar made its appearance, one of the most striking and the most short-lived grammatical schools in history, though a strong rearguard of scholars is still trying to work out why, actually and diagrammatically, 'John is eager to please' is different from 'John is easy to please', and whether 'Will they ever learn?' can be disambiguated from 'Will they never learn?'

It was the age of the word *psychedelic* and of drug-induced new experiences, of *Ms* written or said when the marital status of a woman was unknown, of *U* and *non-U*, and of C. P. Snow's famous *two cultures*. It was also the decade of the National Dairy Council's advertising slogan *Drinka pinta milka day*, and of the arrival of the word *privatiza-*

tion. The Oxford philosopher J. L. Austin introduced the concept of *illocutionary acts.*

The *OED* puts all this vocabulary into focus in such a way that future generations will have a permanent record of the linguistic innovations of the 1950s. The same is broadly true of every decade since the Middle Ages.

Theodora Bynon[4] said that we need the luxury of 'four or five centuries' of time to pass before it is possible to make a 'systematic study of [linguistic] change'. In some respects this is true. The abandonment of the complex arrangements called 'grammatical gender', for example, seems to have happened in some unmappable manner between the eighth century and the twelfth. The gradual loss of this feature is clear, but the detailed way in which it happened is probably no longer ascertainable. Other long-drawn-out changes, like the gradual disuse of the Old English perfective prefix *ge-*, and the displacement of *-inde/ -ande/-ende* by *-ing* as the regular marker of the present participle, were similarly spread out, it would seem, over a very long period of time. Lexical change is usually more easily observable. Let me illustrate this briefly from the *OED.*

I have already mentioned some of the new words of the 1950s in terms of the historical events of that decade. By focusing on a particular letter of the alphabet some further observations can be made. Approximately ninety new expressions of the 1950s are listed in the letter O of Volume 3 (1982) of the *Supplement to the OED.* The largest group, not surprisingly, consists of technical terms from the sciences – *obruchevite* (Min.), *oligomer* (Chem.), *opioid* (Pharm.), *optoelectronics, orocline* (Geol.), *orphan virus* (Path.), and so on – and these, of course, lie outside the central and familiar core of the language. Computers brought the expressions *off-line* and *on-line,* terms now much more familiar than those in the previous group. Several common prefixes continued to generate new words during the decade: *off-beam, off-Broadway, off-campus; outpunch* and *outscore* (verbs); *overheat,* v. (of the economy), and *overkill.* Numerous general expressions made their way into the language: *Oedipus effect* (K. R. Popper), *old boy network, open heart surgery, organization man* (W. H. Whyte), *origami* (paperfolding), *Orwellian, outgoing,* adj. (extrovertish), *over-prescribe,* v., and *over-specify,* v. Each of these words is presented with full credentials and the whole apparatus of historical scholarship in this volume.

People who lived 200 years ago, that is, in the 1780s, had no such advantage. It would have been impossible for them to ascertain, except with all the imperfections and betrayals of memory, what words had come into the language in the 1750s. What, then, is the picture? With the aid of the *OED*, what can we determine to be the new words of the 1750s? In a quick experimental search I found approximately fifty new items of this decade listed under the letter O. Scientific words, somewhat to my surprise, again formed the largest group – e.g. *oblong* (Bot. and Ent.), *octahedral*, adj., *octandria* (Bot.) and derivatives, *oporice* (Pharm.), *orthoceratite* (Zool.), *oryctography* (Palaeontology), and *osculatory* (Math.). The prefixes *out-*, and *over-*, then as in the 1950s, produced a scattering of new formations: *outfort*, v., *out-lung*, v., *outpost*, *outpouring*, and *outsettler*, *over-delicacy* and *overstrain*, sb. *Off-* was apparently unproductive. The most noteworthy of the new words of the decade were *obsolescent* (which of us could have *guessed* when it came into use?), *obstruent*, adj., *obversely*, adv., *octopus*, *oddity*, *odds and ends*, and *optimism*. Curiously, two of the items first recorded from the 1750s are cited first from Johnson's *Dictionary* (1755). These are *obtension*, 'the action of obtending (alleging)', and *obstruent* used as an adjective ('obstructing'), both of them left by Johnson without a contextual example. And, even more curiously, Johnson used the word *obsolescent* in his entry for *hereout* but did not list it in its correct alphabetical place, a further illustration of the kind of irritating minor inconsistency that marred this great dictionary.

So far I have placed emphasis on the value of the *OED* as a permanent record of the language, a record not significantly diminished by the discoveries by scholars of unrecorded words, earlier examples, and the like. For most purposes the huge monument stands as a sufficiently complete record of the language of our predecessors. It is nevertheless no use pretending that it has an uncriticizable evenness of design and of execution from beginning to end.

In a paper elsewhere (*The Incorporated Linguist*, 1984: see p. 20 above), I dwelt a little on the inclusiveness of the *OED*, and in particular on the inclusion there of the whole vocabulary of medieval works like the *Peterborough Chronicle*, the *Ancrene Wisse*, the *Ormulum*, and the *Ayenbite of Inwyt*. It is clear that James Murray and his colleagues aimed at total inclusiveness when they dealt with the vocabulary of routine medieval works of this kind. They also attempted a concordancing of the works of early writers like Chaucer, Malory, and Spenser. Any omissions were attributable to the frailty of the word collectors, not to deliberate design.

> There were no exclusion zones, no censorings, no blindfoldings, except for the absence of two famous four-letter (sexual) words. Dr Murray, his colleagues, and his contributors had dredged up the whole of the accessible vocabulary of English (two words apart) and had done their best to record them systematically in the *OED*. (*Op. cit.*, p. 116)

From the time when this circumstance became clear to me I embarked on a similarly ambitious programme for the inclusion of the vocabulary of our greatest modern writers in the *Supplement to the OED*, among them T. S. Eliot, Virginia Woolf, Evelyn Waugh, W. H. Auden, and even Dylan Thomas and James Joyce (except for most of *Finnegans Wake*). This seems not to have been understood by one or two of the reviewers, those with little taste for *hapax legomena*, nonce words, and other inventions.

In the pursuit of my main aim I had to delve a little into the language of the second half of the nineteenth century as well as that of the twentieth. The language of Thackeray, Swinburne, Henry James, and others had been too uncomfortably close in time for Murray and his colleagues to take it fully into account.

I can best illustrate my own attitude towards literary English, and its preciosities, in the following manner. I have been as much concerned to record the unparalleled intransitive use of the verb *unleave* ('to lose or shed leaves') in G. M. Hopkins's line:

> Margaret, are you grieving
> Over Goldengrove unleaving[5]

as Murray was to record Milton's unparalleled use of the word *unlibidinous*:

> But in those hearts
> Love unlibidinous reign'd[6]

or Langland's unparalleled use of *unleese*, 'to unfasten':

Seriauntz . . . nauȝt for loue of owre lorde vnlese here lippes onis[7]

I want to end by making a different point from one of mere inclusion or exclusion. The beliefs and expectations of one generation seldom exactly coincide with those of another, but elements of the beliefs of one age spill over to the next. Jon Stallworthy elaborates this point of view in his introduction to *The Oxford Book of War Poetry* (1984):

> While America was forging a new society in the fires of the Civil War, Britain was making one of those cautious adjustments to the old society by which she had avoided civil strife for three hundred years. Thomas Arnold, as headmaster of Rugby from 1827 to 1842, had revitalized the public school system . . . The ethos of these schools was essentially chivalric . . . Each school was dominated by its chapel, which suited the philistine respectability of the devout bourgeois, and the curriculum was dominated by Latin, and to a lesser extent, Greek. In 1884 [i.e. the year of the publication of the first fascicle of the *OED*] there were twenty-eight classics masters at Eton, six mathematics masters, one historian, no modern language teachers, and no scientists.   (pp. xxiii–xxiv)

It was in this Victorian climate that the *OED* was prepared. The four-letter words could not be admitted because of the 'philistine respectability of the devout bourgeois'. The terminology of the sciences was admitted only if it could be presented in a manner intelligible to the educated layman. Some 'cautious adjustments' to Murray's policy were needed, and they have been made.

Jon Stallworthy points out that the public-school poets of the early years of this century went to war 'conditioned by their years of immersion in the works of Caesar, Virgil, Horace, and Homer'. This classical training is reflected in their poetry: 'in the poems of 1914 and the first half of 1915, there are countless references to sword and legion, not a few to chariot and oriflamme, but almost none to gun and platoon' (p. xxvii). There were exceptions, of course, including Wilfred Owen.

In the supplementary volumes to the *OED* I had little choice but to adopt Murray's main principles. He was, as it were, my Homer and my Virgil. Nouns are nouns (or rather substantives) in the *Supplement* as they were in the *OED* – they are never described as count nouns or mass nouns, and there are no plurals described as zero plurals. The way in which such words operate is made plain, of course, but in a Murrayan manner, both by him and by me. And so it is with all the other main conventions, including the Pronunciation Key. On the other hand Murray's thinking has not been left entirely unreconstructed. For example, the treatment of scientific terms and of the terminology of the old English-speaking dominions and colonies has been magnified in the *Supplement* beyond anything that Murray and his colleagues would have judged reasonable. And there are numerous other changes, including the superficially 'simple' task of abandoning the obligatory capital that Murray used for the initial letter of every headword.

The unpublished archives of the *OED* show that Murray made extensive use of outside consultants – for opinions about the relationship of the Germanic analogues of English words, for example, he turned repeatedly to E. Sievers, A. S. Napier, J. Zupitza, F. Kluge, and others. Many letters from these scholars survive, as do others from Romance philologists like Paul Meyer. I have continued the tradition, but whereas Murray's replies tended to come from Tübingen, Jena, Leiden, Halle, and Berlin, mine have come more often from Tokyo, Washington, Leningrad, Dublin, and Beijing. Apart from Britain itself the centre of gravity for the study of English no longer lies in Germany and Holland but is to be found much farther afield.

Now the *OED* and the four volumes of the *Supplement* are about to be merged by an intricate operation of microcomputer keyboarding. The keyboarding will begin on 1 November 1984. The resulting electronic database, when it exists, will be capable of permanent updating and of boundless expansion. New expressions like *break-dancing* are being edited now for inclusion in the database as soon as it is ready. The Murrayan plan, a product of the 1870s, will be used as a template for this gigantic electronic structure of the future, making available to everyone the nature, origin, history, pronunciation, and meaning of an enormous range of English words, wherever they occur, and whenever they occurred. It is a noble plan, and it is a stroke of luck that the work of many scholars and men of letters of the last hundred years has provided a suitable foundation on which scholars of the future can build with their capacious computers.[8]

For James Murray the *OED* proved to be a life sentence. The letters

U to Z lay unedited when he died. I look like being more fortunate, as I am now working on the word *up*. I must confess that the journey has been a rough one – as it clearly was for my revered predecessor James Murray – and that it has always been discouraging to see the waves of new words lapping in behind as one dashed one's frame against the main flood.

Notes

1. K. M. E. Murray, 1977, 313.
2. *Times Literary Supplement*, 13 October 1972, 1226.
3. Theodora Bynon, *Historical Linguistics*, Cambridge, 1977, p. 1.
4. Bynon, p. 6.
5. Gerard Manley Hopkins, 'Spring and Fall', 1–2.
6. John Milton, *Paradise Lost*, V, 449.
7. William Langland, *Piers Plowman*, B-text, Prol., 213.
8. The preparation of this merged version of the *OED* and the four volumes of the *Supplement* was completed on schedule, and *The Oxford English Dictionary*, Second Edition, was published on 30 March 1989.

References

Historical Introduction to the *Oxford English Dictionary*, 1933: an amalgamated summary of the prefaces to the fascicles published between 1884 and 1928.

Murray, J. A. H. *The Evolution of English Lexicography*, Romanes Lecture, 1900.

Murray, K. M. E. *Caught in the Web of Words: James A. H. Murray and the Oxford English Dictionary*, 1977.

Timpson, George F. *Sir James A. H. Murray: a Self-portrait, c.* 1958.

Burchfield, R. W. Prefaces to *A Supplement to the OED*, Vol. 1 (A–G), 1972; Vol. 2 (H–N), 1976; Vol. 3 (O–Scz), 1982.

—'O.E.D.: a new Supplement', *Essays and Studies*, 1961, pp. 35–51.

—'The treatment of controversial vocabulary in the *Oxford English Dictionary*', *Transactions of the Philological Society, 1973*, 1974, see p. 83 above.

7 The End of the Alphabet: Last Exit to Grammar

My preface to the final volume (1986) of *A Supplement to the Oxford English Dictionary* ends as follows:

> With the completion of a task assigned to me in 1957, I now retire from the 'great theatre' of lexicography, and will devote myself in the years ahead to a reconsideration of English grammar.

In what follows I want to indicate why, as it happens, this is a propitious moment to make such a change. I shall also deal with some aspects of one fundamental topic in grammar – grammatical concord. Throughout I must emphasize that this, my first exploration of a grammatical topic, is bound to show evidence of uncertainty. The evidence I have been able to collect is inevitably far from complete, and, as a result, I must here remain at the edge of a great subject.

In his *Grammar of the English Language*[1] William Cobbett said that

> In the immense field of . . . knowledge [connected with books], innumerable are the paths, and Grammar is the gate of entrance to them all.

The importance of grammar was obvious to him and is obvious to me. What is less than obvious is how one approaches it and how one masters it in a satisfactory manner.

As a lexicographer I am, of course, accustomed to the placing of words in alphabetical order in columns. The procedures involved in preparing large English dictionaries and smaller ones are very familiar to me, as are the hazards and frustrations. What I am much less accustomed to is the nature of the rules that govern the joining of words across the page. We can all, by instinct, construct sentences more or less effortlessly. We are all aware that primary rules of, say, concord, predication, and mood exist, and can be written down, but we are also aware that hazards and bunkers of one kind or another are strewn around and need to be avoided if communication is to be effective. There are also areas where questions of acceptability and good taste arise.

I said that it was a propitious moment to give up lexicography. There are two main reasons. One is the arrival of keyboarding microcomputers, the twentieth-century equivalent of the fifteenth-century printing presses. I think it unlikely that many of the patient scribes who copied the manuscripts of Chaucer, Gower, and Langland in the first half or so of the fifteenth century retrained themselves in the new technology of printed leaden characters in the 1470s. There seems to me an unqualifiable inappropriateness in my trying to learn the new technology of the green screen when I have spent nearly thirty years editing material manually from large but manageable databases. The maddening opacity of the instruction manuals, the structured programs that are needed to make retrieval possible, the hideous pyramids of information that are being accumulated as the entire contents of learned journals and even of daily newspapers are keyboarded into electronic databases – none of this has any special appeal to someone trained in a different age.[2]

It is also a good moment to move away from lexicography when the pitched battles of commercial firms – in practice in Britain this means OUP, Collins, Longmans, and Chambers, but the pattern is the same elsewhere – are leading to the publication of dictionaries with new titles but old content, and when, by commercial agreements, the initial text of certain dictionaries is being modified by crude techniques of adaptation (normally, of course, with permission) in a desperate bid to reach new markets and new customers.

It goes without saying that grammar is part of a linguistic system, and that it is therefore related to lexicography. Words that form part of the system of grammar – pronouns, conjunctions, prepositions, and so on – are listed in dictionaries and are defined. In the *OED* the history of words like *that*, *what*, *so*, *can*, *be*, etc., is presented in a systematic manner, and at length. The entries are extremely informative and yet, in a curious way, they seem somewhat inadequate because of the sense-by-sense and use-by-use manner in which they needed to be set out.

If one turns to dictionaries of earlier English, for example Bosworth and Toller's *Anglo-Saxon Dictionary* (1882), the same problem arises. Grammatical words are difficult to define and really need a different method of presentation altogether to do justice to them. Anyone who has tried to grapple with *swa* or *þonne* in Bosworth and Toller will know what I mean.

Just as there are excellent reasons for leaving lexicography at the present time, there are similarly excellent reasons for someone trained in older values of scholarship to move into grammar. At a time when some grammarians can express themselves only in a manner which is 'as inviting as a tall wall bottle-spiked' (to use Professor Christopher Ricks's memorable phrase),[3] and when it seems that formal English grammar has been relegated almost to the point of extinction from school syllabuses,[4] a plain need exists for a re-examination of grammar in terms of the needs of educated laymen.

Transformational grammar, systemic grammar, functional grammar, communicative grammar – these, and other modes of grammar, are products of the last three decades or so. They have been of unquestionable value to other grammarians, but some of the practitioners do not appear to have noticed that they constitute a form of unrelieved intellectual apartheid. 'For professionals only' is the *verkrampte* message of these groups of grammarians. The political metaphor can be pressed a little further: the fervent application of intuition and of what may be called second-level ingenuity produces systems of contrastive sentences and of tree-diagrams which can be admired and applauded by other grammarians but which leave the rest of the population disastrously uninformed and uninstructed.

History is filled with examples of migrations of people from one country to another and of the adaptation of individuals and of communities to the realities and circumstances of their new world. I am now finding out what such pioneering involves. At present, though, I feel much more like a shipwrecked sailor than a pioneer, in a strange new country of warring tribes, each one declaring that there is no real alternative to its own system and each pursuing its own targets along different paths and tracks.

In the next few years I shall do what I can to bring English grammar back to a condition in which an ordinary intelligent person, trained in subjects other than mathematical logic or linguistics, can understand the nature of the joinings and linkages that constitute syntax. I shall try to find terminology that has an aura of brightness and a grammatical system that has an imaginative core. I shall not be trying to account for every possible English utterance, nor, at the opposite extreme, will I go through the ritual banality of explaining how a sentence like *the cat sat on the mat* differs from, and is more 'acceptable' than, *the mat sat on the cat*.

The history of lexicography differs from the history of grammar in one important respect. From Cawdrey to Richardson, lexicographers produced dictionaries of varyingly moderate length, trimmed or extended to suit particular markets. James Murray changed all that by producing the commanding monument of the *OED*. Since then small English dictionaries have proliferated on the slopes beneath this great monument: they have multiplied partially because so much verified and thoroughly analysed material lay ready to hand in the voluminous pages of the *OED*. The scholarship of grammar, by comparison, is still at an eighteenth-century stage of evolution. Even the weighty *Comprehensive Grammar of the English Language* (1985) is moderate in size and coverage when the complexity of the subject is pondered on, and when one reflects on the absence from it of any consideration of literary English. The several volumes of Visser, Poutsma, Jespersen, and other grammarians are signal examples of heroic personal scholarship. But no one would claim that these volumes, even if they were in some way amalgamated, would constitute an '*OEG*' to match the grandeur of the *OED*. I do not know whether any institution will ever undertake the preparation of a multi-volume grammatical equivalent to the *OED*. In the absence of such a work, the numerous English grammars at present in existence must suffice, but very much *faute de mieux*.

The second part of this chapter will be concerned with some observations on the nature and treatment of perhaps the most primary of all grammatical relationships, that of grammatical concord. The subject is treated in all the main grammars of English: Mitchell, Visser, Jespersen, Curme, Quirk, and others. My contribution in what follows is more one of emphasis than of doctrine.

Barbara Strang, in an excellent paper published in 1977, said that

> *Prima facie*, concord, especially S–V concord [i.e. subject–verb concord], constitutes an area of linguistic organisation one would expect to be very vulnerable in English (because of its restricted

domain, and because of the many marginal, doubtful and insoluble cases within that domain). (1977, p. 73)

My own assumption is the opposite one: that S–V concord is normal, that English-speaking people regard it as obligatory, and that a reasonably finite list of exceptions can be drawn up. Barbara Strang's paper is a study of the grammar used by eighteen English literature students in their examination scripts at the University of Newcastle upon Tyne in the 1970s. She took it to be axiomatic that the scripts exhibited the kind of English that 'youngish, highly educated people thought appropriate to write on a formal occasion'. She found that, in the mild terror of the examination room, the students' grasp of concord became somewhat brittle:

A whole new set of characters *appear* at the beginning of Book II.

The combination of circumstances that bring about his downfall in the end *are* totally unconvincing. (1977, pp. 79, 80)

In my view such incongruence or discord is central to an understanding of the subject at any period of English. It is contextual, minor, and reducible to rules. An imperfect hold of concord in English is part of the nature of our language, both in its written and its spoken form, from earliest times down to the present day, and not only in the special circumstances of the examination room. It is a vulnerable area only in the sense that *all* grammatical areas are vulnerable.

Let me restate some of the primary rules. In present-day English agreement in number between subject and verb is paralysingly normal:

(1) The *climate was* not brilliant. (Brookner, 1984, p. 15)[5]

One just cannot say *The climate were not brilliant*, at any rate not in standard English. This is true even if another phrase containing a noun in the plural intervenes:

(2) The wooden *platform* between the pillars *was* green and rotten. (Fuller, 1983, p. 10)

If the subject is plural, the verb must also be plural:

(3) The *supplies were* all laid out. (Wilson, 1978, p. 127)

Two nouns joined by *and* normally form a plural subject and require a plural verb:

Unreason and *inevitability* go hand in hand. (Brookner, 1984, p. 21)

Except that a composite subject may occasionally be thought of as a single subject and is then followed by a singular verb:

(4) The *innocence* and *purity* of their singing *comes* from their identification with the character. (Levin, 1985)

(5) *Tarring* and *feathering was* too good for Meakin as far as I was concerned. (Lodge, 1962, p. 126)

See also Quirk, section on *coordinative apposition* (1985, §10, p. 39), Jespersen (ii.6, pp. 522–3).

The rules set down in (4) and (5) have remained unchanged since Anglo-Saxon times (Mitchell, 1985, §26–29). Examples:

(6) Se halge gast cymþ. (sing. S + sing. V)

(7) We sind Godes gefylstan (helpers). (pl. S + pl. V)

(8) His gebyrd (quality) and goodnys sind gehwær cuþe. (pl. S + pl. V)

(9) Flæsc and blod ne onwreah (did not explain) ðisne geleafan (belief). (pl. S thought of as a unit)

Similar examples from Middle English and in the period between 1500 and 1800 are listed by Visser (1963, I.§94). Examples (pl. subject thought of as a unit):

(10) Siþen þe *sege* and þe *assaut watz* sesed at Troye. (*Sir Gawain, c.* 1380)

(11) All torment, trouble, wonder, and amazement / Inhabits heere (Shakespeare, *The Tempest*, v.i.105)

And it is obvious that modern English would require a singular verb in the following context:

(12) There is no doubt that drug abuse, and heroin abuse in particular, has increased sharply. (*The Times*, 27 Feb. 1985)

since *heroin abuse* is subsumed within the general subject *drug abuse* and is not additional to it.

Thus nouns in the singular linked by *and* can be followed by either a plural verb (the norm) or a singular verb (occasionally, but acceptably). There are other linking expressions that from the earliest period have left the choice of number in the verb to be the contextual decision of the speaker or writer, for example OE. *mid* and *samod mid* and modE. *accompanied by, as well as, not to mention, together with*, etc.:

(13) He *mid* his aðume (son-in-law) and *mid* his dohtor to hyre *urnon*. (plural V)

(14) þa se uðwita (scholar) Graton *samod mid* þam cnihtum *feoll* to Iohannes fotum. (singular V)

Similar examples are provided by Visser (1963, I.§95, 96), for example:

(15) Hadrian, *as well as* Trajan, *is* recorded as disputing in these exercises. (Gibbon, 1776–88)

To which one might add: *Along with* the insecurity there is a general sense of unease and mistrust, of conspiracy and treason, that *runs* through *Henry VI.* (Rowse, 1985)

Quirk, in his section on *quasi-coordination* (1985, §10.40), lists some additional minor types.

In all these the verb is in the singular if the first subject is felt to be dominant but in the plural if both subjects are judged to be of equal standing.

The following example of an extended subject followed by a verb in the singular shows congruence at its most stretched:

(16) That slender elegant blondness, and the equally stylish cut of the working-clothes, jeans-and-shirt, not to mention the expert make-up and hint of very expensive scent, *was* positively debilitating. (Price, 1982, p. 117)

In the same book, a few pages later, an extended subject is followed by a verb in the plural:

(17) The garden, and the quiet of evening, with the smells of honeysuckle and lavender, *were* the same. (Price, 1982, p. 123)

As in Old English the freedom to choose either a singular verb or a plural one remains, and no dredging up of rules can affect the choice.

It is well known that in British English collective nouns may be correctly followed by either a singular or a plural verb.

(18) Each *generation* of gallery visitors *finds* it easier to recognize Cubist subject-matter. (*Illustrated London News*, 1980)

(19) The *jury* retired at five minutes past 5 o'clock to consider *their* verdict. (Bainbridge, 1984, p. 197)

Mitchell (1985, §1520) and Visser (1963, I.§77) provide ample supporting evidence from earlier centuries for the same phenomenon, for example:

(20) *Folc wæs* on salum. (collective with singular V)

(21) *Weorod* eall *aras; eodon* unbliðe. (collective with singular V immediately followed by plural V)

Visser's list of collectives includes *army, audience, choir, clan, company, court*, *crew*, *flock*, *folk*, and so on, seventy-four in all. All are shown to have been used both with a following singular verb and with a following plural verb.

Indefinite pronouns (*each, either, every, everybody, neither, nobody, none, no one*, etc.) also belong in the optional area. Contextual considerations have always determined whether the accompanying verb is to be singular or plural, and sometimes (as in 22 and 24) there is a clash of agreements within a given sentence.

(22) *No one* in *their* senses *wants* to create instability. (Denis Healey, 1985)

(23) *None* of those people *was* very interesting. (Tuohy, 1984, p. 162)

(24) *Neither* of these figures *illuminates* the case against Trident, nor are *they* intended to. (David Steel, 1985)

(25) I have written about almost every subject under the sun except astrology and economics, *neither* of which *are* serious subjects. (Howard, 1985)

In Old English (which also used *fela* and *unrim* in this manner), and in the period between 1066 and 1800, all of these indefinite pronouns are found with either a plural or a singular verb.

One of the peripheral areas of difficulty that I have found to be of some interest is that in which a subject and a complement of different number are separated by the verb *to be*. Visser (1963, §104) calls this phenomenon 'concord of copula connecting nouns of different number'; Quirk *et al.* (1985, §10.46) call it 'subject–complement and object–complement concord'. Their examples include:

(26) His meat was locusts and wild honey. (Bible)

(27) Their principal crop is potatoes.

(28) Good manners are a rarity.

Such see-saw constructions are extremely common in modern English, as the following examples confirm:

(29) Gustave is other animals as well. (Barnes, 1984, p. 50)

(30) The only traffic is ox-carts and bicycles. (*Illustrated London News*, March 1980)

(31) Cassettes smuggled in from Turkey . . . are the focus of private film shows. (Boyes, 1985)

(32) The curtains were blue and white gingham. (Carter, 1967, p. 44)

(33) The eyes beneath them were no colour, like a rainy day. (Carter, 1967, p. 73)

(34) These huge biographies are usually a mistake nowadays. (Stone, 1985)

(35) Shirts were really my speciality. (Wilson, 1978, p. 126)

From the above, and from other evidence not presented here[6], it will be obvious, I think, that in the field of grammatical concord the options available to English speakers from the Old English period onward have hardly changed at all. Congruence, concord, or agreement – whatever one calls the phenomenon – is normal, but for a thousand years or so the language has permitted choices in a limited number of listable areas.

As one might expect, grammarians from the eighteenth century onward have not always let the optional areas go without adverse comment. For example, Cobbett (1823, §246) says that 'it is the meaning that must determine which of the numbers we ought to employ' when two or more singular subjects are joined by *with*. But immediately afterwards (1823, §247) he urges his readers to avoid constructions like *the great evil is the taxes* and to use some other form of words instead (*the great evil is produced by the taxes*, or the like). He condemns (1823, §253) the lack of grammatical concord in *the quality of the apples were good*, a typical example of 'attraction' or 'proximity'.

And so we are left with the basic proposition that grammatical concord is desirable in number and person, but that in many circumstances notional concord arises from the presence of collective nouns, some of the indefinite pronouns, and other causes of 'abnormality', and especially from the phenomenon known as 'attraction' or 'proximity'. Of these only the last has been fairly consistently opposed by grammarians from the eighteenth century onward. We must, I expect, regard Marlowe's *The outside of her garments were of lawn* and Shakespeare's *The posture of your blows are yet unknown* as having drifted now into a discarded area. But for nearly all the remainder it must be accepted that options have been available in this area for a thousand years or so. And the existence of options at the fringes has not endangered the central rule of agreement. Concord has to coexist with discord at the margin, and the margin easily accommodates such discord.

(36) A *group* of four young men, in denim overalls, *was* standing close to him. (Ackroyd, 1982, p. 75)

(37) In the church Emma was able to pick out a *group* of what *were* presumably relatives in the front pews. (Pym, 1980, p. 204)

(38) To me, the whole *complex* of cleanness, which is to say all soap, all hygiene, *is* inhuman and incomprehensible. (Golding, 1959, p. 17)

(39) The *work* of Ludwig Wittgenstein (in philosophy) and of Ferdinand de Saussure (in linguistics) *has* been of fundamental importance. (Burchfield, 1985, p. 3)

One can sense that Cobbett and some of his predecessors and followers would have gnashed their teeth at the 'irregularity' of the options underlying the constructions in these examples. But the gnashing would have been in vain. And, *pace* Barbara Strang, the brittleness does not arise only in the examination room. It is a component of the language as a whole, in its guarded as well as in its unguarded moments.

Notes

1. Cited from the Oxford University Press reprint (1984) of the 1823 edition, with an introduction by myself.
2. Despite what I said I have now (1988) mastered an Apricot personal computer and have assembled in it a large and growing database of grammatical evidence for the period since 1980.
3. *London Review of Books*, 6 June 1985, p. 9.
4. My own observation, based on the inability of many undergraduates who come to Oxford to distinguish some of the ordinary parts of speech or to analyse the most elementary sentences.
5. References for 1–39: Ackroyd, Peter, *The Great Fire of London* (1982) [cited from 1984 reprint]. Bainbridge, Beryl, *Watson's Apology* (1984). Barnes, Julian, *Flaubert's Parrot* (1984). Boyes, R. in *The Times*, 19 Feb. 1985. Brookner, Anita, *Hotel du Lac* (1984). Burchfield, Robert, *The English Language* (1985). Carter, Angela, *Magic Toyshop* (1967) [cited from 1981 reprint]. Fuller, John, *Flying to Nowhere* (1983). Golding, William, *Free Fall* (1959) [cited from 1961 reprint]. Healey, Denis in *Observer*, 24 Feb. 1985. Howard, Philip in *The Times*, 22 Feb. 1985. Levin, Bernard in *The Times*, 2 Feb. 1985. Lodge, David, *Ginger, You're Barmy* (1962) [cited from Penguin edition 1984]. Price, Anthony, *The Old Vengeful* (1982) [cited from Panther edition 1984]. Pym, Barbara, *A Few Green Leaves* (1980) [cited from 1981 reprint]. Rowse, A. L. in *The Times*, 4 May 1985. Steel, David in *The Times*, 8 Feb. 1985. Stone, Norman in *Sunday Times*, 10 Feb. 1985. Tuohy, F., *Collected Stories* (1984). Wilson, A. N., *Unguarded Hours* (1978) [cited from Hamlyn edition 1983].
6. The standard authorities deal with numerous other classes where congruence or incongruence both occur: readers are referred to Mitchell (1985, §25ff.), Visser (1963, §62–128), Quirk *et al.* (1985, §10.34–10.50), and other standard grammars, for further information.

References

Bosworth, J., 1882. *An Anglo-Saxon Dictionary* based on the Manuscript Collections of the late Joseph Bosworth. Ed. and enlarged by T. Northcote Toller. Oxford: Clarendon (latest reprint 1980, Oxford University Press).

Cobbett, W., 1823. *A Grammar of the English Language* (repr. 1984).

Jespersen, O., 1913. *A Modern English Grammar: Part II, Syntax*. Especially §6.31–6.83.

Mitchell, B., 1985. *Old English Syntax*, Vol. I. Especially §25–47.

Quirk, R. *et al.*, 1985. *A Comprehensive Grammar of the English Language*. Especially §10.34–10.50.

Strang, B., 'Some Features of S–V Concord in Present-Day English', *English Studies Today*, Vol. 4. Rome, pp. 73–87.

Visser, F. Th., 1963. *An Historical Syntax of the English Language*, Vol. I. Especially §77–128.

8 The *OED*: Past and Present

Valediction

The first valedictory oration recorded in *OED* is one to the 'People of Bewdeley' in the mid-seventeenth century, described by the theologian Richard Baxter in a work entitled *Plain Scripture-Proof of Infants' Church Membership and Baptism* (1651). The dictionary gives details of other valedictions: a valedictory play by Dryden (1694), valedictory songs by Thomas Harmer (1764), and other examples, including some valedictory observations by the wily one-legged old villain Silas Wegg to Mr Boffin in Dickens's *Our Mutual Friend*. Leaving wiliness, one-leggedness, elderliness, and villainy aside, Silas Wegg's observations to Mr Boffin, the Golden Dustman, have a certain poignancy. He is about to lose his stall where he has been selling halfpenny ballads:

> My stall and I are for ever parted. The collection of ballads will in future be reserved for private study, with the object of making poetry tributary to friendship. (Bk 1, chap. 15)

'The pang it gives me to part from my stock and stall,' says Mr Wegg, reminded him of the emotion undergone by his own father when he gave up his occupation as a waterman in order to take up 'a situation under Government'. His words, according to Mr Wegg, were:

> Then farewell, my trim-built wherry,
> Oars and coat and badge farewell!
> Never more at Chelsea Ferry
> Shall your Thomas take a spell.

I completed the editing of the final volume of the *Supplement to the Oxford English Dictionary* on 25 March 1985, and when the last proofs of the volume have been dealt with I shall bid farewell to the 'oars and coat and badge' of lexicography and devote myself in the years ahead to a reconsideration of English grammar. In the last thirty years, grammar for me has been a tributary of lexicography, the Cherwell, as it were, not the Thames. The order is about to be reversed.

In 1957 my five-year lecturership in English language at Christ Church, Oxford, came to its contractual end. I had given lectures on numerous medieval linguistic topics and on the history of the English language to Oxford undergraduates. I had more or less re-edited the *Ormulum*, a late-twelfth-century set of metrical homilies written in a semiphonetic manner, with Professor J. R. R. Tolkien as my supervisor.[1] I had taught numerous undergraduates. For some years I had assisted Dr C. T. Onions, the last survivor of the *OED* editors, in an informal way, with points arising from his work as editor of *Medium Ævum*, and as editor of three other works – Sweet's *Anglo-Saxon Reader*, *A Shakespeare Glossary*, and *The Oxford Dictionary of English Etymology*.[2] From him I learned the meaning of astringency and its relevance to scholarship. He introduced me to the works of Du Cange, Tobler-Lommatzsch, Meyer-Lübke, and numerous others that stood like stars in a distant heaven to the young lecturer in English language but which, until then, I had scarcely if ever consulted. He was entranced by the uncovering of new linguistic evidence, among which I recall was a definitive article by E. J. Dobson on the etymology of the word *boy*, but impatient with theory and especially with modern linguistics. He was sufficiently impressed by my work on the *Ormulum* to publish an article of mine in which I showed that Orm had not used *unntill* (as the editors of the work and of the *OED* believed) but its northern variant *inntill* in line 1399; and in which I gave details of a word used by Orm, *apperrmod* 'bitterness' (from Old Norse *apr*, from Old East Norse **appr* 'bitter'), hitherto unknown, even to the editors of *OED*, because it had been misread as *awwerrmod*.[3] On such slender evidence, and on the basis of some brilliant work done within his knowledge by other New Zealand scholars, especially Kenneth Sisam, J. A. W. Bennett, and Norman Davis, he invited me to become the editorial and subscriptions secretary of the Early English Text Society (EETS), a post I held from 1956 to 1968. And it was on his recommendation that in 1957 Dan Davin, then assistant secretary to the Delegates of the Oxford University Press, and another New Zealander, invited me to prepare a new *Supplement to the Oxford English Dictionary*.

The prospect was alarming. I had glossarial experience from preparing my glossary to the *Ormulum* and from vetting those supplied by the editors of EETS texts. I had a reasonable working knowledge of all the languages that were related to medieval English (like Old Norse) or had influenced it in a substantial way (like Latin and Old French). But I had never defined a word in my life and, as a closet scholar and university lecturer, had no experience of the kind of organization needed to establish and maintain a whole department of scholars.

My innocence was such that when I reported to the Oxford University Press on my first day, 1 July 1957, and was shown to a small house nearby in which a bare little room with a desk and a telephone was to be my work place, I expected the telephone to ring, and that someone – presumably Dan Davin – would summon me and tell me how to go about compiling a large-scale dictionary on historical principles. It quickly dawned on me that I would simply need to organize the whole project myself from scratch. There were no courses, no conferences, no seminars, no handbooks or manuals of lexicography. All that lay to hand were the remarks of Dean Trench, F. J. Furnivall, and especially J. A. H. Murray, on, first, some deficiencies in English dictionaries and then, in the prefaces of the *OED* fascicles and in the *Transactions of the Philological Society*, descriptions of various methods adopted for the assembling of the evidence for the *OED*, together with some account of the editorial policy.

My quite primary problem was my total inexperience of defining techniques. How did one define a function word like a preposition or a conjunction? I did not even know the formalities adopted to deal with nouns, verbs, and adjectives, essential phrases like 'having the form of', 'one versed in', 'resembling or pertaining to', 'the art or process of', 'one whose trade is', 'ability or capacity to', and all the scores of other formulaic devices that form the protective equipment of lexicographers. Professor Gabriele Stein has recently shown us how Thomas Elyot in his Latin–English *Dictionarie* (1538) was all at sea in this respect.[4] He adopted a nonsubstantival mode of defining nouns, for example, an equalizing verb + *whan*: '*Eruptio*, is whan an host issueth hastily out of a campe or fortresse, and falleth on their ennemies.' Or an equalizing verb + *where*: '*Flegmen*, is where with moche goynge the bloudde issueth out of the toes.' He defined adjectives as if they were nouns: '*Vsurarius, a, um*, that which is occupyed.'

That is how children, and nonlexicographical educated adults, still define words. In 1957 I was in that unenviable state, a glossator but not a lexicographer, familiar with the *OED* as a source of information, but unaware of the professional ways in which one described a word by defining it, and in which one left a word distinguished as far as possible from other words of similar meaning by the avoidance of circularity and by not being tempted to particularize too closely. And it had hardly dawned on me that there was a chasm between the comfortable familiar complexities of Old East Norse and the *Ormulum* on the one hand and the hunting out and editing of modern words like *stereophonic*, *super-market*, and *zap* on the other.

I started by reading that day's issue of *The Times* and working systematically through it, from the advertisements to the weather forecast, and everything in between, copying out examples of words and meanings found there that were not dealt with in the *OED*. The results were a revelation. The *OED* was shown at once to be a product of the Victorian and Edwardian period, and not up-to-date at all. The reigns of George V and George VI had witnessed wars, scientific discoveries, and social changes of immense importance, but these were very poorly reflected in the *OED* and its 1933 *Supplement*, *body-line bowling*, *Bolshevism*, *questionnaire*, and such unmissable items apart. The early centuries of English vocabulary had been scrutinized and analysed with meticulous care. But the language that had come into being in the period since 1879 (when J. A. H. Murray undertook the *OED*) had been collected and dealt with only in the manner of a Sunday painter. Subject for subject, word class for word class, the first *OED Supplement* of 1933 was a riffraff assemblage of casual items, in no way worthy of the magnificent monument to which it formed an extension.

The reception of the *OED*

Elisabeth Murray's book *Caught in the Web of Words* (1977) is a very engaging account of the life of her grandfather, Dr J. A. H. Murray, and of the difficulties that confronted him and that he overcame as work on the dictionary proceeded. Inevitably it is biased in favour of her grandfather, and the Delegates and their senior officers emerge as counting-house clerks obsessed with the cost of the project and intent on comparing the size of the growing monster with that of Webster's transatlantic dictionary. It is a classic account of one of the traditional battles of the nineteenth and twentieth centuries – that between commercial profit on the one hand and patient scholarship on the other. It appears that then as now the publishers saw bankruptcy at hand if the historical lexicographers continued unchallenged with their unparalleled 'engine of research'.[5]

After all, most scholarly monographs were and are produced by writers employed by someone else, usually a university, whereas the *OED* placed an average of eighteen people on the payroll on an open-ended project with unguarded schedules. The lexicographers conducting the operation, especially Dr Murray, trod the tightrope successfully, and this was one of their greatest achievements. The unpublished archives of the period[6] throw some light on the kind of practical difficulties faced by Dr Murray. In a letter of 19 March 1903 to Charles Cannan, Secretary to the Delegates of the Oxford University Press, he commented on the salary to be offered to a new member of staff:

> There is the initial difficulty of the salary: £3 a week is not much for a man of his education, but considering that it is more than Mr Balk, Mr Maling, & Mr Sweatman receive, after many years of experience, . . . it would be manifestly unjust as well as impolitic to take him on at that rate. You would have to raise salaries all round.

Some future historian of the *OEDS* will find scores of such letters in the files in the period since 1957, not all of them so passive and accepting as the one Dr Murray wrote. In other words the day-to-day practicalities of salaries and conditions of employment, and related matters, now as then, are part of the process of completing a great lexicographical project, and often as agonizing and as time-consuming as the scholarship itself. And it is no secret that the financial guardians of publishing houses still keep a stern eye on the waywardness and procrastination of their resident lexicographers. The estimated losses of revenue resulting from the publication of each volume of the new *Supplement* are very considerable – another subject for a future historian to re-explore.

The policy of the *OED* that emerged from the papers and recommendations of Dean Trench, F. J. Furnivall, and others and that was finally imposed by Dr Murray was almost unreservedly acclaimed when the first fascicles began to appear. An anonymous reviewer in the *Nation* (18 August 1887), speaking of the third fascicle:

We have here the same sanity of statement that marked the two preceding parts; the same refusal to make conjecture do the work of investigation; the same willingness to confess ignorance when knowledge is not attainable, which of itself tends to inspire confidence in whatever conclusions are asserted with positiveness. (p. 137)

The same reviewer speaks with pleasure of how successfully the editor had established 'the boundaries between the known and the unknown and the unknowable'.

By 1902 another reviewer, this time in the *Academy* (4 January 1902), was able to say:

It is in the presentation of the sense-histories of English words that this great lexicon triumphs so conspicuously over all others. You are enabled to trace the life of a word from source to sea. Not that this progression is always simple and graduated. Meanings overlap and coexist in the most curious way, one running ahead of another, to be itself overtaken. (p. 648)

Various aspects of the dictionary came in for particular praise, for instance in the *Scotsman* (5 October 1903) on the publication of the fascicle *lock* to *lyyn*:

The history of the suffix '-ly' is given in articles which for lucidity and conciseness form an admirable epitome of all that wide research has brought to light.

I commend to the attention of my hypothetical future historian the treatment of prefixed and suffixed elements in *OEDS*, and also the manner in which overlapping senses have been repeatedly encountered and dealt with by the use of branching displays and signals in the manner of those in the parent work.

Not everything was praised by the reviewers. For example, a reviewer in the *Guardian* of 23 August 1893 objected to the unnecessarily encyclopaedic nature of the note s.v. *Covenant*, sb., sense 7:

Why does the editor go behind the Authorised Version, and discuss the various renderings in the various versions of the Heb. *bĕrīth* and the Gr. διαθήκη? This long, closely condensed note, full of the most painstaking research, must have cost a good many days' hard work, and yet it does not throw one scintilla of light on the meaning of the English word 'covenant', and while it would have been quite in place in a concordance of the Bible or in a theological dictionary, it is quite irrelevant to the purpose of the *New English Dictionary*.

The reviewer was probably right, and yet one can imagine the pain that this attack must have inflicted on Dr Murray himself, as the note in question was almost certainly his own work.

Dr Murray allowed himself to have three coeditors, and thus ran the risk of conflict of views and eventually of performance. This whole area of the relationship of the editors has probably received insufficient attention. Dr Onions was altogether too discreet to reveal the main lines of disagreement, but from time to time he did emphasize to me that Dr Murray was an astringent scholar in all respects and that his scholarship, and the way in which he organized his life, sometimes brought him into conflict with his coeditors and especially with the more flamboyant and less economical William Craigie. On 3 December 1902, for example, Murray (who worked in the scriptorium at his residence, Sunnyside, Banbury Road) wrote to Craigie (who worked at the Old Ashmolean in Broad Street) as follows:

Dear Mr Craigie,

My attention has been called to the articles *Railroad* and *Railway*, now in Revise, which I did not see in copy . . . I am very sorry to see that these articles are (in my opinion) in their treatment of the attributive use of these words, not in accordance with the principles and method of the Dictionary, and that much valuable space appears in consequence to be consumed on what is of no practical value. The attributive or collocative use of a neuter sb. is the ordinary English way of expressing the genitive relation, and is a grammatical, not a lexicographic matter. *Railway director* is simply our ordinary way of saying *director of a railway*, and the one phrase has no more business in the Dictionary than the other, or than such a phrase as *man's life, manufacturer's employees*, or *officer's valet*.

The letter continues for ten pages in much the same vein, with much underlining of key phrases and an insistence that Craigie's policy 'would take a lifetime's misspent energy'. The bitterness, almost a sense of treachery, emerges most clearly towards the end:

I should like also to add that no part of my work is so onerous and unpleasant to me as that of looking through your copy, which has consumed many many hours of this year.[7]

It would be foolish if I were to say that I have sailed through *OEDS* without similar problems. Some of these have arisen because of my insistence that this very class of words, 'obvious' attributive uses, should be extended and expanded to show that the twentieth century is at least as productive in this respect as those that immediately preceded it. Furthermore, my view that the language of great writers, including poets, should be registered, even once-only uses, virtually in concordance form, has been resisted both by some of my colleagues within the project and by one or two reviewers. But the resistance did not come from those who had subjected themselves to the study of the works of the great writers of the past as part of the discipline of studying English language and literature.

One of the day-to-day pleasures of historical lexicography is the receiving of small items of new information from the general scholarly public. For Murray hardly a day passed without the arrival of letters like the following from J. A. Herbert (British Museum, the person who copied out all the manuscripts of the *Ancren Riwle*), 1 April 1911:

> My colleague H. I. Bell drew my attention to this very modern use of the phrase *what's what*; so I send it on the chance of its being useful to you.

Hundreds, possibly thousands, of such letters stand in the files, often from unexpected places and about unusual subjects. For example, Professor Charles H. Hull of Cornell University, on 14 October 1921, wished to draw the attention of the editor to an 1842 use of the word *shoe* in the retting and breaking of flax. Such letters have reached us in great abundance ever since, and continue to do so. On 6 August 1985, for example, Mr W. J. Rasbridge of Radley in Oxfordshire pointed out to us a use of the word *navigation* in a work by Daniel Defoe. In the sense 'a constructed canal', it antedated the earliest use recorded in *OED* by more than thirty years. Letters like this one are of uncountable value, even though they represent only a fraction of the material in the quotation files.

OEDS 4

The prefaces to the four volumes of *OEDS* taken together constitute a formal description of the manner in which *OEDS* has been prepared, and the main theoretical and practical considerations that have been brought into play. I have also set down my views in numerous other places, details of which are recorded in the footnotes to the four prefaces. The most recent pieces, one in *The Incorporated Linguist*[8] and the other the preface to *OEDS 4*, can be taken to represent my most cherished views. I have reconfirmed by hard experience the truth of the statement in the General Explanations of the *OED* that 'the vocabulary of a widely-diffused and highly-cultivated living language is not a fixed quantity circumscribed by definite limits'.

Like Dr Murray I have attempted to compile a *Lexicon totius Anglicitatis*, bounded only by practical considerations and by some uncrossable boundaries, and like him I have doubtless failed. My colleagues and I have largely kept to the detailed policy of the *OED* as to the pronunciation system, the setting out of etymologies, the manner of defining, the numbering of senses, and numerous other matters of substance, in order that the tail might be seen to belong to the animal to which it is attached.

There are two main ways in which *OEDS* does not resemble the *OED*. Murray insisted on aiming at an average of one quotation per century for any given meaning. But such a policy would have been entirely inadequate for a proper presentation of the proliferating new vocabulary of the present century. We have moved towards a policy of including at least one quotation per decade. We have also been far less reticent about the inclusion of sexual vocabulary and have not held back when presenting illustrative examples of such words.

The enormous growth in the publishing of new books and journals in the present century is reflected in the very large number of publications quoted in *OEDS*. By 1972, for example, the Bodleian Library was perhaps eight times the size it was in 1885, and the British Museum library seven times larger than in 1880.[9] Both of these libraries, and also the great libraries abroad, have doubtless increased at a remarkable rate since then. Our reading of sources has been adapted to keep pace with the enormous increase in the number of publications. For the last three years we have also had unrestricted access to three immense computerized databases – LEXIS/NEXIS, DIALOG, and the Oxford University computerized literary concordances and other products of the University's optical character reading device, the Kurzweil Data Entry Machine (KDEM). *OEDS 4* is a bulging compendium of modern vocabulary between *Se* and *Z*. It deals with the latest terminology of the world of computers, for example, *SNOBOL*, *transputer*, and *wysiwyg*. It throws light on the social and political history of our century by treating words like *self-fulfilling prophecy*, *sputnik*, *supercalifragilisticexpialidocious*, *test-tube baby*, and *Zen Buddhism*. The chilling terminology of drugs and of nuclear weapons is included, as are many of the harmless elements of demotic English, *watcha*, *willya*, *yeah*, *yep*, and so on. Cross-references, some of them made a quarter of a century ago – for example, Azande, pl. of Zande – have at last all found their targets.[10]

Notes

1. The edition remains incomplete and unpublished.
2. He was not infirm but found visits to the Oxford libraries irksome. I tidied up many typescripts for him, for example by verifying footnote references at source; and I recall that, with not much success, I urged him to amplify the glossary in Sweet and to add numerous items to the *Shakespeare Glossary*. The work that I did with G. W. S. Friedrichsen on the *Oxford Dictionary of English Etymology*, ed. C. T. Onions, Oxford, Clarendon Press, 1966, was of a different order altogether. Dr Friedrichsen and I needed to verify virtually every linguistic form and every date throughout the book.
3. R. W. Burchfield, 'Two Misreadings of the *Ormulum* Manuscript', *Medium Ævum* 21, 1952, pp. 37–9.
4. Gabriele Stein, 'Forms of Definition in Thomas Elyot's *Dictionarie*', in *Kontinuität und Wandel: Festschrift für Leonard Alfes* (Siegen: Fachbereich Sprach- und Literaturwissenschaften Universität-Gesamthochschule-Siegen, 1985), pp. 195–205.
5. 'The Dictionary . . . must now be the largest single engine of research working anywhere in the world' (Charles Cannan, letter to Sir James Murray, 23 January 1905, in *OED* files).
6. Including many held, and now being catalogued, in 37a St Giles', the headquarters of the *OED* department.
7. This letter is quoted in part, but with a different emphasis, in K. M. E. Murray, *Caught in the Web of Words*, New Haven, Yale University Press, 1977, p. 288. In the dictionary itself s.v. *railway* Murray added a note about the infinite number of collocations arising from the development of railways in the nineteenth century.
8. See Note 8, p. 20.
9. Quoted from my article 'Data Collecting and Research', in *Lexicography in English*, ed. Raven I. McDavid and Audrey Duckert, *Annals of the New York Academy of Sciences* 211, 1973, pp. 99–103.
10. *OEDS* had only a brief independent existence before it was merged electronically with the *OED*. See Note 8 on p. 176.

Index